100 SCIENCE LESSONS

YEAR 1

Scottish Primary 2

Published by Scholastic Ltd,
Villiers House,
Clarendon Avenue,
Leamington Spa,
Warwickshire CV32 5PR

567890 34567890

Series Consultant
Peter Riley

Authors
Carole Creary
Gay Wilson

Editor
Joel Lane

Assistant Editor
David Sandford

Series Designers
David Hurley
Joy Monkhouse

Designer
Rachael Hammond

Cover photography
Martyn Chillmaid

Illustrations
Kirsty Wilson

British Library Cataloguing-in-Publication Data
A catalogue record for this book is available from the British Library.

ISBN 0-439-01802-1

Teachers should consult their own school policies and guidelines concerning practical work and participation of children in scientific experiments. You should only select activities which you feel can be carried out safely and confidently in the classroom.

Acknowledgements
The National Curriculum for England 2000
© The Queens Printer and Controller of HMSO. Reproduced under the terms of HMSO Guidance Note 8.
The National Curriculum for Wales 2000
© The Queens Printer and Controller of HMSO. Reproduced under the terms of HMSO Guidance Note 10.

Contents

Introduction

100 Science Lessons is a series of year-specific teachers' resource books that provide a wealth of lesson plans and photocopiable resources for delivering a whole year of science teaching, including differentiation and assessment.

The series follows the QCA *Science Scheme of Work* in the sequencing of topics. However, instead of having six or seven units as in the QCA scheme, the book for each year contains eight units. These units are the familiar topics: 1. Ourselves, 2. Animals & plants, 3. The environment, 4. Materials, 5. Electricity, 6. Forces & motion, 7. Light & sound, 8. Earth & beyond. They appear in the same order in every book, but have sub-titles which describe the emphasis of the work in that year. For example, in this book Unit 1 is Ourselves: Me and my body.

By having eight units, this resource builds on the QCA scheme to accommodate the demands of the curricula for Wales, Scotland and Northern Ireland. It also creates opportunities to visit each topic in every year: after visiting a topic in synchrony with the QCA scheme, you can make a further visit the following year for extension or consolidation of the previous year's work. The grid on page 208 shows how the topics are mapped out through the whole series.

Each unit is divided into a number of lessons, ending with an assessment lesson. The organisation chart at the start of each unit shows the objectives and outcomes of each lesson, and gives a quick overview of the lesson content (main activity, group activities, plenary). The statements from the national curricula for England, Wales, Scotland and Northern Ireland (given in the tables on pages 198–207) provide the basis for the lesson objectives used throughout the book.

ORGANISATION (16 LESSONS)

	OBJECTIVES	MAIN ACTIVITY	GROUP ACTIVITIES	PLENARY	OUTCOMES
LESSON 1	● To know that different materials have different properties.	Sorting materials into two groups, according to given criteria and then to their own criteria.	Sorting materials according to three given criteria. Name materials to match properties on cards.	Review names and properties of materials.	● Can name the properties of some common materials.
LESSON 2	● To be able to identify some common materials.	Match labels to samples of common materials.		Discuss the different forms that materials, especially plastics, can take.	● Can identify and name some common materials.

LESSON PLANS

Each lesson plan is divided into four main parts: Introduction, Main teaching activity, Group activities and Plenary. In many of the lessons, the introduction is supported by background information and a vocabulary list that will help in delivering the lesson and support assessment of the work. The lesson introduction sets the context for the work; the Main teaching activity features direct whole-class or group teaching, and may include instructions on how to perform a demonstration or an experiment in order to stimulate the children's interest and increase their motivation. There is then usually a choice of two activities to engage groups of children. (In those lessons where a whole-class investigation takes place, there is a single Group activity related to this.) Advice on differentiation and formative assessment linked to this work is provided. Finally, there are details of a plenary session.

About 60% of the lesson plans in this book, including those for the assessment lessons, are presented in full detail. Many of these are followed by outlines for closely related extension of the lesson; these plans are presented as grids for you to develop. They contain the major features of the detailed lesson plans, allowing you to plan for progression and assessment.

Detailed lesson plans

The lessons in this book have been designed to encourage and develop the children's investigative skills. Children at this stage are not expected to carry out a fair test without a great deal of help, though they may be able to recognise when a test is not fair. It is, however, important that they begin to understand the process and practise the skills of making predictions, planning a fair test, choosing appropriate resources, collecting data and drawing conclusions. Even lessons that focus on knowledge and understanding are approached in an investigative way through questioning, in order to develop the children's thinking skills. Careful observation and the use of secondary sources are also encouraged as ways of gaining science knowledge.

Objectives

The objectives of the lessons are derived from the statements in all the UK science curriculum documents. They are stated in a way that helps to focus each lesson plan and give a unique theme to each unit. At least one objective for each lesson is derived from the statements related to content knowledge. In addition, there may be objectives relating to scientific enquiry; but you may choose to replace these with others to meet your needs and the skills you wish the children to develop. The relationship of the curriculum statements to the coverage of each unit's lessons is indicated in the grids on pages 198–207.

Wherever relevant, the focus and content of each unit coincides with that of the matching unit in the QCA *Science Scheme of Work*. However, we have not distinguished in the lesson objectives which content is specific to any one curriculum, and have left it to your professional judgement to identify those activities that are best suited to the age and ability of your class and to the minimum requirements spelled out in your local curriculum guidance. If you wish to check whether a particular activity cross-references directly to your curriculum, please refer to pages 198–207.

Resources and Preparation

The Resources section provides a list of everything you will need to deliver the lesson, including any of the photocopiables presented in this book. Preparation describes anything that needs to be done in advance of the lesson, such as preparing a weather chart or a dark box. As part of the preparation for all practical work, you should consult your school's policies concerning the use of plants and animals in the classroom, so that you can select activities for which you are confident to take responsibility. The ASE publication *Be Safe!* gives useful guidance on what things are safe to use in the classroom.

Background information

The Background section provides relevant facts and explanations of concepts to support the lesson. In some cases, the information provided may go beyond what the children need to learn at Year 1/Primary 2; but you may find this further knowledge valuable in helping you to avoid reinforcing any misconceptions that the children may have.

Vocabulary

Each fully detailed lesson plan has an associated vocabulary list, containing words that should be used by the children in discussing and presenting their work, and in their writing. The words relate both to scientific enquiry and to knowledge and understanding.

It is important that children develop their science vocabulary in order to describe their findings and observations and to explain their ideas. Whenever a specialist word is used, it should be accompanied by a definition, as some children in the class may take time to understand and differentiate the meanings of words such as 'dissolve', 'waterproof' and 'melt'.

Introduction

The lesson introductions contain ideas to get each lesson started and to 'set the scene'. You may also wish to draw on the background information or make links with other lessons in your scheme of work.

Main teaching activity

This section presents a direct, whole-class (or occasionally group) teaching session to follow the introduction. This will help you to deliver the content knowledge outlined in the objectives to the children before they start their group work. It may include guidance on discussion, or on performing one or more demonstrations or class investigations to help the children understand the work ahead.

The relative proportions of the lesson given to the introduction, main teaching activity and group activities vary. If you are reminding the children of their previous work and getting them on to their own investigations, the group activities may dominate the lesson time; if you are introducing a new topic or concept, you might wish to spend all or most of the lesson engaged in whole-class teaching.

Group activities

The group activities are very flexible. Some may be best suited to individual work, while others may be suitable for work in pairs or larger groupings. In the detailed lesson plans, there are usually two group activities provided for each lesson. You may wish to use one after the other; use both together, to reduce demand on resources and your attention; or, where one is a practical activity, use the other for children who complete their practical work successfully and quickly. Some of the group activities are supported by a photocopiable sheet.

The group activities may include some writing. These activities are also aimed at strengthening the children's science literacy, and supporting their English literacy skills. They may involve writing labels and captions, developing scientific vocabulary, writing about or recording investigations, presenting data, explaining what they have observed, or using appropriate secondary sources. The children's mathematical skills are also developed through number and data-handling work in the context of science investigations.

Differentiation

For each of the lessons, where appropriate, there are suggestions for differentiated work for the more able and less able children in the class. Differentiated group activities are designed so that all the children who perform these tasks can make a contribution to the plenary session. At this stage many of the activities are suitable for all abilities, with children contributing at their own level.

Assessment

Each lesson includes advice on how to assess the children's success in the activities against the lesson objectives. This may include questions to ask or observations to make to help you build up a picture of the children's developing ideas and plan future lessons. A separate summative assessment lesson is provided at the end of each unit of work.

Plenary

This is a very important part of the lesson. It is important not to let it get squeezed out by mistiming other activities in the lesson. Suggestions are given for drawing the various strands of the lesson together in this session. If an investigation has been tried, the work of different groups can be compared and evaluated. The scene may be set for another lesson, or the lesson objectives and outcomes may be reviewed.

Homework

On occasions, small tasks may be suggested for the children to do at home. These are tasks, such as collecting things to add to a class display or observing the Moon, that cannot easily be done in school time.

Outcomes

These are statements related to the objectives; they describe what the children should have achieved through the lesson.

Links to other units

The lesson can be linked to other lessons in the same unit to provide progression or reinforce the work done. It may also be linked to lessons in other units in the book, and suitable links of this kind are suggested. You may like to consider these links in planning your scheme of work – for example, linking Lesson 3 (about the senses) in Unit 1: Me and my body with Lesson 2 (about using the senses to sort materials) in Unit 4: Properties of materials.

Links to other curriculum areas

These are included where appropriate. They may include links to subjects closely related to science, such as technology or maths, or to content and skills in subjects such as art, history or geography.

Lesson plan grids

These short lesson plans, in the form of a grid, offer further activity ideas to broaden the topic coverage. As the example below shows, they have the same basic structure as the detailed lesson plans. They lack the introduction, background information and vocabulary sections, but these are supported by the previous and related detailed lesson plans. Notes suggesting a main teaching activity and group activities are provided for you to develop. There are no photocopiables linked to these lesson plans.

LESSON 15

Objective	● To know that some materials are changed in shape by forces.
Resources	Biscuit ingredients, rolling pins, bowls, biscuit cutters, baking trays, an oven, the recipe on page 32.
Main activity	Working in groups of four, the children can make the biscuit dough, roll it out, cut biscuits and decorate them – using, practising and reinforcing all the forces vocabulary and ideas learned in Lesson 8.
Differentiation	Some children will need extra support to link what they are doing to the ideas in Lesson 8.
Assessment	Talk to the children as they are rolling and shaping their biscuits to find out whether they understand that they are using a force to change the shape of the dough.
Plenary	Discuss what the children have been doing and relate this to other work on changing shapes by using a force. Ask them to identify actions and forces that they used with the playdough and are using again here.
Outcome	● Know that they can change the shape of some materials by using a force.

RESOURCES
Photocopiable sheets
Photocopiable sheets are an integral part of many of the lessons and are found at the end of the relevant unit, marked with the 'photocopiable' symbol: . They may provide resources, a means of recording (including collage, writing or drawing), or activities (such as matching).

Classroom equipment and space
A wide range of resources are needed for the lessons in this book. However, every attempt has been made to restrict the list to resources that will be readily available to primary schools. You may wish to borrow some items from the science department of your local secondary school.

Each lesson plan includes a resources list. When you have planned which lessons you wish to use, you could make up your own resources list for the term's or year's work. Encourage your colleagues to do the same for other years, so that you can compare lists, identify times when there may be a high demand for particular resources and make adjustments as necessary.

ICT
Many of the lessons in this book can be enhanced by the use of ICT. As new products are entering the market all the time, few are specified in this book. However you may like to plan your ICT work under these headings:

Interactive programs
These are available for the youngest children in the school, and some are useful to reinforce early skills with older children:
- *My World* series from Semerc (includes *All About Ourselves, Skeleton* and *Healthy Eating*)
- *My Amazing Human Body* from Dorling Kindersley.

Information retrieval
Some children may be starting to find information from secondary sources, including CD-ROMs. Where this is the case, it is important that the children have a focus for their enquiries, that the materials offered are at an appropriate level, and that the task of information retrieval is sufficiently challenging.

Visual recordings
A visual record of an investigation may be made by taking photographs (with a conventional or digital camera) or recording an activity with a video camera, and storing the information on the computer for use in a presentation. Visual records should be annotated to provide a complete record, not just a picture of the children's experiences.

Desktop publishing
Some children may be able to design and produce booklets of their work using their own written material, graphs, charts or photographs, and information retrieved from other sources.

Presentations
Presentations may be made using video sequences that have been recorded during an investigation with a digital or video camera.

ASSESSMENT

The assessments in this book indicate the likely progress of children in Year 1/Primary 2. The statements relate specifically to work in this book, and are arranged in groups to reflect different levels. In this year's work, it is expected that most children will achieve National Curriculum Level 1/Scottish Level A; but some may not progress so well, and achieve only Level W/working towards Scottish Level A, while others may progress further in some aspects to achieve Level 2/Scottish Level B.

You may find it useful to determine what the children already know before embarking on each unit. If appropriate, look at the previous book in the series, find the corresponding unit and check with your colleagues what work has been covered. Talk to the children about what they know, and use the results to plan differentiated activities and provide materials as you teach the unit.

The last lesson in every unit focuses on summative assessment. This assessment samples the content of the unit, focusing on its key theme(s); its results should be used in conjunction with other assessments you have made during the teaching of the unit. The lesson comprises one or two activities which may take the form of photocopiable sheets, a 'question and answer' session or practical activities. This will give you an idea of how the children are progressing relative to an average expectation of Level 1 attainment in England/ Level A in Scotland by the end of Year 1/ Primary 2. You may wish to start the lesson by reviewing the vocabulary learned in the unit with the children.

A sample of the children's work from the assessment lessons in this book, kept in a general portfolio, will be very useful in supporting your teacher assessment judgments.

SUPPORT FOR PLANNING

Developing your scheme of work

This book is planned to support the QCA *Science Scheme of Work* and the statements of the UK national curricula. In planning your school scheme of work, you may wish to look at the units in this book or throughout the series along with those of the QCA scheme. You may also wish to address the objectives in your curriculum planning more directly to those of the curriculum documents. The grids on pages 198–207 show how the statements of the national curricula for knowledge and understanding and science enquiry for England, Wales, Scotland and Northern Ireland provide the basis for the lesson objectives used throughout the eight units in this book. In the tables, each statement is cross-referenced to one or more lessons to help with curriculum planning.

Planning progression

The Series topic map on page 208 shows the focus of each of the units in the books in this series, to help you work out your plan of progression. By looking at the charts of curriculum coverage on pages 198–207 and the organisation chart for each unit, you can plan for progression through the year and from one year to the next, covering the whole of the work needed for Reception and Key Stages 1 and 2/Primary 1–7.

You may choose to use all or most of the lessons from the units in this book in their entirety, or make a selection to provide a 'backbone' for your own curriculum planning, and supplement this with lessons you have already found successful from other sources. The pages in this book are perforated and hole-punched, so you can separate them and put them in a planning file with other favourite activities and worksheets.

TEACHING SCIENCE IN YEAR 1/PRIMARY 2

The units in this book introduce children to the work in the national curricula, and build on the early learning work done in Reception/Primary 1. It is expected that most children will attain NC Level 1/Scottish Level A as they work through this book, though some may still be working towards this level, and some may attain Level 2/Level B in some areas.

An underlying theme of this book is the application of science knowledge to our everyday world. As the children are maturing, this approach allows them to consider the ways in which science can alter our everyday life. This should help them see that it is important to know about science (to become scientifically literate) and to form opinions that, in future, can help in the sensible development of their world. This idea is only introduced in this book, but should help to prepare the children for work in later years on this topic.

A brief description of the unit contents follows, to show more specifically how the themes are developed:

● **Unit 1: Ourselves** focuses on 'Me and my body', including knowledge of the main external parts of the human body, differences and similarities between humans, the purpose of the senses, how we move and grow, and the importance of food and water.

● **Unit 2: Animals & plants** focuses on 'Growing and caring'. It looks at the requirements of living things and how to distinguish living from non-living things. The children learn to recognise and name some common animals and their main external parts, and learn how they move and feed and that they produce offspring. They also learn to recognise and name some common plants, know the main parts of plants, know that most plants grow from seeds and know some of the requirements for healthy plant growth. They begin to understand the importance of plants as a food source.

● **Unit 3: The environment** focuses on 'Environments and living things'. It looks at the habitats of plants and animals, and how these are affected by the weather and the seasons. The children will learn how to care for living things indoors.

● **Unit 4: Materials** focuses on 'Properties of materials', exploring ways to identify some common materials. It looks at the range of materials in the environment and their different uses. The children learn how materials can be changed in shape, and investigate some simple properties.

● **Unit 5: Electricity** focuses on 'Using and misusing electricity', including some of the dangers of electricity. It includes a simple complete investigation using batteries.

● **Unit 6: Forces & motion** focuses on 'Introducing forces' as pushes and pulls that move objects and can change their direction and shape.

● **Unit 7: Light & sound** focuses on 'Sources of light and sound'. The children learn about various light and sound sources, and about keeping safe. They make sounds in a variety of ways and investigate how sound travels.

● **Unit 8: Earth & beyond** focuses on 'Stargazing'. It uses basic observation work to develop the children's knowledge of the Earth, Sun and Moon, the pattern of day and night, and how this pattern affects living things.

Me and my body

ORGANISATION (12 LESSONS)

	OBJECTIVES	MAIN ACTIVITY	GROUP ACTIVITIES	PLENARY	OUTCOMES
LESSON 1	● To know that there are different external parts of the human body.	Draw round a body and label it.	Label a simple picture of a body. Collage a body shape.	Recap on names of body parts. Compare two body outlines.	● Can locate and name the main external parts of the human body.
LESSON 2	● To know that there are differences and similarities between bodies (hair, ears, eyes, and so on). ● To draw and interpret a pictogram (of hair or eye colours).	Collect data about hair colour and make a class pictogram.	Collect data about eye colour and make a group pictogram. Make a self-portrait using a mirror.	Interpret and evaluate the pictograms. Discuss how individuals vary.	● Can describe how the external features of people vary. ● Can make a pictogram. Can interpret a pictogram.
LESSON 3	● To know about the human senses.	Name the five senses. Discuss how each is useful.	Identify which senses would be useful in different contexts. Describe a hidden object in sensory terms for others to guess what it is.	Discuss how our senses give us pleasure and warn us of danger.	● Can explain that we have senses to make us aware of our surroundings. ● Are aware of the five senses: sight, hearing, smell, taste and touch.
LESSON 4	● To identify familiar smells.	Smell pots to identify the contents.		Talk about the importance of the sense of smell.	● Can identify some familiar smells.
LESSON 5	● To identify familiar tastes.	Blindfolded tasting.		Make a 'yum' and 'yuk' chart. Discuss types of taste.	● Can recognise some familiar foods by taste. ● Can identify some flavours.
LESSON 6	● To know that the skin is sensitive to hot and cold.	Can you feel it?		Discuss the skin as a sense organ.	● Know that the skin is sensitive to touch. ● Know that we can feel all over our bodies.
LESSON 7	● To know that the human body can move in a variety of ways.	Examine a model or picture of a skeleton. During gymnastic activities, consider the action of joints.	Play 'Simon Says'. Make a jointed paper figure.	Discuss the role of the skeleton in movement.	● Can demonstrate different ways in which the body can move. ● Know that joints help us to move, and can name and indicate the main joints.
LESSON 8	● To know about how they have grown from birth to the present day.	A mother and baby visit the classroom. Discuss how the children have changed since birth.	Match early to current pictures of children. Identify what a child can do as a baby and later on.	Consider future growth and other changes.	● Can describe how they have grown from babyhood.
LESSON 9	● To know that there are different stages in the human life cycle.	Use pictures and invited visitors to discuss phases in the human life cycle.	Sequence a set of pictures of people at different ages. Role-play a family with three generations.	Consider ageing and other changes.	● Know about the different stages in a human life. ● Can describe some of the changes.

ORGANISATION (12 LESSONS)

	OBJECTIVES	MAIN ACTIVITY	GROUP ACTIVITIES	PLENARY	OUTCOMES
LESSON 10	● To know that food and water are needed for animals, including humans, to stay alive. ● To carry out a simple survey.	Discuss how food and water are necessary to sustain life. Make a tally chart of favourite foods.	Make a block graph of favourite foods. Make a 3-D collage or model of their favourite meal.	Discuss the need to eat sensibly for health. If appropriate, discuss famine and drought.	● Know that animals need to eat and drink to stay alive. ● Can undertake a simple survey. Can construct a block graph.
LESSON 11	● To compare data from two classes.	Collect data from their own and another class, then draw two block graphs.		Interpret and compare the two graphs.	● Can compare data from two different graphs.

	OBJECTIVES	ACTIVITY 1	ACTIVITY 2
ASSESSMENT 12	● To assess whether the children can name parts of the human body, and identify the organs associated with the five senses. ● To assess the children's ability to name some of the ways in which we move.	Match labels to body parts.	Show that they can move in a variety of ways.

LESSON 1

OBJECTIVE
● To know that there are different external parts of the human body.

RESOURCES
Main teaching activity: Large sheets of plain wallpaper, chalk or large crayons, two sets of large labels of body parts (for back and front) as listed in Vocabulary.
Group activities: 1. Photocopiable page 26. **2.** Collage materials, adhesive, scissors, Blu-Tack.

Vocabulary

arm, leg, hand, foot, head, body, elbow, knee, neck, shin, chin, shoulders, chest, hips, eyes, ears, mouth, nose forehead, thigh, abdomen

BACKGROUND
None of the UK science curriculum documents, including the QCA *Science Scheme of Work*, gives a definitive list of the parts of the body that children should be able to name. A decision has to be made about expectations for Year 1/Primary 2, particularly as foundation stage children will already have been working on identifying and naming parts of the body. Typically, they can sing 'Heads, shoulders, knees and toes', play finger rhymes and point to the relevant parts of themselves. There is no reason why Year 1/Primary 2 children should not continue to sing a song that they enjoy; but less familiar body parts could be added, such as elbows and shins. It is important that as well as reinforcing what has been learned at the foundation stage, teaching should extend the children's knowledge of body parts.

You may feel that this would be a good opportunity to introduce the proper names for human genitals (such as 'penis', 'testicles' and 'vagina'). Male genitalia are obvious, but because female genitalia are less so, some little girls get quite worried that they have 'something missing'. Whether you discuss this with the children will depend on your school policy.

INTRODUCTION
Singing a familiar song such as 'Heads, shoulders, knees and toes' is a good introduction to this lesson.

MAIN TEACHING ACTIVITY
Talk to the whole class about familiar parts of the body. Ask them to indicate each part on their own body. Discuss the fact that we usually have the same parts in the same places, and yet we all look different. Say some less familiar part names, such as 'shin', 'chin', 'elbows' or 'hips', asking the children to place a hand on the correct part of their body.

Look at one child from the back and front. Ask other children to come up, choose labels and stick them on to this child in the correct places. Have some spare labels on which to write the names of any extra body parts that the children may suggest.

Spread four large sheets of wallpaper out on the floor and choose two children to lie on their backs on two of them. Using chalk or large wax crayon, draw round each child. Move the children to the other two sheets of paper, ask them to lie face-down and draw round them again. If possible, choose two children who are physically different (for example, the tallest and the shortest in the class). Label the sheets 'front' and 'back'. From the selection of labels, ask a number of children to pick one and place it on the relevant part of any of the four outlines. If some of the labels have not been chosen, help the children to put them in the correct places. Have blank labels ready to add any other body parts that the children may suggest. Some labels may be repeated on both the back and front body pictures – for example, 'shoulder', 'neck' and 'thigh'. Labels such as 'calf', 'back' and 'bottom' will only appear on the back view. While the labels are being placed, remind the children of the fact that we nearly all have the same body parts in the same places.

If appropriate, when all the ready-made labels have been placed, add some less familiar body parts to the list, such as 'knuckles', 'ankles', 'calf', 'forehead' and 'nostrils'.

GROUP ACTIVITIES

1. Give the children a copy each of photocopiable page 26. Ask them to find the correct word for each label on the body outline and write it in the appropriate box.
2. Ask the children, in groups of about six, to collage the big body outlines (back and front) for a display and attach all the body part labels identified by the class (using Blu-Tack, so that they can be removed and replaced).

DIFFERENTIATION

1. Extend the number and range of body parts to be identified for those who already know all the main ones. Some children may be able to make and place more labels for themselves; others will need to have every label read to them, and in some cases, be helped to place them. The less able could perhaps work with more able children, who can help them identify the correct label.
2. All children should be able to take part in Group activity 2.

ASSESSMENT

Note those children who can name all the main parts of the body. Note those who have made more progress and can name and place a range of less familiar parts.

PLENARY

Using the collaged figures, recap on the names of body parts. Remove and shuffle the labels, then replace them with the children's help in order to reinforce what they have learned, with particular emphasis on the less familiar names. Compare the pictures of the two children. Discuss the fact that they have the same body parts, even though they look quite different. Ask the children to think about how they are different. Ask the class to sing 'Heads, shoulders, knees and toes', replacing the usual words with the names of other body parts that they have identified.

OUTCOME

● Can locate and name the main external parts of the human body.

LINKS

Literacy: writing labels.

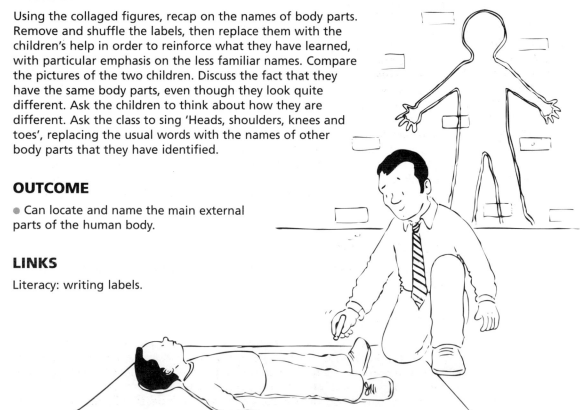

LESSON 2

OBJECTIVES

● To know that there are differences and similarities between human bodies (hair, ears, eyes and so on).
● To draw and interpret a pictogram (of hair or eye colours).

RESOURCES

Main teaching activity: Large sheets of paper (for pictograms), small squares of paper (for recording hair colour).
Group activities: 1. Large sheets of paper, small squares of paper, plastic mirrors. **2.** Plastic mirrors, drawing and colouring or painting materials.

Vocabulary
different, same, similar, pictogram, data, hair, eyes, ears, skin, self-portrait, unique, identical twins

BACKGROUND

It is important that the children know that all humans usually have two eyes, two ears, two legs and so on, whatever their race or skin colour. This lesson provides a good opportunity to talk sensitively about those of us who might differ in some way or have a disability. Differences in skin colour are the result of adaptation to the level of sunlight found in different parts of the world. The children should realise that although the body parts are the same, there are subtle differences that enable us all to be recognised as individuals. Making a graph or chart of the eye colours of children is a good activity, but don't suggest that they chart the eye colours of the rest of their family. Some children who are adopted or not living with both biological parents may be unaware of the fact at this stage.

INTRODUCTION

Remind the class that we nearly all have the same features in the same places – eyes, ears, mouth, hands, feet and so on – and that we talked about this in the last lesson.

MAIN TEACHING ACTIVITY

Compare two or three children with different colouring. Ask the other children to identify similarities and differences between them. Reinforce the fact that we all have the same features in the same places, but that we are all different from each other – even those with similar colouring. Compare two or three children with similar colouring: *How are … and … the same? How are they different? How do we recognise them as individuals?* Look at the shape of eyes, noses or mouths. *Are they all the same height?* Can the children identify some other differences, such as the shape of their teeth? *Even if they had the same colour hair and eyes and the same sort of haircut, would we still be able to recognise them as individuals? If so, how?* Discuss the fact that we are all unique – even identical twins, who might be mistaken for each other physically, show differences in their movement, expression and behaviour.

Sort the children into groups according to whether they have fair or dark hair. Line them up and count how many are in each group. Look at each group and ask the children whether it could be split into smaller groups – and if so, how. Perhaps there could be separate groups for light brown, dark brown and black hair, or for blonde and red hair. Line the children up again and re-count. Talk to the children about how this 'living graph' could be recorded on paper. Ask them to suggest ways of doing this. Discuss the purpose of a graph or pictogram and how it can give us information.

Ask each child to draw a small picture of his or her own head, showing the hair colour. Make a class pictogram of hair colour under the colour headings decided on during the discussion.

GROUP ACTIVITIES

1. Remind the children how they made the pictogram showing their hair colour. Ask them to look carefully in a mirror and draw a picture showing their eye colour, then work together to agree on colour headings and make a pictogram with the eye pictures.
2. Ask the children to look in a mirror and draw or paint a self-portrait, including as much detail as possible.

DIFFERENTIATION

1. Some groups may be able to substitute coloured squares for pictures and make a block graph of their eye colours. Some children will need more support in interpreting the data on the pictograms (see Plenary).
2. The drawing or painting activity is accessible to all children.

ASSESSMENT

Note those children who are able to construct and interpret a pictogram relatively independently. Are there others who require much more help, and will need further opportunities to work with graphs in order to develop their understanding?

PLENARY

Ask the children questions about the information on the graph (pictogram) to assess their ability to interpret the data. *What can you find out from this graph? How many people have dark brown hair? How many blondes are there?* Invite a visitor (such as your headteacher) to the classroom. Encourage the children to ask him or her questions about the graph. How much could the visitor find out about the hair colours in the class if the children weren't there? This will help the children to understand the purpose of gathering data and making graphs. *Can you think of any way the graph could have been made better, to give even more information?* Look at the self-portraits and discuss how the children vary. Compare those with the same colouring. Ask the children to identify some unnamed self-portraits. Reinforce the idea that we are all unique and that even though some of us may have virtually identical skin, hair and eye colouring, we could never be mistaken for each other (except in the case of identical twins).

OUTCOMES

● Can describe how the external features of different people vary.
● Can make a pictogram. Can interpret a pictogram.

LINKS

Maths: graphing data in a practical context.

LESSON 3

OBJECTIVE

● To know about the human senses.

RESOURCES

Main teaching activity: A picture of a garden.
Group activities: 1. Photocopiable page 27. **2.** A card screen, a collection of different objects or materials.

BACKGROUND

Vocabulary
look, see, sight, hear, listen, taste, flavour, smell, sense, feel, touch, light, sound

We see because light enters the eye and signals are sent along the optic nerve to the brain, which interprets the signals so that we 'see' images. Many children (and some adults!) believe that light comes out of the eye and focuses on whatever they are looking at, so that they can see it. Help your class to understand that we need light in order to be able to see by asking them how much they can see when it is dark.

Sounds are made by things vibrating. Our ears change the vibrations into signals that are sent to the brain, which interprets them as sounds.

Taste is situated on the tongue, and can vary between individuals. One person might judge a food too sweet while another thinks it is not sweet enough. Using a magnifying glass, you can actually see the small papillae ('taste buds') on the tongue that are responsible for tasting. We smell things because olfactory sensors in our noses can detect minute particles in the air, released during various processes or for various purposes. Like taste, smell is subjective: different individuals may be more or less aware of various smells and react differently to them.

Children are used to touching and feeling things with their fingers, but may not really appreciate that the whole of their skin is sensitive to touch. Sensitive cells (touch receptors) just below the skin enable them to feel things all over their bodies, though there is a particular concentration of them at the fingertips.

INTRODUCTION

Ask the class whether they know the names of the five senses, and where each sense is located on the body. Ask them to respond to: *We see with our... We hear with our...* and so on.

MAIN TEACHING ACTIVITY

At this stage, many children will still be developing the language that enables them to describe their observations. List some of the words that they might use, referring to particular senses. For example: 'rough', 'smooth' or 'cold' would go with touch; 'light', 'dark' or 'colour' would go with sight. Using one of the following contexts, think about which sense would tell you most about where you were or what was happening:
● Role-play someone cooking for the children. *Which sense would tell you something was cooking? What could it tell you about the ingredients? Could it tell you if the food was burning?* Other role-play situations that could be explored include: listening to a radio or Walkman; doing a jigsaw; a doctor using a stethoscope; eating an ice-cream or a bar of chocolate; stroking a cat or a dog.
● Present a picture of a garden. *Which senses would you use here?* Sight would help you to appreciate all the colours and shapes in the garden, while smell would tell you more about things in the garden (such as flowers or new-mown grass).

GROUP ACTIVITIES

1. Give each child a copy of photocopiable page 27. Ask the children to match each picture to the sense that would be most useful. Some children may match more than one sense to a particular picture; if so, ask them to give their reasons for doing this.
2. The children take turns to hold an object behind a screen and describe it by its smell, its appearance, the sound it makes and so on. Can the others guess what it is?

DIFFERENTIATION

1. Differentiate by outcome. Some children may only identify one sense for each picture. Others may see that two are useful – for example, the TV set matches to sight and hearing, the flower to sight and smell.
2. Children on each side of the screen could be given an identical set of objects to help with identification.

ASSESSMENT

Check the children's work on matching senses to pictures. Which of them need more opportunities to do this in order to develop their understanding? Are some children able to describe their 'behind the screen' object easily, while others need more practice in putting their thoughts into words and developing their vocabulary?

PLENARY

Talk about how our senses tell us about our surroundings. They may give us pleasure, or they may warn of danger.
    Discuss some pleasurable experiences and which senses are employed.
How do our senses warn us of danger? Consider sirens, bells, burning smells, a stone in a shoe, bad food, traffic lights and so on.

OUTCOMES

● Can explain that we have senses to make us aware of our surroundings.
● Are aware of the five senses: sight, hearing, smell, taste and touch.

LINKS

Unit 4, Lesson 2: using the senses to sort materials.

LESSON 4

Objective	● To identify familiar smells.
Resources	Rubber, lemon juice, soap, vinegar, talcum powder, coffee, fresh sawdust; small pots with lids, cotton wool, labels. Make very small holes in the lids. Put a few drops of each liquid on cotton wool to prevent liquids spilling; cover powders with a thin layer of cotton wool to prevent them being inhaled.
Main activity	Place small amounts of the materials in the pots. Invite the children to smell the pots and identify the contents. They could match labels to the appropriate pots.
Differentiation	Some children may need to experience the materials first and then choose a given material from the selection. Others may be able to guess the materials from previous experience.
Assessment	Note those children who are able to identify the substances correctly.
Plenary	Talk about smells: favourite smells; nasty smells; smells that remind us of people or places; smells that may warn us of danger.
Outcome	● Can identify some familiar smells.

LESSON 5

Objective	● To identify familiar tastes.
Resources	Small pieces of orange, lemon, ginger biscuit, carrot, apple, crisp etc. (Fruit gums are a fun alternative.) Be aware of any food allergies (for example, to artificial colourings or nuts) or dietary restrictions.
Main activity	With eyes closed or blindfolded, the children taste a familiar food and try to identify it. (With sweets, they try to identify the flavour.)
Differentiation	Most children should be able to achieve in this activity. Some children may know the colour of the sweets, but be unable to name the flavour.
Assessment	Note those children who are able to identify the substances correctly.
Plenary	Talk about likes and dislikes. Make a collective 'yum' and 'yuk' chart. Discuss vocabulary such as 'sweet', 'sour' and 'salty'.
Outcomes	● Can recognise some familiar foods by taste. ● Can identify some flavours.

LESSON 6

Objectives	● To know that the skin is sensitive to touch. ● To know that we can feel all over our bodies.
Resources	Blindfolds for half the class.
Main activity	The children work in pairs and take turns to blindfold each other. The child without the blindfold gently touches the other child on the cheek, hand, arm, leg, shoulder, foot and top of head. The blindfolded partner says when he or she can feel the touch and where it is.
Differentiation	All the children should be able to take part in this activity.
Assessment	During the plenary session, ask the children where they could feel a touch on their bodies and where they felt it most clearly.
Plenary	Discuss the fact that we can feel all over our bodies; that we feel with our skin; and that the most sensitive parts of our bodies include our fingertips and mouth. Explain that there are more of the special cells that enable us to feel in these parts of us.
Outcomes	● Know that the skin is sensitive to touch. ● Know that we can feel all over our bodies.

LESSON 7

OBJECTIVE

● To know that the human body can move in a variety of ways.

RESOURCES

Main teaching activity: Space to move around, a model human skeleton or picture of a skeleton, a *Funnybones* story by Janet and Allan Ahlberg (Mammoth).
Group activities: 1. Space to move around. **2.** Photocopiable page 28 copied (to A3 size) onto thin card for each child, paper fasteners, scissors, single hole punches, materials for decoration.

BACKGROUND

Learning to look after our bodies cannot begin too early, and understanding something of how the body works is a necessary part of this. Young children can begin to think about how their joints are different and how the joints help them to move. Knees and elbows are both hinge joints, allowing the limb to bend in one direction and locking when straight. If our knees bent in both directions, we would be unable to stand or walk. Hips and shoulders are ball and socket joints, which allow a greater degree of movement. The skeletons of young children are more cartilaginous than those of adults, which gives them greater flexibility: their joints are more supple, allowing them to move in ways that most adults can only dream of!

Many children at this stage will still be exploring their bodies and what they can do. Some children will be more adventurous than others, and appear to be totally unaware of any danger. Others will be more timid and reluctant to try anything different. It is important that children are allowed to develop at their own pace. The daredevils need to be made aware of how their movements may affect both their own safety and that of others. The reluctant may be gently encouraged to spread their wings with a little support. Holding a hand as the child takes his or her first steps along a balance beam can help to inspire the confidence for a solo attempt.

INTRODUCTION

Build on work done at the foundation stage: ask the children to quickly name different ways of moving. Read one of the *Funnybones* stories to the children.

MAIN TEACHING ACTIVITY

Look at a model or picture of a human skeleton. Identify some of the joints. Can the children find the same joints on their own bodies? If you have a model skeleton, move some of the limbs and demonstrate how the joints work. What do the children notice about the way in which the elbow works, compared with the shoulder? Talk about the different types of joints (see Background).

Look specifically at walking. Ask the children to think about how their legs move: *Do they bend? Where do they bend? What are these joints called?* (Hip, knee, ankle.) *How easy is it to walk without bending your legs? Will your legs bend backwards? What would happen if they did?*

Ask the children to bend and stretch their arms. *Will they bend backwards? What about the joints at your shoulders?* Ask them to touch their hands together in front of them, and then see how far back they can move their arms. *Can you touch your hands behind you?* Ask them to sit on the floor or stand and hold on to something, then see how far and in which directions they can move their legs, swinging them from the hip. *Which limbs do you use to climb the climbing frame? Which joints do you use?*

GROUP ACTIVITIES

1. Play 'Simon says' (run, skip, hop, jump and so on). The children should obey the instruction only if told that 'Simon says' to do so.
2. Give each child a copy of page 28 on thin card. They should cut out the pieces, punch holes where indicated (using a single hole punch) and join the limbs together with paper fasteners, so that they can make the figure move. They could decorate their figure, giving it a face and so on.

DIFFERENTIATION

1. All the children can join in this game.
2. Some children may be able to cut out the shapes for the figures, but others may need the shapes to be pre-cut. You may need to show some children how to use the paper fasteners.

ASSESSMENT

During the plenary session, ask the children to indicate a number of joints on their bodies. Can they all name and locate the main joints: hip, shoulder, knee, ankle? Ask them to describe how these joints help us to move.

PLENARY

Ask the children: *Why do we need to move in different ways? Why don't our legs bend backwards?* Look at a model or picture of a skeleton and talk about how our skeletons help us to move. This may provide an opportunity to talk sensitively about people who cannot move so easily for one reason or another. You may have a child in the class who has suffered a broken limb and can tell the class what it felt like.

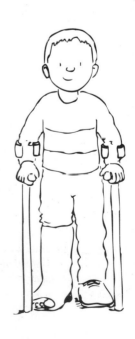

OUTCOMES

● Can demonstrate different ways in which the body can move.
● Know that joints help us to move, and can name and indicate the main joints.

LINKS

Unit 6, Lesson 1: types of movement (as an introduction to forces).

LESSON 8

OBJECTIVE
● To know about how they have grown from birth to the present day.

RESOURCES

Main teaching activity: If possible, a baby brother or sister to visit the class with his or her mother; a tape measure, bathroom scales.
Group activities: 1. Photographs of the children now and as babies, home videos (if available), measurements taken of the children at birth (if available) such as weight and height.
2. Photocopiable page 29.

PREPARATION

Send a note home a week or so before this lesson, asking to borrow recent and early photographs and similar records (see Resources) of the children for use in this lesson.

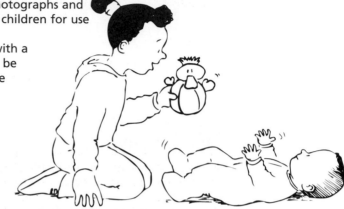

If you are able to invite a parent with a small baby into the classroom, it may be possible to arrange for the baby to be bathed so that the children can appreciate how tiny they once were. This could also provide an opportunity to introduce the correct names for the external genitalia. You will need to consult your school's policy on sex education beforehand.

Vocabulary

baby, grow, crawl, walk, run, feed, milk, bottle, birth, born, talk, physical independence, confidence, taller, change, womb, abdomen

BACKGROUND

Children should be helped to understand that the changes that happen to them as they grow are not simply physical. For example, not only do they become taller, have larger hands and become able to run faster, but they also increase in independence and confidence, understand more and know more. Not everyone develops at the same rate, and there may be children at different stages of development within the same class. One of the most notable changes during these early years is the acquisition of language skills: children can now begin to communicate their own ideas to others. Cognitive development is accelerated when ideas can be put into words. Children should be encouraged to express and explain their ideas at every opportunity.

INTRODUCTION

Ask all the children to stand up and look at each other. Compare heights, colouring and so on fairly quickly (see Lesson 2 on page 14). Now ask them to sit quietly for a moment with their eyes closed and think about what they were like when they were babies.

MAIN TEACHING ACTIVITY

Ask the children: *How have you changed?* Ask individuals to tell the class about some of the things they can do now that they could not do when they were smaller. *How many of you have younger brothers and sisters, and how are they different from you? What do your baby brothers and sisters need to have done for them that you can do for yourself? Did you have to be fed and washed and have your nappies changed when you were a baby? What were some of the other changes in your life from birth to now? Are any of you already losing your milk teeth? Do babies have teeth when they are born?*

Invite a baby brother or sister of one of the class to visit the classroom with his or her mother. Choose one or two of the children to measure the length of the baby and the height of the baby's big brother or sister. Take various other measurements of the baby, such as the circumference of the head, the weight and the size of the hands and feet, and compare these measurements with those of the sibling. Some children may have similar sets of measurements from when they were born: how do these compare with the baby in the class and with themselves now? Look for other differences between the children in the class and the visiting baby, such as teeth and nappies.

Look at pictures of the children when they were babies and pictures of them now. *How have you changed? What has helped you to grow?* Talk about the need for food, drink, exercise and warmth: explain that all these things have helped them to grow, and will continue to keep them growing healthy and strong. Ask the children to list some of the things they can do now but could not do when they were babies. *Do you need looking after as much now as you did when you were born?*

GROUP ACTIVITIES

1. Play 'Who's who?' The children have to match pictures of each other as babies to present-day pictures. Discuss how they have changed.
2. Give each child a copy of photocopiable page 29; ask them to put ticks and crosses in the appropriate boxes.

DIFFERENTIATION

1. All the children should be able to join in this activity.
2. Some children may need help to read the photocopiable sheet. Some children may be able to add categories of their own in the spaces on the sheet.

ASSESSMENT

Review the photocopiable sheets from Group activity 2. Note which children have correctly identified changes between babyhood and their own age. Which children were able to add categories of their own?

PLENARY

Discuss the fact that we were all born and that we have all grown from babyhood. Even the oldest adult we know was once a baby in his or her mummy's womb, was born, grew up and became old. Explain that a womb is the special place in a mother's abdomen where babies grow until they are ready to be born. Recap on what we need to grow up strong and healthy. Ask the children what will happen to their bodies next. Ask them to think about the children in Year 2/ Primary 3: *How are they different from you? Can they do anything that you can't do?* Talk about losing early teeth ('milk teeth') and getting taller: *Do we all do that?* Talk about brothers and sisters who are even older than Year 2/Primary 3 children: *How are they different? How have they changed?*

OUTCOME

● Can describe how they have grown from babyhood.

LESSON 9

OBJECTIVE

● To know that there are different stages in the human life cycle.

RESOURCES

Main teaching activity: Photocopiable page 30, enlarged to A3 size.
Group activities: 1. Photocopiable page 31, scissors, adhesive, colouring materials, blank paper. **2.** Props for role-play, such as a walking stick, spectacles, hats, a feeding bottle, a feeding cup, a rattle, a shopping basket, a skipping rope, a card book, a picture book, a novel and so on.

PREPARATION

If possible, ask a co-operative parent with a small baby and an older person (perhaps a grandparent) to visit. If you are able to invite adults in, ask them to bring photographs of themselves as children.
  If you wish, you could prepare two or three sets of sequencing cards from page 31 by photocopying them onto stiff card and laminating them for durability. They could be used to play 'Snap'-type games.

BACKGROUND

For most young children, anyone over 20 is ancient: they cannot really imagine that they will ever be that old.

Different people develop and age at different rates. Our body shape changes during puberty, and secondary sexual characteristics appear. The texture of hair and skin may change. The change in pitch of a boy's voice is very noticeable, but a girl's voice will also change. Our roles may change from being cared for to caring. We do not continue to grow in height after our early adult height has been achieved, but we do continue to change. As we get older still, our hair colour may change (though this is often disguised); men may lose their hair. Our movements slow down as our bodies lose their suppleness, and the roles of caring and cared-for person may once more be reversed. Some children may have experienced the death of a family member, and this may be an opportunity to talk sensitively about death. Care should be taken, as some children get very worried about death and think, for example, that if it has happened to Granny, it might happen just as soon to Mummy.

INTRODUCTION

Look at a picture of an extended family and identify the different members: Mum, Dad, Grandad, Grandma, sons, daughters and so on.

MAIN TEACHING ACTIVITY

Ask the class how they know that the people in the picture on photocopiable page 30 are different ages. Who do they think is the youngest and who is the oldest? Ask the children how old they think the different people might be. Can they guess what the relationships between the people might be?

Introduce the visitors (if you have them). Allow the children to ask them questions about some of the things that they can no longer do as well as they used to – for example, run up the stairs, thread a needle or read without spectacles. Can they hear as well as they used to? Are their joints as supple as they used to be? Is there anything they do better? For example, they are taller and can reach higher objects than when they were children.

Compare the different ages of the people in the picture. *What are the differences?* The baby is smaller and moves differently from the grown-ups. It needs looking after. The parents are bigger, can look after the baby and can talk. The father grows hair on his chin and talks in a deep voice. The mother has breasts so that she can feed the baby. The grown-ups can do things for themselves. Some people always wear spectacles to help them see better; nearly all old people need them, at least for reading. Old people may not hear very well, and they may have difficulty moving. Their faces may show more lines and wrinkles. They may not have all their teeth. Some very old people may need to be looked after because they can no longer look after themselves.

GROUP ACTIVITIES

1. Give each child a copy of photocopiable page 31 or a set of sequencing cards (see Preparation). The children can cut out and sequence the pictures, then paste them into a book or onto paper. They could also play 'Snap' with the cards.
2. Encourage the children to take part in structured role-play, acting as different generations within a family group.

DIFFERENTIATION

1. Less able children could have fewer pictures to sequence, and may need help with cutting out. Some may get on better with a set of prepared cards.
2. All the children should be able to take part in the role-play. Some will be able to demonstrate more subtle changes or differences between the ages and stages within a given role.

ASSESSMENT

Note which children know the stages in the human life cycle – and in particular, order the pictures correctly.

PLENARY

Talk about the way in which people grow up, grow old and eventually die. Discuss the fact that our bodies change as we grow up and continue to change as we age, and that this is quite natural. Ask the children to describe how they think they will change as they grow. Emphasise that people may change in different ways and at different rates.

OUTCOMES

● Know about the different stages in a human life.
● Can describe some of the changes.

LESSON 10

OBJECTIVES

● To know that food and water are needed for animals, including humans, to stay alive.
● To carry out a simple survey.

RESOURCES

Introduction: A selection of pictures of foods, food packets and food wrappers.
Main teaching activity: Pictures of well-nourished and malnourished children; a large sheet of paper (or board). Many aid organisations produce useful teaching packs containing information and photographs.
Group activities: 1. Squared paper for graphs. **2.** Paper plates, a variety of materials for collage or modelling (for example: tissue paper to roll into peas, sugar paper to make lettuce or cabbage leaves, foam sheeting to cut into chips, red and brown paint for tomato ketchup and brown sauce, felt for meat slices, string for spaghetti).

Vocabulary

favourite, graph, fruit, vegetable, food, life, living, essential, death, malnourished, starvation, famine, drought, hunger, thirst

BACKGROUND

It is difficult to demonstrate to children that we need food and drink to stay alive, since a 'fair test' would logically mean feeding one group a wholesome, nutritious diet and starving another group until they became very ill or died. However, most children will have seen pictures on television of children involved in wars or natural disasters who are starving, and many aid organisations produce information packs dealing with food or water shortages. Take care not to reinforce the stereotypical view that all starving children come from Africa or India.

Growth requires good nutrition, and a balanced diet is needed to maintain good health. There are no 'bad' foods, just some that we should eat or drink in moderation. Children need to know that they need to drink in order to replace fluids lost through excretion, and that they should drink lots of water and not just sweet drinks. Some children may become distressed if certain foods are labelled as 'bad' or 'not to be eaten', since these may be the foods they are given. Not all children of this age have a choice about what they eat. Conduct any discussion sensitively – for example, some children may come to school without breakfast; some may only have one meal a day; and some may feed themselves with whatever they can find in the house. Others may eat far too much or live on sweets, crisps and fizzy pop. It is important that children learn the need for a balanced diet, but it is equally important not to make very young children feel guilty about what they eat or do not eat.

INTRODUCTION

With the whole class, look at the pictures of foods and the packets and wrappers. Name some familiar items. Are there any foods the children don't recognise?

MAIN TEACHING ACTIVITY

Ask the children what they like to eat. *What is your favourite meal? Why? What is your favourite drink? Do you know any living thing that doesn't eat or drink?* Explain that plants make their own food, but still need water. This provides an opportunity to think about things that are living and non-living (see Unit 2, Lesson 1 on page 36). Ask whether anyone in the class has a pet. *How do you care for your pet? What would happen if it were not fed and given water to drink?* Discuss the children's ideas about why we need to eat and drink. *What do you think might happen to us if we had no food or drink?* Look at the pictures and compare the malnourished people with those who look well-fed. *What has happened to those who have not had enough to eat?*

Ask the children whether they have ever felt really hungry. *What does it feel like?* Explain the difference between just feeling hungry and real starvation: that some people in situations of famine may have nothing to eat for days on end, and may die from lack of food.

When the children are hungry, what do they like to eat best? Use the board (or a very large sheet of paper) to create a tally chart. Ask each child for one food that they like to eat when they are hungry, and mark the chart accordingly. If you wish, you could restrict the choice of foods to one category (such as breakfast cereals).

GROUP ACTIVITIES

1. Working in groups of two or three, the children can use the survey data collected in the tally chart to make a block graph of favourite foods.
2. Using the materials provided, individuals can model the various components of their favourite meal and stick them onto a paper plate.

DIFFERENTIATION

1. Less able children could make the graph using the data for just the five or six most popular foods.
2. Some children could work independently to select materials for a model meal, while others will need help.

ASSESSMENT

Can the children say (in simple terms) why we need food and water to stay alive? Check the children's block graphs to see whether they have been able to transfer the information from the tally chart of favourite foods.

PLENARY

Review the fact that all animals need to eat and drink to stay alive. Discuss the need to eat sensibly in order to grow and stay healthy. It may be appropriate to talk about children who do not have enough to eat, or who do not have access to clean drinking water. Beware of giving the impression that this only happens in 'Third World' countries: there are many families in the Western world who live in less than adequate conditions.

OUTCOMES

- Know that animals need to eat and drink to stay alive.
- Can undertake a simple survey. Can construct a block graph.

LINKS

Unit 2, Lesson 1: characteristics of living things.

LESSON 11

Objective	• To compare data from two classes.
Resources	Tally charts, clipboards, co-operation of a second class.
Main activity	Discuss the data that the children are going to collect, eg favourite drinks or foods. Different groups could collect different data. The children should collect data from their own class and another class using tally charts, then construct two block graphs.
Differentiation	The children should work in mixed-ability groups in order to help each other collect the data and construct the graphs.
Assessment	From the children's work, note those who have been able to make a tally chart and transfer the data to a block graph.
Plenary	Ask the children to interpret the data gathered from another class and compare it with the data collected in their own class.
Outcome	• Can compare data from two different graphs.

LESSON 12

OBJECTIVES

● To assess whether the children can name parts of the human body, and identify the organs associated with the five senses.
● To assess the children's ability to name some of the ways in which we move.

RESOURCES

Activity 1: Photocopiable pages 32 and 33, pencils, colouring materials.

INTRODUCTION

You may wish to start the assessment lesson in a fun way by singing 'Heads, shoulders, knees and toes', 'Put your finger on your nose' or another familiar song about body parts.

ASSESSMENT ACTIVITY 1

This activity may be done with the whole class, or with groups over a period of time. In the latter case, organising the children into ability groups will give you the opportunity to focus on those children who need extra help with reading. Give each child a copy of photocopiable page 32. Read through the words with the children, asking them to put their finger on each word as you read it out. Ask them to draw a line matching each word to the appropriate part of the body.

Answers

Senses: see – eye; hear – ear; smell – nose; taste – mouth; feel – skin (some children may draw a line to a hand, while others may draw it to any exposed area of skin). Body part labels: check that the label lines are reasonably close to the part being identified, particularly less obvious parts such as the elbow, knee or shoulder.

Looking for levels

Most children should be able to label ten of the body parts and four of the sense organs correctly. More able children may get all the answers right. Less able children may only label the more obvious parts, such as the head, arm, leg, hand and foot; they may only identify one or two sense organs.

ASSESSMENT ACTIVITY 2

Write the following movement words on the board: walk, run, hop, skip, jump, crawl, roll, bend, stretch, twirl. Give each child a copy of page 33. Borrow a child (who can skip) from another class. Read through the words on the board with the children. Explain that as they see each movement, they should write its name in the spaces on the sheet – starting with 1 and going down to 10. Whisper the name of a movement from the list to the borrowed child and ask him or her to demonstrate that movement to the class. Repeat until all the movements have been carried out. Be careful to say the movements in a different order from that on the board, but remember which order you said them in.

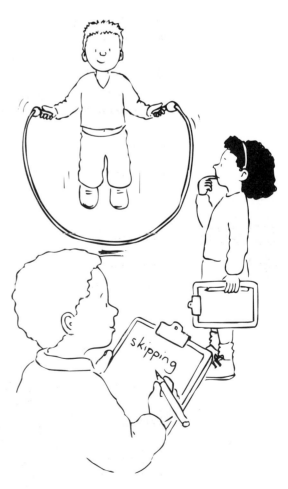

Answers

The children should have written the names of the movements in the appropriate order.

Looking for levels

Most children will be able to identify the more common movements such as walk, run, hop, skip, jump and crawl. More able children will know all the movements. Less able children may have difficulty with all but the most familiar (such as walk, run and jump).

Body parts

Choose the correct word to write in each label box.

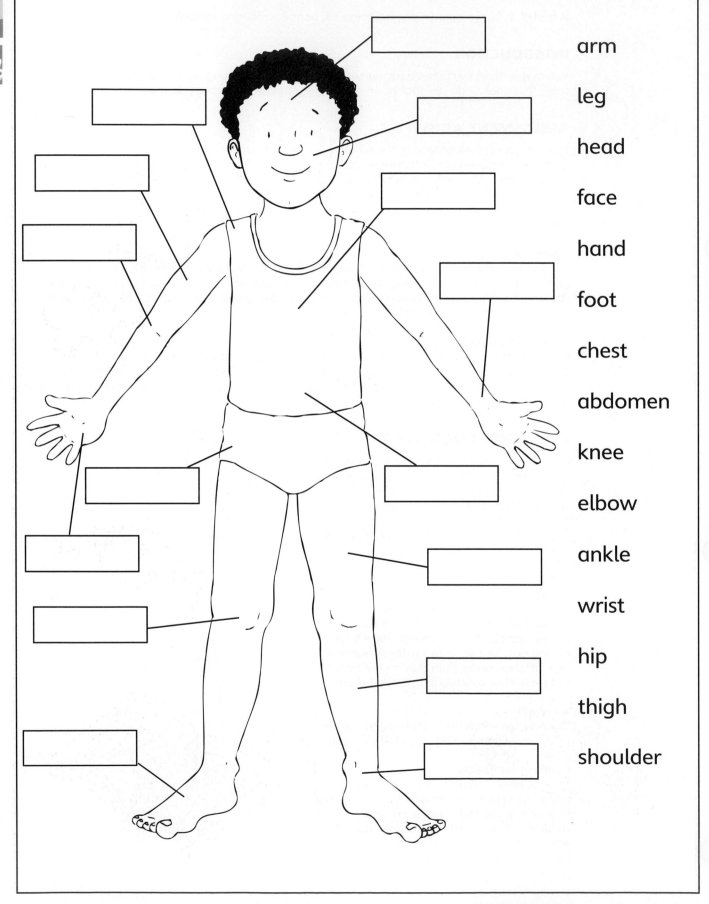

arm

leg

head

face

hand

foot

chest

abdomen

knee

elbow

ankle

wrist

hip

thigh

shoulder

The senses

Draw a line to match each thing to the sense or senses you would use for it.

taste

smell

touch

sight

hearing

Joints

Cut out the pieces, then join them together with paper fasteners to make a jointed figure.

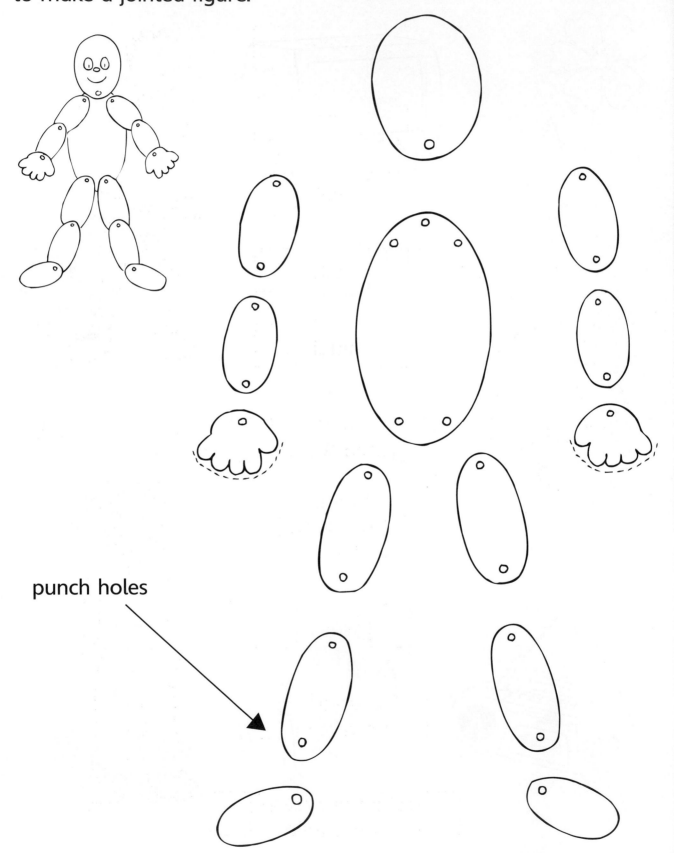

punch holes

What can they do?

✔ or ✗ what each person does.

☐ crawl ☐

☐ cry ☐

☐ walk ☐

☐ talk ☐

☐ laugh ☐

☐ feed themselves ☐

☐ eat using teeth ☐

☐ wave ☐

☐ wear a nappy ☐

☐ take themselves to the toilet ☐

The family

Name

How we grow

teenager

toddler

old person

older adult

young adult

school child

baby

Cut out these cards and arrange them in the right sequence.

Name

Me and my body

Draw a line to the part of the body with which we:

see

hear

smell

taste

feel

Draw a line to match each name to the body part:

shoulder

abdomen

leg

elbow

fingers

foot

head

hand

toes

arm

neck

chest

knee

Me and my body

1	
2	
3	
4	
5	
6	
7	
8	
9	
10	

Growing and caring

ORGANISATION (16 LESSONS)

		OBJECTIVES	MAIN ACTIVITY	GROUP ACTIVITIES	PLENARY	OUTCOMES
LESSON	1	● To know how to distinguish between a living thing, something no longer living and something that has never been alive. ● To know that living things have certain requirements.	Look at various items to compare the features of living things, no longer living things and things that have never been alive.	Sort pictures of living and non-living things. Make an observational drawing of a chosen object, living or non-living.	Review the Group activity work.	● Can distinguish between a living thing, something no longer living and something that has never been alive. ● Know that living things need food and water.
LESSON	2	● To recognise and name some common animals.	Look at pictures of of animals. Go for an animal observation walk.	Draw pictures of the animals seen on the walk. Make a model animal.	Talk about what animals were found and where. What conditions do they require?	● Can recognise and name some common animals.
LESSON	3	● To recognise and name the main external parts of the bodies of animals.	Look at animal pictures and identify different features: wings, fins, beaks, shells, feelers etc.		Talk about similarities and differences between animals, and how they are adapted to where and how they live.	● Can name some external parts of animals such as wing, fin, tail, beak and feelers.
LESSON	4	● To know that animals can move and feed in different ways from humans.	Watch animals moving and feeding, live and on video. Notice how they swim, fly, run etc. Compare different ways of feeding.		Discuss which animals run, fly, crawl etc. Discuss which animals eat plants, insects, meat etc.	● Can describe how some animals move and feed.
LESSON	5	● To know that animals produce offspring and these offspring grow into adults. ● To match adult animals with their offspring.	Match pictures or models of young animals to adults. Name adult and infant forms of some animals.	Sort and match baby and adult animals in a model farmyard or zoo. Match pictures of adult and baby animals.	Discuss adult animals that have different male and female names. Discuss young animals that are very unlike their adult form (eg tadpoles).	● Know that animals produce offspring and that these offspring grow into adults. ● Can match adult animals with their offspring. ● Know the name of both the adult and infant forms of some common animals.
LESSON	6	● To know that plants have roots, stems, leaves and flowers.	Look closely at some flowering plants, both in and out of their pots.	Draw and label a picture of a plant. Make a model plant.	Label a large plant picture. Discuss the functions of plant parts.	● Know that flowering plants have roots, stems, leaves and flowers.
LESSON	7	● To recognise and name some common plants.	Go for a walk to observe different plants in the local environment.		Review the children's observations; compare plants seen.	● Can recognise and name some common plants.
LESSON	8	● To know that most plants grow from seeds.	Look at and sort seeds. Sow seeds in a garden or in pots; follow up by observing growth.	Grow cress seeds or mung beans to observe germination. Make a seed collage.	Recall what happened when they planted their seeds and the sequence of events.	● Can describe how a seed germinates and grows into a plant. ● Know that different plants come from different types of seed.

ORGANISATION (16 LESSONS)

	OBJECTIVES	MAIN ACTIVITY	GROUP ACTIVITIES	PLENARY	OUTCOMES
LESSON 9	● To observe the changes in a growing plant. ● To make simple measurements. ● To take information from a chart.	Observe, measure and 'train' the growth of peas or beans. Record growth on a chart.	Keep a diary of the plant's growth. Make a class book about the plant's growth.	After plant growth, mark dates on a calendar; draw a timeline; discuss how the plant grew and changed.	● Can describe the growth of a plant. ● Can make simple measurements. ● Can take information from a chart.
LESSON 10	● To know that roots change as they grow. ● To know that different plants can have different types of roots.	Plant bean seeds in jars of gravel or pebbles. Observe and record the changes. Look at the roots of some common plants.	Cut open and examine some root vegetables. Make a 3-D frieze of trees with roots.	Examine the roots and shoot of a bean.	● Can describe how the roots of a plant grow. ● Know that different plants may have different root systems.
LESSON 11	● To know that green plants need light to grow. ● To carry out a simple investigation.	Observe the changes in a plant kept in the dark, compared with one kept in the light.	Make an observational drawing of the plant kept in the dark.	Consider the arrangement and function of leaves in a healthy plant.	● Know that light is necessary for green plants to grow healthily. ● Can carry out a simple investigation with help.
LESSON 12	● To know that plants need water to survive.	Investigate what happens to a plant deprived of water.	Draw a picture of what the plant might look like after more time without water. Use reference materials to find out about plants that grow in deserts.	Discuss why plants need water to survive. What happened to the plant deprived of water?	● Know that a plant needs water to survive.
LESSON 13	● To know that plants provide a range of foods. ● To be able to match some foods to their plant of origin.	Relate various foods often eaten by children to the plants from which they come.	Draw a chart of the foods, matched to the original plants. Devise a menu for a meal consisting of foods made from plants.	Discuss the importance of plants in the diet of humans and other animals.	● Know that plants provide a range of foods. ● Can match some foods to their plant of origin.
LESSON 14	● To know that some foods are prepared directly from plants. ● To know that there is a wide variety of fruits.	Sort a collection of fruits. Make a fruit salad.		Discuss how plant foods may be eaten raw, processed or cooked.	● Know that some foods are prepared directly from plants. ● Know that there is a wide variety of fruits. ● Be able to handle knives safely.
LESSON 15	● To know that some foods are processed by humans, and some are taken directly from the plant.	Discuss the contents of a cress sandwich, their origin and how they have been changed. Make and enjoy!		Consider other plant foods used in sandwiches, and how they have been changed.	● Know that some foods that are made from plants have been processed and changed by humans, and some are taken directly from the plant.

	OBJECTIVES	ACTIVITY 1		ACTIVITY 2	
ASSESSMENT 16	● To recognise and name some common animals. ● To know that plants have roots, stems, leaves and flowers.	Match labels to pictures of some familiar animals.		Draw a plant and label the flower, stem, leaf and root.	

LESSON 1

OBJECTIVES

● To know how to distinguish a living thing from a non-living thing.
● To know that living things have certain requirements.

RESOURCES

Main teaching activity: A collection of living and non-living things (stones, buttons, fridge magnets; a living fish, mouse or gerbil; a snail, a woodlouse, a collection of plants in pots, a wooden spoon, a dried flower, cornflakes).
Group activities: 1. Photocopiable page 56 (or magazines with pictures of living and non-living things), A3-sized paper, scissors, adhesive. **2.** Art paper, drawing materials.

Vocabulary

dead, alive, move, grow breathe, feed eat, drink, food water, feel, see, hear

BACKGROUND

There are seven basic requirements for life: respiration, reproduction, excretion, movement, nutrition, sensitivity and growth. Children do not need to know all of these at this stage; they might, for example, use the word 'breathing' for respiration and 'eating and drinking' for nutrition. They may find these requirements easy to recognise in animals, but not so easy when it comes to plants. Allow them to take responsibility for caring for plants or animals in the school. Having an animal in the classroom permanently is not something that many teachers are willing to do. It takes a great deal of commitment, and finding someone to look after creatures at weekends and in the holidays is not always easy. Unless you are really committed, it is better to borrow animals for a day or two, so that the children have a chance to observe, discuss and look after them without the difficulties of looking after them full-time. Children must be made aware, from the beginning, that all living things should be treated with respect. Many adults do not set a good example in this respect, showing aversion to creatures such as spiders and wasps, often killing them for no good reason. Try not to pass on your particular aversions – remember, one person's feared animal is another person's best friend!

Beware of reinforcing misconceptions when talking about plants. We say that we are 'feeding' a plant when we give it a dose of fertiliser, but in fact we are only providing trace minerals that help it to make its own food by the process of photosynthesis. Plants do not 'move' in the sense of travelling, but many will grow quickly towards a light source; there are time-lapse videos that show this very well. Plants, like animals, take in oxygen and give out carbon dioxide in the process of respiration – but they also take in carbon dioxide and give out oxygen in the process of photosynthesis (during the hours of daylight). They reproduce by producing seeds or spores, which do their 'travelling' for them.

INTRODUCTION

Look closely at the things collected. Add a child to the collection. Why do the children think some of these things are alive?

MAIN TEACHING ACTIVITY

Talk to the children about how we might know whether something is alive or not. Encourage the children to volunteer their ideas. This is a good way of finding out the level of their understanding and whether they have any misconceptions. Ask them what we need to do to keep animals and plants alive and healthy. Remind them that humans are animals too.

Ask the children to sort the things that are living from those that are not. Choose one correct thing from each set, such as a fish and a stone. Compare the two things. Look closely at the living thing. *What does it do?* Encourage the children to describe such processes as moving, breathing, drinking and feeding. *Do all animals do these things?* Think of a different animal and check that it does the same things. Humans are animals too. *Do they do all these things? What would happen to animals if they were not able to feed and drink?* Now look at the stone. *Is it alive? Why not? How is it different from the living thing you have just looked at? Can it move? What does it eat? Does it have babies?*

Next, look closely at a plant. *Is it alive? What does it need to keep it alive and healthy?* (Light, water and air.) *What would happen if it had no water?*

Look at all the things and check that each one has been sorted into the right set. *Should anything be in a different set?* Pick up the dried flower. *What about this? It is not alive – but has it ever been alive? Can you find anything else in the set that was once alive?* (The cornflakes and the wooden spoon.) Suggest that these go in a different set. Label the three sets 'Living', 'No longer living' and 'Never been alive', and leave them out as part of a class display. The children might add to the display over the next few days. (Remember that borrowed pets must go back fairly soon.)

GROUP ACTIVITIES

1. Ask the children to cut out the pictures from photocopiable page 55 (or choose pictures from old magazines or catalogues), sort them into sets of 'Living', 'No longer living' and 'Never alive', then stick the sets onto appropriately labelled sheets of A3 paper.

2. Ask the children to choose an object from the collection (either living, no longer living or never alive) and draw it very carefully. Use their pictures for a suitable display.

DIFFERENTIATION

These activities are accessible to all the children.

ASSESSMENT

Observe how the children sort the things. Use their work in Group activity 1 to assess their understanding.

PLENARY

Look at some of the work the children have produced from Group activity 1. Ask them to explain why they have sorted the pictures in the way they have. Look at some of the observational drawings and draw the children's attention to any significant details that have been observed (such as whiskers on a mouse or the grain on a piece of wood).

OUTCOMES

● Can distinguish between a living thing, something no longer living and something that has never been alive.
● Know that living things need food and water.

LINKS

Art: observational drawing.
Maths: sorting into sets.

LESSON 2

OBJECTIVE

● To recognise and name some common animals.

RESOURCES

Main teaching activity: Pictures or photographs of animals that the children might recognise, including humans, a dog, a cat, a goldfish, a butterfly and a familiar bird such as an owl or parrot.
Group activities: 1. Appropriate reference books; drawing, collage and painting materials.
2. Modelling materials.

Vocabulary

caring, feeding, animal names as appropriate

BACKGROUND

Many children will not realise that humans are part of the animal kingdom, and that the animal kingdom includes insects, birds, fish and so on as well as mammals. Each type of creature is adapted to live and feed in a particular way, and children at this age can begin to think about the more obvious differences between species and how they are adapted to their habitats. For example: fish have fins to help them swim in water; birds have wings so that they can fly and various types of beaks to get seeds or nectar from plants, catch insects and so on; ducks' feathers are waterproof so that the duck does not become waterlogged and sink.

PREPARATION

If possible, a few days before the lesson place a few half grapefruit shells under a hedge or in a garden area to attract snails and slugs. A piece of tree trunk in a shady place will attract woodlice and spiders, but this will need to have been there for some weeks for best results. Some small creatures such as snails, spiders or woodlice can be kept in a vivarium for a few days and then returned to where they came from.

The ASE booklet *Be Safe!* gives a comprehensive list of animals that are suitable for the classroom, together with advice on how to care for them. However, unless you are fully committed to caring for an animal over a long period, don't try! (See notes on caring for animals, page 38.) A goldfish is easy to look after and will provide interest. Be aware that you may have children in the class who are allergic to fur and feathers. There may also be a school policy about keeping animals in the classroom, which you will need to consult.

INTRODUCTION

Look at some pictures of animals (see Resources). How many can the children name? How many of these animals have they actually seen? Many children may recognise a giraffe or elephant, but never have seen one; they may have no real idea of the size of the creature.

MAIN TEACHING ACTIVITY

Ask which of the animals we might find in the locality. *What else might we find there?* Divide the children into small groups, then go outside and look for animals (especially any you have elicited – see Preparation). Look for birds in trees or on rooftops. If you have a bird-table, it may be better to observe it from a suitable window: it is unlikely that you will get any visitors while the children are in the vicinity, though the children should be encouraged to sit or stand quietly to make their observations. The children can look under stones or logs, or under window-ledges, for small creatures. If there are flowers, the children may see butterflies or bees. Can they see any cats or dogs in the street? Make a list of all the animals found.

GROUP ACTIVITIES

1. Draw pictures of the animals seen on the walk. Use the pictures to make a class frieze showing where the various animals were found: birds in trees and on roofs, snails under stones and in grass, a cat on the wall and so on.
2. Make a model animal. For example, use clay to make models of dogs and cats. Each child can cut out two fish shapes from thick paper and staple them together, leaving a small gap so that the fish can be stuffed with crumpled newspaper, and decorate the fish with silver paper scales. The group can then put together a fish mobile to hang from the ceiling.

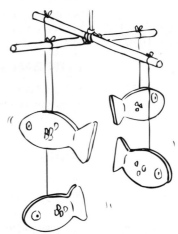

DIFFERENTIATION

1. More able children could add a sentence to their pictures. Some children may be able to find out more information about a particular animal using books, CD-ROMs and so on.
2. All the children should be able to take part in this activity.

ASSESSMENT

Ask the children to name some of the animals they found on their walk. Can they describe any of them?

PLENARY

Talk about the variety of different animals found. *Where were they found? How were they different?* Talk about how some animals are only found in certain places – for example, woodlice prefer dark, damp places.

OUTCOME

● Can recognise and name some common animals.

LINKS

Unit 3, Lessons 10, 11 and 12: more opportunities to feed and observe creatures in the local environment.

LESSON 3

Objective	● To recognise and name the main external parts of the bodies of animals.
Resources	An animal (if available); pictures of animals or a collection of model animals (including fish, insects and birds).
Main activity	Look at an animal (if possible), then at models or pictures of various animals, and ask the children to name parts. Ask them what parts various animals have in common with humans (such as ears, eyes or legs), and how some animals differ from humans (number of legs, fins rather than arms and legs, wings instead of arms etc). *What other parts do some animals have?* (Feelers, shells, beaks, tails etc.)
Differentiation	Some children may only be able to identify the more obvious features. More able children could use reference books or CD-ROMs to find out, for example, whether birds have ears or worms have eyes.
Assessment	Note which children are able to name the parts of animals in the Main activity.
Plenary	Talk about how all animals are basically the same: they all grow, feed etc. Talk about how different animals are adapted to their way of life and habitat (for example, fish have fins for moving through the water; birds have wings for flying through the air).
Outcome	● Can name some external parts of animals such as wing, fin, tail, beak and feelers.

LESSON 4

Objective	● To know that animals can move and feed in different ways from humans.
Resources	Snails, worms or fish in a tank; videos of animals moving and feeding; a bird- table.
Main activity	Watch videos of animals moving. *How do animals without legs move?* Watch worms, fish or snails in a tank. In a PE session, ask the children to move smoothly like a snail; quickly like a spider; with a slow, slinky movement like a cat stalking, and so on. Watch snails (live or on video) feeding on lettuce leaves, and compare with humans feeding. *Do we sometimes eat the same things? Do animals cook their food? How do animals put food in their mouths?* Elephants use their trunks, but monkeys and humans use their hands. *Why do some animals have really big teeth?*
Differentiation	All children should be able to take part in this activity.
Assessment	During the plenary session, ask children to describe how particular animals move and feed.
Plenary	Discuss different movements made by animals. Talk about animals that run, hop, skip, jump, fly, swim and crawl. Discuss different ways that animals feed on plants, insects, fish etc.
Outcome	● Can describe how some animals move and feed.

LESSON 5

OBJECTIVES

● To know that animals produce offspring and these offspring grow into adults.
● To match adult animals with their offspring.

RESOURCES

Main teaching activity: Models of adult and baby animals. Very good, reasonably priced models are now available. They can be used for a range of sorting and naming activities, and will more than repay the investment. You will also need pictures of adult and baby animals, books about animals, videos of animals with babies. The pictures should include a human adult and baby, horse and foal, cow and calf, hens and chicks and so on, as well as cases where the babies are very different from the adult (caterpillar and butterfly, tadpole and frog).
Group activities: 1. Model animals, a model farmyard or zoo (or a layout of one on a large sheet of paper). **2.** Photocopiable page 56, scissors, adhesive.

PREPARATION

It may be possible to invite someone with a baby animal, such as a lamb, to make a visit to the classroom.

Vocabulary
calf, cow, chick, hen, cockerel, foal, horse, duckling, duck cub, tiger, pup, seal

BACKGROUND

Although all creatures have young, they don't always look like the adult. Not all baby animals are cared for by their parent or parents. Some, such as snakes, most fish, crocodiles and spiders, are independent at birth and fend for themselves immediately (though crocodiles do sometimes carry their newly hatched young in their jaws from their nest in the sand to the water). Most warm-blooded creatures are cared for by at least one parent, and in many cases by both parents. All creatures need to be treated with care and sensitivity, and children should be made aware of this from the beginning. Hatching chicks in the classroom is fascinating for the children, and a good lesson in caring for living things. It is possible to keep them until they begin to fledge, so that the children can see the change from fluffy yellow ball to adult cockerel or hen. An incubator can sometimes be borrowed from a secondary school or from a Local Education Authority loan service. Alternatively, several schools in a cluster could combine to buy one. It is vital, though, that arrangements are made for the chicks to be returned to a suitable environment when they are no longer needed in the classroom.

INTRODUCTION

Remind the children about when they were babies and how they have grown up. Talk briefly about how they have changed.

MAIN TEACHING ACTIVITY

Discuss the fact that all animals have babies. Draw the children's attention to the fact that the babies often have different names from their parents – for example, tadpole and frog. Ask them whether they know the names of some animals and their babies (for example, sheep and lamb, duck and duckling). Look at pictures or models of adult animals and ask the children to identify them. Look at a corresponding set of baby animals. Ask the children to match each baby to the appropriate adult. Can they give the babies their proper names? Introduce pictures of a frog and a butterfly. Do any of the children know what their babies are called and what they look like? Ask them to match pictures of a tadpole and a caterpillar to the correct parents.

GROUP ACTIVITIES

1. The children sort baby animals and match them to their parents, using models in a model farmyard or zoo. Encourage them to label both the adult and the baby as they sort, especially where the baby animal has a very different name from the adult (as in the horse and foal or the sheep and lamb).
2. Give each child a copy of photocopiable page 56. Ask the children to cut out the pictures of the baby animals and stick each one onto the picture next to its parent.

DIFFERENTIATION

1. More able children may be able to do some research in books to find the names of more unusual animal babies and discover that some of the adults have male and female names (such as 'hen' and 'cockerel' or 'ewe' and 'ram'. They may be able to say which animals have living babies (mostly mammals) and which lay eggs. Some children may be able to label their work independently; others may need to have labels given to them.
2. All children can take part in this activity, but some may need help with cutting out.

ASSESSMENT

Observe how the children have sorted the model animals. Use the photocopiable sheet to assess their understanding.

PLENARY

Discuss what the children have done. Show the animal pictures and models again, and ask the children to match adults and babies. Can they name the parents and their babies, including parents that have different male and female names? Some children could select the correct labels to put with the various family groups (for example, 'cow', 'bull', 'calf'). Talk about the fact that adults and babies often don't look alike (for example, a baby chick and a mother hen). Ask the children whether they can name any animals whose babies are very different from their parents (for example, a tadpole and a frog). *Do human babies look like grown-ups? How are they the same? How are they different?* Finish the session by singing 'Old MacDonald Had a Farm', with the children suggesting the names of baby animals and then the parents to match them in each successive verse.

LESSON 8

OBJECTIVE

● To know that most plants grow from seeds.

RESOURCES

Main teaching activity: Plant pots, compost, plant labels (lolly sticks or pieces cut from yoghurt pots), a watering can or jug, white paper plates, newspaper or plastic sheets, a camera (optional), photocopiable page 58 (if required); a variety of seeds including a coconut, conkers, acorns, beans, and seeds for onion, French marigold, mustard, cress and radish. Beware: some of the most impressive seeds can be very poisonous! The ASE booklet *Be Safe!* gives a comprehensive list of seeds that are suitable for use in the classroom and seeds that should be avoided. Children should always be taught that they must never eat any seeds they find in the wild or in gardens.
Group activities: 1. Cress seeds and kitchen towel (or mung beans, blotting paper and a glass jar), saucers, a magnifier. **2.** A selection of seeds of different sizes and colours, such as beans, lentils, dried edible peas, sunflower seeds, popping corn and melon seeds; stiff paper, PVA glue. Seeds such as those mentioned are available from garden centres for growing, but you could try a local health food store or pet shop for larger quantities to use in craft work.
Plenary: A calendar.

BACKGROUND

After the lesson, the growing plants will need to be revisited over a period of time to make observations. Some seeds, such as cress or mung beans, germinate very quickly: you can usually see some results within a few days. Most annuals germinate quite quickly, but will take several weeks before they produce flowers and then seeds. French marigolds will produce seeds before the summer holidays if started off in a warm place in February or March. This will allow the children to see the whole life cycle of a plant, from a growing seed to an adult plant producing seeds. If this is not possible, you could produce 'the one I made earlier' by buying bedding plants (of a similar variety to those sown by the children) from a garden centre, where they will have been forced into growth much earlier than is normal.

> **Vocabulary**
>
> grow, plant, seed, poisonous, germinate, root, shoot

The children will also enjoy collecting acorns, horse chestnuts and citrus seeds. These will all germinate, but will take a longer time to do so than the seeds of an annual plant. Acorns and conkers usually need to spend the winter outside, where they are exposed to frost, before they can germinate in the next spring.

In order to avoid reinforcing misconceptions, it is important to remember that before they can grow, seeds need to germinate. This is the process whereby the seed produces its first shoot (plumule) and root (radicle), using its stored food reserves. We all talk about seeds 'growing'; but to be correct, we should talk about seeds germinating and plants growing. The plant does not really begin to grow until it has produced its first green leaf and begun to photosynthesise. Most plants need moisture and warmth to germinate and water, warmth and light to grow successfully. Soil is not a requirement for growth. For example, many tomato crops are now grown hydroponically (with their roots suspended in a liquid nutrient). Think of all the hyacinths grown in water pots on classroom window sills, and the cress seeds germinated on cotton wool or blotting paper.

A classroom window sill may not be the best place to keep any plant. A botanist friend of ours believes it to be one of the harshest habitats in the world: the plants cook in full sunlight during the day, then freeze when the heating goes off at night. All plants need some light, but most do not require full sunlight.

INTRODUCTION

Look at some of the seeds you have collected. *Where do acorns and conkers (horse chestnuts) come from?* Do the children appreciate that a coconut is actually a seed from a palm tree? Look at some much smaller seeds, such as cress or onion seeds.

MAIN TEACHING ACTIVITY

Put a variety of seeds on white paper plates, so that they can be seen easily. Provide a plate for each group. Make sure the children understand that they must not attempt to eat any of the seeds. Discuss the different types of seeds. *How do we know what the different seeds will grow into?* Look at the pictures on the seed packets. *Do we believe that is what the seeds will grow into? How could we find out?* Ask the children to suggest how the seeds could be planted.

If you have a garden area, some seeds could be sown directly into the ground. Different groups of children could choose a different variety to sow and care for, write labels and mark where the seeds are. Remind them to 'water in' the seeds on planting. Before they start handling soil or compost, make sure that any cuts the children may have are covered. If you are working indoors, make sure that the tables are well covered with newspaper or plastic sheets. Encourage the children to fill the plant pots with compost and put a small number of seeds in each pot, then water them in and make sure that each pot is labelled with the seed type and date of sowing. They can put the pots in a safe but accessible place and wait, checking daily for the appearance of any shoots.

The children could use photocopiable page 58 to keep a simple record of the progress their plants make. If you have access to a camera, the growth of the plants could be recorded in a series of photographs for a class book or display.

GROUP ACTIVITIES

1. The children put some cress seeds on a damp kitchen towel (or some mung beans on damp blotting paper lining a glass jar), then watch them closely over the next few days. They can use a magnifier to watch for the first signs of the root and shoot. Tell them that when they appear, the seeds have 'germinated': taken the first step towards becoming plants.
2. The children use lots of different seeds to create a group collage: either a picture (such as a big flower) or a pattern. They should draw their picture or pattern first, then choose an appropriate type of seed to fill in each area. Do not provide pieces of paper that are too large, or the children will need tons of seeds!

DIFFERENTIATION

1. This activity should be accessible to all of the children. More able children could make an independent pictorial record; others could join in a group or class record of how the seeds germinate and then begin to grow.
2. All of the children should be able to take part in this activity.

ASSESSMENT

During the plenary session, ask the children to describe what they would do if they wanted to grow, for example, some radishes. How would they plant them and care for them?

PLENARY

Ask the children to recall the sequence of events involved in planting the seeds. Talk about what they think will happen next. *How long do you think you might have to wait before you see anything happening?* Look at a calendar and estimate when you might see the first shoots, and when the flowers might appear. Mark the estimated date; later, mark the actual date. *How accurate was our estimate?*

OUTCOMES

- Can describe how a seed germinates and grows into a plant.
- Know that different plants come from different types of seed.

LINKS

Unit 3, Lesson 16: caring for a growing plant indoors.
Art: collage.

LESSON 9

OBJECTIVES

● To observe the changes in a growing plant.
● To make simple measurements.
● To take information from a chart.

RESOURCES

Main teaching activity: A version of the 'Jack and the Beanstalk' story; a large plant pot or tub, compost, pea or bean seeds, three or four 1.5m canes, a plant pot to cover the tops of canes for safety, garden twine, a camera (optional), newspaper or a plastic sheet.
Group activities: 1. Strips of thick paper or card (about 15cm × 40cm) to make zigzag books, drawing materials. **2.** Paper to make a large class book.
Plenary: A calendar.

Vocabulary

seed, shoot, root climb, germination, pollination

BACKGROUND

Peas or beans are a good choice of seed for this investigation, since they germinate and grow quite quickly and the adult plants are quite tall, allowing the children plenty of opportunities for measuring and recording. Beware: most pea seeds have been treated with fungicide, and children should not be allowed to handle these. If you make a wigwam of canes in a large pot, you can have a competition between three beans to see which gets to the top of the canes first. Since germination can never be guaranteed, plant two beans by each cane; if both germinate, remove the weaker-looking plant to leave one bean per cane. Bean plants will twine themselves around the cane. However, peas will need a little more support for their tendrils to hang on to: either use twiggy branches instead of canes or make a web of string around a wigwam of canes, so that the pea plants can be woven in and out (see diagram). Peas and beans will both grow indoors, but don't do well in hot conditions. They tend to be healthier if you can grow them outside, or at least put them outside during the day. The children need to take great care as they tend the plants, and particularly when they are measuring them, that they don't knock off the tips of the shoots. If this happens, the plant will shoot again from lower down; but this will take time and the measurements will become somewhat confusing. If you grow the plants indoors, you (or the children) will need to act as bees if you want a crop. Use a soft paintbrush to transfer pollen gently from one flower to another. You will need to do this on several occasions to ensure a good set of seeds. If you can grow the plants outside, then nature will take care of itself. Choose an early variety and sow the seeds between mid-March and early April if you intend to get a crop before the summer holidays. Keep the young plants indoors until all danger of frost has gone.

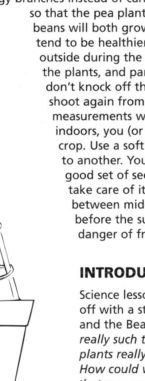

INTRODUCTION

Science lessons are often very effective if started off with a story stimulus. Read the story of 'Jack and the Beanstalk' to the children. *Are there really such things as magic beans? Do bean plants really get that big or grow that quickly? How could we find out?* Have the resources that you are going to use for the activity available, so that the children can begin to make suggestions about what to do.

MAIN TEACHING ACTIVITY

You will need one initial lesson to set up the investigation, with shorter periods each day to chart the progress of the plants.

Spread some newspaper or a plastic sheet on the floor and have the children sitting around it. Choose two or three to fill a large pot or tub with compost and construct a wigwam from three or four canes to support the growing plants. Choose different children to plant two seeds at the base of each cane and water them well. Discuss with the children why they are planting two seeds rather than just one. (One seed may not germinate, so you have a 'spare'.) If both germinate, take the weaker one out. You could then have a little fun by putting a different coloured flag (red, blue, green) at the top of each cane and letting the children predict which bean will reach the top of its cane first. Make a chart with the children's names under the colour they have chosen. (Watch out for sabotage if the race gets close!)

Discuss how you are going to measure the growth of the plants. *What equipment will you need? How are you going to record the measurements? Will you need to make a chart? What else will you need to notice?* For example, if you use beans, the children might count the number of leaves each time they measure the height (peas grow too many leaves after a while). They might also record the date on which they see the first flowers. *Why does a plant have flowers? Why do bees and other insects visit flowers?* Talk about how the flowers need to be pollinated if the tiny eggs inside the plant are to be fertilised and grow into seeds (beans or peas).

In subsequent shorter lessons, watch how the shoots uncurl as they come out of the compost. Note how the leaves are curled at first, and how they unfold and become flatter. Later, note how the bean shoots twine around the canes or how the peas hold on to the sticks with little curly tendrils. Look carefully to see how the new leaves come from the tip of the shoot, while the 'old' leaves at the bottom gradually get bigger. Look for the first flower buds and watch how they open. The children can add entries to their diaries or a class book (see below) when there is something significant to record. Daily records can be kept on a simple chart, and information from this used to update the diaries or class book from time to time.

GROUP ACTIVITIES

1. The children can make a simple zigzag book and use it as a diary to record the growth of the plants. They should make sure all entries are dated. Discuss with them what it will be appropriate to record in their diaries, and how often they are going to check the plants. Every second or third day should be sufficient to note changes, but the plants may need watering more often if they are in a warm environment.

2. Make a class book about the beans or peas, with children contributing drawings, writing, poems, facts they have found out and any photographs taken.

DIFFERENTIATION

1. Organise the children into small mixed-ability groups to take turns to measure the plants. Some children may need help in making their zigzag book.

2. More able children may contribute written records or stories to the class book, while less able children may present their observations or thoughts in a pictorial way.

ASSESSMENT

Use the children's diaries or contributions to the class book to assess their understanding. Ask them to describe how the plants grew.

PLENARY

After the initial lesson, you may wish to recap on what you have done and organise the first groups to make the observations. The final plenary may occur when you harvest the first peas or beans, or at the end of the topic if time runs out. The discussion will vary depending on the maturity of the plants. Look at the records and mark the dates on a calendar to see how long the plants took to grow. Make a timeline to show when the first shoots appeared, the first flowers and so on. Talk about how the shoots changed as they grew, and how the leaves changed in size and number.

OUTCOMES

● Can describe the growth of a plant.
● Can make simple measurements.
● Can take information from a chart.

LINKS

Literacy: writing records and stories.
Maths: measuring, counting.

LESSON 10

OBJECTIVES
- To know that roots change as they grow.
- To know that different plants can have different types of roots.

RESOURCES

Main teaching activity: A clear container, gravel or small pebbles, four or five germinated bean seeds, black paper, an elastic band, water, photocopiable page 59, coloured pencils, saucers. Useful containers can be made from plastic soft drinks bottles: simply cut off the top to the desired height and bind the new rim with sticky tape to cover any sharp edges. For Session 3: some weeds, such as dandelions and groundsel, dug up carefully to show the roots (or small pot plants if you do not have access to weeds); a clear container, water.
Group activities: 1. A collection of root vegetables (carrots, parsnips and so on). **2.** A display board, old (clean) tights, newspaper, paints and brushes, blue and brown sugar paper, textured wallpaper, different shades of green paper, scissors, pastel paints or crayons.
Plenary: Kitchen towel, a ruler, black paper.

PREPARATION

About a week before the lesson, put enough beans for each group to have four or five each on a damp kitchen towel to germinate. For Group activity 2, cover a display board (or other suitable large area) with brown sugar paper at the bottom and blue sugar paper at the top, representing the ground and the sky.

> ### Vocabulary
> root, shoot, seek, absorb

BACKGROUND

Not all plants have similar root systems. Some plants develop a strong main root or tap root that grows deeply into the ground, while others may have many fine roots that spread out just below the surface. A tap root anchors the plant firmly in the ground. Common examples of this type of root are carrots and parsnips. Dandelions also have a long tap root, which explains why they are so difficult to pull up. Roots usually grow downwards, towards water and in the dark. Their job is to absorb water and nutrients from the growing medium, which is usually soil or compost. The water then passes up through the plant and out through pores (stomata) on the underside of the leaf. As well as absorbing nutrients, the roots anchor the plant securely in the ground to prevent it being blown or washed away. They also play a part in helping to prevent soil erosion by holding the soil together and preventing it from being blown or washed away. Evidence shows that where wholesale logging has taken place without the trees being replaced, the soil has quickly been eroded and the land has become barren.

INTRODUCTION

Look at the germinated beans and talk about the roots and shoots that have emerged. *How are the roots different from the shoots?*

MAIN TEACHING ACTIVITY

You will need to revisit this activity over a period of time to observe the changes. Three sessions (to be undertaken by the whole class, working in groups) are suggested below.
Session 1. Talk with the class about what roots do and why they are important. Ask the children for their ideas. Help them to understand that the roots take up water and help to anchor the plant in the soil.

Each group should fill a clear container with gravel or small pebbles, then fill it with water to just below the top of the pebbles. They should place four or five germinated beans on top of the pebbles, round the edge of the jar, making sure that the beans do not get waterlogged (see illustration). They should wrap black paper around the container to keep out the light, fasten it firmly in place with an elastic band, then place it somewhere safe and leave it for a week.
Session 2. The children should remove the black paper from the jar and look carefully at what is happening. *In which direction are the shoots growing? What is happening to the roots? How much have they grown?* They should start

Fill container with pebbles and water.

Wrap in black paper and fasten with elastic bands.

to fill in the record sheet (photocopiable page 59), using a coloured pencil to draw the roots. They should put the black paper back around the container and leave it for a few more days.
Session 3. The children should look at the roots again. *How have they changed now?* They should fill in the changes on the record sheet.

Working with the whole class, dig up some weeds (being careful not to damage the roots). Include a dandelion if possible (but be warned: the roots can go down a surprisingly long way). Gently wash the roots in water to get rid of all the soil or compost, and spread them out on a saucer so that the pattern of growth can be seen. (Alternatively, the roots show up very well if you fill a clear container with water and allow the plant to sit on top.) Gently remove one of the beans from the jar and place it on a saucer. Compare the different root systems. *How are they different? How are they the same? Is there one main root, or are there lots of branches?*

GROUP ACTIVITIES

1. With the group, look at a carrot, a parsnip, and some other root vegetables. They can use a magnifier to see the smaller roots coming from the central tap root. Cut across one tap root, then cut another lengthways. Observe the difference. Ask the children to draw what they see.
2. Make a large 3-D wall display showing views above and below ground (see illustration). In groups, the children can stuff pairs of old brown tights with scrunched-up pages of newspaper, then paint them roughly with streaks of brown, green and grey. Twist the tights together and staple them to the brown sugar paper to look like thickly growing, gnarled and twisted roots. The children can use appropriately painted textured wallpaper to make tree trunks and branches. Staple these loosely to the blue part of the display board, and stuff behind them for a 3-D effect. Ask the children to cut leaves from paper in different shades of green, adding details with pastel paints or crayons. Add these to the picture.

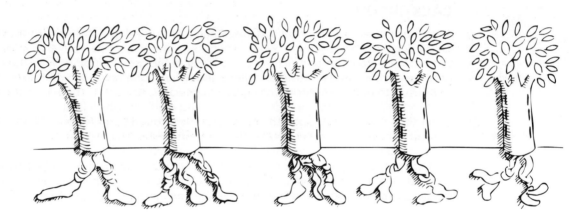

DIFFERENTIATION

1. Some children could make prints of the cut roots to show the different effects of cutting them across and lengthways.
2. All the children can join in this activity.

ASSESSMENT

Ask children to draw a simple plant including the roots. Can they say what roots do? (Absorb water and keep the plant in the ground).

PLENARY

Discuss how the roots of the beans have grown. Take a bean from the jar and gently dry the roots on some kitchen towel. Lay the whole plant on some black paper. *Which is longer, the root or the shoot? Why do roots branch into lots of smaller rootlets?* (So that there is a bigger surface area to absorb water and nutrients.)

OUTCOMES

● Can describe how the roots of a plant grow.
● Know that different plants may have different root systems.

LINKS

Art: making a frieze, 3-D modelling.

LESSON 11

OBJECTIVES
● To know that green plants need light to grow.
● To carry out a simple investigation.

RESOURCES

Main teaching activity: Card for a countdown calendar; a small collection of pot plants; two small plants of a similar type (or two small trays of cress); a dark cupboard or black bin bag.
Group activity: Photocopiable page 60, drawing materials.

PREPARATION

If small trays of cress will be used, sow three of these (one for a spare in case of accidents) about ten days before they are required. Make a 'countdown calendar' (see illustration below), so that the children can tick off the days until they take the plant out of the cupboard or bag.

Vocabulary

light, dark

BACKGROUND

There is often confusion between growing plants and germinating seeds. Seeds do not generally need light to germinate. They are usually in the soil, where it is dark. The initial germination uses the food reserves in the seed. However, green plants need light if they are to grow. They are the only living things that are able to make their own food. They do this through the process of photosynthesis in the leaves. Plant leaves are green because of the presence of chlorophyll, a pigment that traps light energy and so allows photosynthesis to take place. Water is absorbed through the roots; carbon dioxide is absorbed through the leaves. Using these in the presence of light energy, plant cells are able to synthesise sugars, which are then stored as starch.

The by-products of photosynthesis are also important to life on Earth. Large forests are often called 'the lungs of the Earth'. They can absorb vast quantities of carbon dioxide, which is given off by animals and produced by many of our power stations, vehicles and manufacturing processes. As they photosynthesise, plants give off oxygen, which animals need to sustain life. All green plants including Green algae floating near the surface of the world's oceans also carry out this process.

At this stage, children do not need to understand the above information; but it is useful knowledge for you to have in order not to reinforce any misconceptions.

INTRODUCTION

Talk about where plants usually grow: in the garden, in the house, in fields, in forests and so on.

MAIN TEACHING ACTIVITY

You will need two sessions for this activity: one to set up the investigation and another to observe the results. This is a whole-class investigation, but it could be done by groups if you have the space and resources.

Session 1. Look at a collection of healthy green plants in the classroom. Ask the children where the plants are greenest (the leaves). Talk about how healthy the plants are, and recap on the names of the different parts. Ask the children what we need to do to help these plants grow healthily. *We need to water them – but not too much. Where is the best place to put them? Does it make a difference whether they are put in a bright place or a dark corner? Do you think the plants will grow better and keep healthier in the light or the dark? Could we do an experiment to find out? Do you have any ideas about how we could carry out an investigation using the*
classroom plants? One plant could be put in a really dark cupboard that is not opened very often, or put in a black plastic bin bag (make sure it is well labelled to avoid accidents). Ask the children to explain why another plant should be kept out in the classroom. Make sure they understand that they need a plant that is grown in the light to compare with the one in the dark. If the plants are well watered before the experiment, there should be no need to water them again (unless the room is very warm) during the few days that it takes for some

We put the plants in the cupboard on _____

We will take them out on _____

Mon	Tue	Wed	Thur	Fri	Sat	Sun

changes to take place. Decide how long you are going to leave the plant in the cupboard. (A week should be long enough.)

Session 2. On the agreed day, take the 'dark' plant from the cupboard or bag. Compare it with the plant left out in the light. *How are they different? How has the plant kept in the dark changed?* (It will have turned yellow, and may have grown longer and more straggly in the search for light.) *What do you think has caused the change?* Leave the plant in the light for a few days and note how well it recovers. (It should turn green again quite quickly.) Review the list of things that a plant needs in order to grow healthily.

GROUP ACTIVITY

Give each child a copy of photocopiable page 60. Ask the children to draw and colour the plant (or tray of cress) before it is put in the dark. They should use the same sheet to record the changes at the end of the experiment.

DIFFERENTIATION

This activity should be accessible to all the children. Some children may be able to record in more detail than others, and write a sentence or two about how they carried out the investigation.

ASSESSMENT

At the end of the experiment, ask the children to describe what would happen to a plant that was left in the dark (or use their recordings to assess their understanding of how a plant needs light to remain healthy).

PLENARY

Talk about how the absence of light has made a difference. Look closely at the healthy plant, and observe how the leaves are spread out so that they can all receive as much light as possible. Look at some different plants: are their leaves arranged in the same way? Ask whether anyone knows why light is so important for plants. Tell the children that green plants can make their own food, but they need light to help them do this.

OUTCOMES

- Know that light is necessary for green plants to grow healthily.
- Can carry out a simple investigation with help.

LESSON 12

OBJECTIVE

- To know that plants need water to survive.

RESOURCES

Main teaching activity: A flowering pot plant, such as a busy lizzie (*Impatiens*), which reacts quickly to a lack of water; a bowl or tray, a watering can, a camera (if available).
Group activities: 1. Drawing materials, paper. **2.** Simple picture reference books and CD-ROMs with information about plants growing in deserts.

Vocabulary

grow, wilt, revive, crisp, limp, droopy, wither

BACKGROUND

Most plants need a steady supply of water to survive, although many plants are adapted to living in very dry and arid parts of the planet. Plants take water in through the roots, from where it travels up the stems and into the leaves. Special tubes within the stem (called xylem vessels) carry the water up to the leaves, where it is used in the process of photosynthesis. The water also helps to keep the plant cells turgid (firm), keeping the plant upright so that it can make maximum use of the sunlight. Having served its purpose, excess water is excreted through pores (called stomata) on the underside of the leaves: the water evaporates through the pores and more water is automatically drawn up through the xylem vessels (a process called transpiration). If conditions change and the plant becomes short of water, the leaves will droop or wilt in order to preserve water within the plant. A busy lizzie plant will react quite quickly. If you start the experiment fairly early in the day, you may well have a result before home time – especially if you can put the plant on a warm, sunny window sill. The rates of transpiration and photosynthesis are increased in bright conditions, so the plant will lose water at a faster rate.

Most plants revive quite quickly if water becomes available again within a short time, but will die if deprived for long periods. Some plants can survive longer than others. Plants such as succulents and cacti are specially adapted to store water in fleshy stems or leaves. They can withstand the extreme conditions found in deserts (or on classroom window sills!) for long periods of time.

INTRODUCTION

Look at a healthy flowering pot plant such as a busy lizzie (*Impatiens*). Note how the stems are stiff and straight, and how the leaves are crisp and fresh. *Are the flowers standing up from the leaves?* Feel the compost in the pot: it should be damp.

MAIN TEACHING ACTIVITY

Talk with the whole class about the things a plant needs to keep it healthy. Remind the children what they have learned (see Lesson 11) about a plant needing light. Ask them why they think a plant needs water. *What do you think might happen if the plant was left without water?* Suggest that you could carry out an investigation to find out, and ask the children for ideas about how you could do it. This is a simple investigation, and most children should be able to tell you that you simply leave the plant unwatered for a day or two and watch what happens. Discuss where you might leave the plant during this time. Remind the children that they often feel thirsty when they are hot and sweaty. *Do you think plants might be the same? Where would be a hot, bright place to put the plant?* Place the plant in the chosen place, check it every hour or so throughout the day.

Encourage the children to observe what happens as the plant begins to dry out. *How have the leaves changed? Why have they gone floppy and droopy? Are the stems still stiff and upright? How could we revive the plant and make it look crisp and healthy again?* If possible, take photographs of the plant 'before' and 'after'.

Encourage the children to water the plant. The best results are achieved by standing the pot in a bowl of water. *How long does the plant take to revive? Do all the leaves recover?* Sometimes weaker or older leaves will not recover, and will be shed. Busy lizzies are very quick to take up water and revive almost miraculously, as long as they have not wilted too far.

GROUP ACTIVITIES

1. Ask the children each to draw a picture of what they think the plant would look like after some time without water. Remind them to think carefully about how the leaves will look. Will they still be crisp, or will they be limp and droopy? Will some of the flowers drop off?
2. The children can work in small groups, using reference materials to find information about and pictures of plants that grow in deserts and need little water. Each group should report back to the class on what they have found out.

DIFFERENTIATION

1. All children should be able to take part in this activity.
2. Most children will appreciate that water is necessary for plants to live. Some children may need help to access reference books or CD-ROMs. They could work in mixed-ability groups in order to help each other.

ASSESSMENT

Assess the children's understanding from their responses in the Plenary session.

PLENARY

Talk about what happened to the plant when it was deprived of water. Ask the children why they think the leaves hang down on a plant when it is short of water. It is not necessary for children at this stage to know about transpiration or photosynthesis in detail, but they may know that plants wilt in order to try and save water. Talk about what happened when the plant was watered again. Ask them to explain why the leaves perked up. Remember, at this stage we are not looking for accurate scientific explanations but for the children's own ideas.

OUTCOME

● Know that a plant needs water to survive.

LESSON 13

OBJECTIVES
● To know that plants provide a range of foods.
● To be able to match some foods to their plant of origin.

RESOURCES

Main teaching activity: A collection of foods and the plant parts that they are made from. For example: cornflakes or popcorn – a corn cob; a tin of baked beans – dried beans; bread, wheat, cereal or pasta – ears of wheat; crisps or chips – potatoes; a jar of jam or tin of fruit – the corresponding fruit.
Group activities: 1. Photocopiable page 61, writing and drawing materials, hand lenses.
2. Cards, writing and drawing materials.

Vocabulary

food, plant, processed, manufactured, raw, cooked, changed, origin

BACKGROUND

Many young children do not realise that a high proportion of the foods they eat are derived from plants. In fact, many do not know that the carrots, peas and so on that come from the supermarket have grown from plants. It is a good idea, if possible, to take the children somewhere where they can see vegetables growing. If there are allotments in the area, it is worth getting in touch with the local allotment society; it is likely that an allotment holder will be willing for the children to go along and maybe even pick a vegetable or two. If this is not possible, try to buy some vegetables from the organic section of the supermarket, or in the local market, that still have their leaves on and maybe have some earth still clinging to them.

It is possible to grow enough potatoes in a bucket for the class to cook and share. Half-fill a large bucket or pot with compost and plant one potato. Place the bucket in good light and keep it watered. As the shoots appear, add more compost to cover them until the bucket is full. Leave for six to eight weeks. When the potatoes are ready, empty the bucket on to a large plastic sheet and harvest your crop!

INTRODUCTION

Ask the children what they had for breakfast or lunch. Make a list. Can the children say how many of these foods were made from plants (wholly or in part)? *What about a chocolate biscuit, the bread in a sandwich, rice pudding? Do any of you have a piece of fruit in your lunchbox?* Add 'Yes' or 'No' to each food on the list, according to whether there is plant material in it. Ask the children: *Can you name any of the plants? Can you think of any plants or parts of plants that you eat raw? Are these sometimes cooked as well?*

MAIN TEACHING ACTIVITY

Put out the foods collected and ask the children to name them. Discuss when they are eaten, and how often the children eat them. *Do you all eat the foods in this collection? Do you all like them? Which are your favourites?* Talk about the fact that these foods are all made from plants. Now put out the plants. Can the children match each food to the plant that it is made from? Can they think of any other foods made from some of the plants?

GROUP ACTIVITIES

1. Give each child a copy of page 61. Ask the children to draw a chart of some of the foods in the collection, matched to the original plant parts. Remind them to look carefully at the plants and draw as much detail as they can. They might like to look more closely with a hand lens.
2. Each child can devise and create a menu card for a meal consisting of foods made from plants. There should be more than one course. For example, fruit juice, cereal and toast with jam or marmalade would be a suitable three-course breakfast. If they include a pizza or a salad, they should say what toppings are on the pizza and what is in the salad.

DIFFERENTIATION

1. More able children may be ready to understand that there is often more than one ingredient in a food, and that different ingredients may be made from different plants (for example, baked beans in tomato sauce).
2. Less able children might present their menu card in pictorial form.

ASSESSMENT

Ask the children to name some foods made from plants. Use the photocopiable sheet to assess their understanding of how particular foods are linked to their plant of origin.

PLENARY

Recap on the various foods and their plant of origin. Talk about why plants are so important in our diet; explain that they are not only healthy, but add variety and colour. Ask the children whether humans are the only animals that eat plants. *Can you name some others?* (Sheep, cows, rabbits and so on.) *What do they eat? Do they only eat plants, or do they eat other things like meat, fish, eggs and cheese?* Discuss the fact that many people in the world do not eat meat or fish, but remain healthy.

OUTCOMES

- Know that plants provide a range of foods.
- Can match some foods to their plant of origin.

LINKS

Unit 1, Lesson 10: humans need food and water to live.

LESSON 14

Objectives	● To know that some foods are prepared directly from plants. ● To know that there is a wide variety of fruits.
Resources	A range of fruits (such as apple, pear, banana, kiwi fruit, mango, orange and pineapple), chopping boards, school dinner knives, a fruit salad bowl, sugar, water, dishes, spoons.
Main activity	Look at the collection of fruits. Ask the children to identify them, then to sort them by various criteria (colour, shape, whether we peel them and so on). Show the children how to use the knives safely. Some hard fruits, such as a pineapple, may have to be cut ready for the children to cut into smaller chunks. Cut the fruit up together and prepare the fruit salad.
Differentiation	This activity is accessible to all. Some children may be able to find out where the various fruits come from, using reference materials.
Assessment	As the children are sorting, note how many fruits they can identify. Observe how safely they handle a knife.
Plenary	Remind the children that the fruit salad has been made directly from the fruits, which have not been cooked or changed (except by chopping). Draw a contrast with some other foods from plants that the class have looked at.
Outcomes	● Know that some foods are prepared directly from plants. ● Know that there is a wide variety of fruits. ● Be able to handle knives safely.

LESSON 15

Objective	● To know that some foods from plants are processed by humans and some are taken directly from the plant.
Resources	Cress (grown in the classroom or purchased), bread, a spread made from vegetable oil, empty bread packets.
Main activity	Discuss the various foods that go into making a cress sandwich. Explain that they are all foods from plants. *Which one looks like the plant? Which ones don't? Why?* Make the sandwiches and share them.
Differentiation	Some children may be able to examine the bread packets to find out what else is in the sandwich bread as well as wheat.
Assessment	During the plenary session, note which children can distinguish between foods taken directly from plants and foods that have been processed.
Plenary	Ask the children to think of and name some of the other foods from plants that they sometimes have in sandwiches, such as jam, peanut butter, tomatoes, salad or chocolate spread. Which ones can they still recognise as being parts of plants?
Outcome	● Know that some foods made from plants have been processed and changed by humans, and some are taken directly from the plant.

ASSESSMENT

LESSON 16

OBJECTIVES

● To recognise and name some common animals.
● To know that plants have roots, stems, leaves and flowers.

RESOURCES

Activity 1: Photocopiable page 62, pencils (or scissors and adhesive). **Activity 2:** Photocopiable page 63, pencils.

INTRODUCTION

Talking to the whole class, ask the children to tell you about some of the things they have learned in this unit. Ask: *What can you remember about plants and animals? Do all animals eat and drink? Do plants need water too?*

ASSESSMENT ACTIVITY 1

Give each child a copy of page 62. Read through the words with the children, asking them to put their finger on each word as you read it. Some children may need more help with reading the labels as they do the activity. The activity is meant to sample the children's ability to recognise some common animals, not to test whether they can read the labels. The children could cut out the labels and paste them into the correct boxes, or copy each word into the correct box. If they have successfully matched all the names of the animals to the pictures, ask them to turn the sheet over and draw and name as many other animals as they can think of.

Answers

Mark on the sheet whether the names and animals have been matched correctly. On the back of the sheet, some children may have drawn farm animals (such as pigs, hens or goats) and some may have drawn wild animals (such as tigers, elephants or crocodiles). As long as these are different from the animals on the front of the sheet and the child can name them correctly, they are acceptable.

Looking for levels

Most children should be able to match all the animal names to the correct pictures. Less able children may not recognise any but the most common animals (such as dog and cat), and may not remember that humans are also animals. More able children will successfully draw and name three or four other animals on the back of their sheet. The most able will be able to write the names of their animals independently; some may tell you the names of their animals, and some may ask you for the names.

ASSESSMENT ACTIVITY 2

Give each child a copy of photocopiable page 63. Read through the words with the children and ask them to draw the picture.

Answers

Accept any drawing of a recognisable plant showing all the features on the list.

Looking for levels

The expectation for Year 1/Primary 2 children is that they should all be able to name the main parts of a flowering plant. Less able children may not be able to add the bud to their drawing. More able children may be able to label the petals.

Sort it!

Cut out the pictures and stick each one in the right set: **living**, **no longer living** or **never alive**.

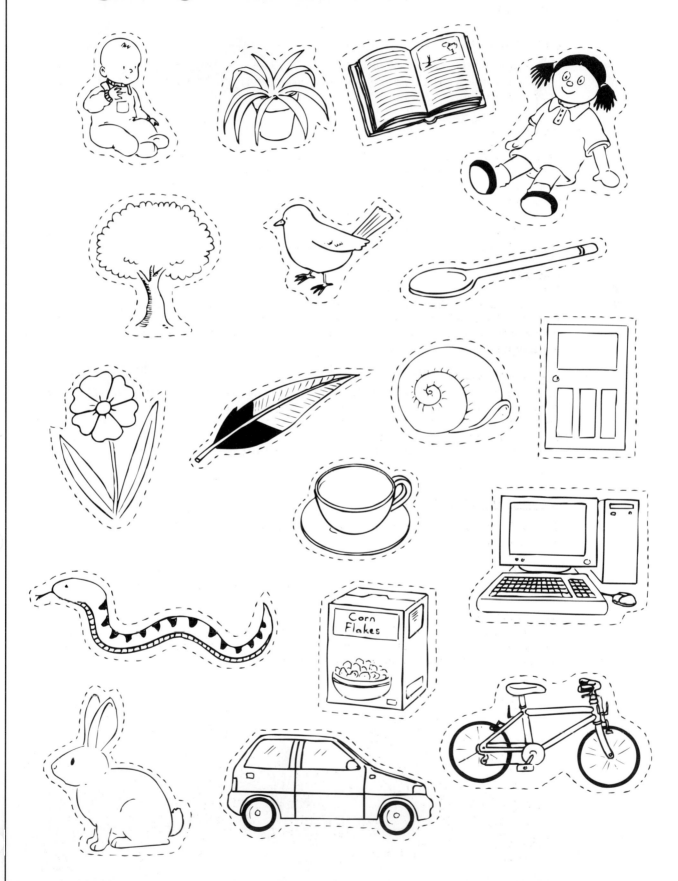

Parents and babies

Cut out each baby animal and place it in this farmyard picture next to its parent.

Make a flower

petals

leaves

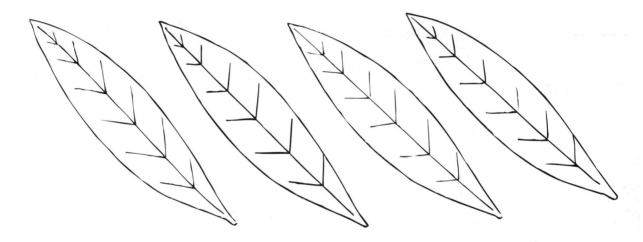

central disc

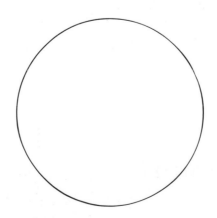

Seed diary

Our seeds were _____

They should grow to look like this.

We sowed the seed on

_____

We saw the first shoots on

_____

The first proper leaves appeared on

_____

We saw the first flower buds on

_____

The first flower opened on

_____

It looked like this:

We collected some seeds on

_____

Name

Roots

Look carefully at the roots of the bean. Draw how they have grown.

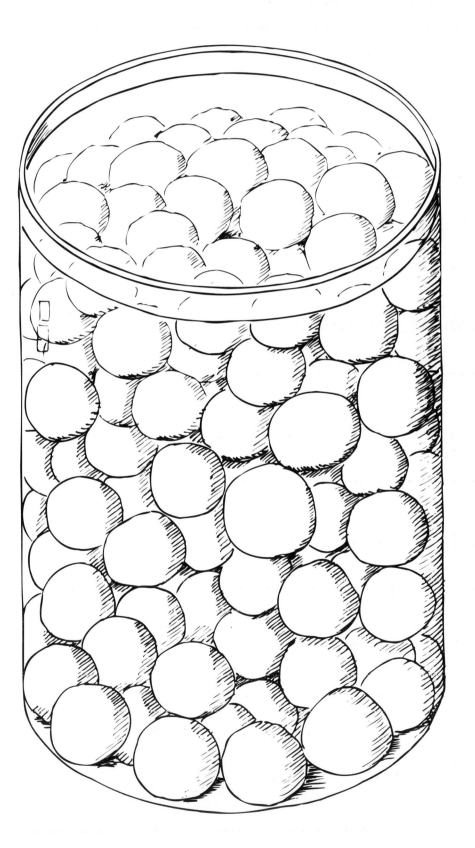

UNIT 2 ANIMALS & PLANTS

In the dark

Our plant looked like this before it went in the dark:

After _____ days in the dark, it looked like this:

Where does it come from?

Food	Plant it came from

Growing and caring

Cut out and stick the labels in the correct spaces, or choose the right word and write it in the box by each picture.

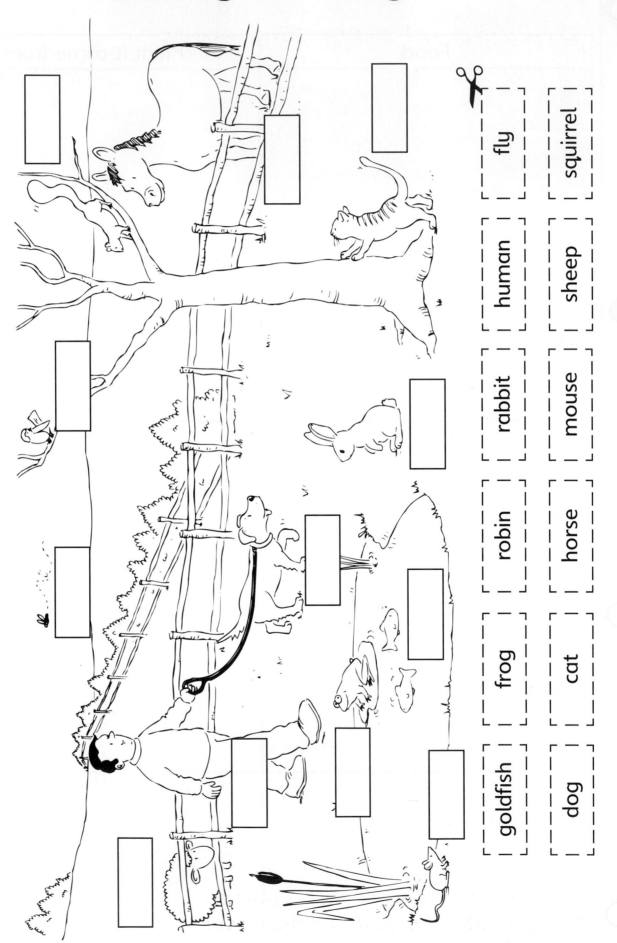

fly

squirrel

human

sheep

rabbit

mouse

robin

horse

frog

cat

goldfish

dog

Growing and caring

Draw a plant with all these things labelled:

flower

stem

leaf

root

Put a bud on a stem in your drawing.
Can you label the petals on the flower?

Environments and living things

ORGANISATION (17 LESSONS)

	OBJECTIVES	MAIN ACTIVITY	GROUP ACTIVITIES	PLENARY	OUTCOMES
LESSON 1	● To know that the environment is the surroundings in which plants and animals live.	Walk around the outside of the school, looking at different areas and what lives there.	Draw or paint their favourite area seen on the walk. Contribute to a large class picture of the school's environment.	Review the idea of the environment. Discuss how to improve the environment within and around the school.	● Know that the environment is all around us, and that it is where plants and animals live.
LESSON 2	● To know that there are simple features of the weather that can be observed. ● To use data collected to construct a pictogram or block graph.	Keep a simple class weather chart, including comparative judgements of temperature.	Make and keep a weather diary. Find out about extreme weather conditions in other parts of the world.	Use the data collected on the weather chart to make a pictogram or block graph.	● Know that there are different types of weather. ● Can enter simple information on a chart. ● Can use the information from a chart to construct a pictogram or block graph.
LESSON 3	● To measure rainfall over a period of time.	Make a simple rain gauge and use it to measure rainfall each day.		Draw conclusions from data over a week.	● Know how to use a simple rain gauge. ● Can enter information on a simple chart.
LESSON 4	● To make and use a simple wind meter to measure the strength and direction of the wind.	Make and use a simple wind meter to indicate the direction and relative strength of the wind.		Discuss other ways of telling the direction of the wind.	● Can retrieve information from a chart. ● Know that the strength and direction of the wind can be measured.
LESSON 5	● To know how the environment changes as the year passes through the seasons (autumn).	Look outdoors for signs of autumn. Draw round a shadow. Begin a 'seasons hoop' mobile.	Add autumn pictures to the seasons mobile. Record observations on a sheet.	Review work done and predict changes in the next season.	● Can describe some changes associated with autumn.
LESSON 6	● To know how the environment changes as the year passes through the seasons (winter).	Look at the changes in the environment, including day-length. What are the signs of winter?		Review work done and compare with previous season.	● Can describe some changes associated with winter.
LESSON 7	● To know how the environment changes as the year passes through the seasons (spring).	Look at the changes in the environment. What are the signs of spring?		Review work done. Compare with autumn and winter; try to explain the changes.	● Can describe some changes associated with spring.
LESSON 8	● To know how the environment changes as the year passes through the seasons (summer).	Look at the changes in the environment. Complete the seasons hoop.		Review the changes over the year; try to explain them.	● Can describe some changes associated with summer. ● Know that we have four seasons each year.

ORGANISATION (17 LESSONS)

	OBJECTIVES	MAIN ACTIVITY	GROUP ACTIVITIES	PLENARY	OUTCOMES
LESSON 9	● To know that plants change according to the seasons.	'Adopt' a tree in the local area; observe and record seasonal changes in it.	Fill in a simple record sheet. Find out what type of tree it is and compare it with other trees.	Discuss what was observed and the usefulness of keeping a record.	● Know that plants change according to the seasons.
LESSON 10	● To know the names of some common animals (minibeasts) in the local environment.	Carry out a 'minibeast safari', collecting and observing specimens.	Draw some of the creatures seen; add labels. Make a minibeast model.	Discuss what was observed. Introduce the concept of an animal's habitat.	● Know the names of and can recognise some common animals in the local environment.
LESSON 11	● To know the names of some common animals (birds) in the local environment.	Feed and observe some birds; keep a 'bird tally'.		Make a class tally chart and discuss what it shows.	● Can identify some common birds in the local environment.
LESSON 12	● To know that a habitat is a relatively small part of the environment and is the home of a plant or animal.	Observe the animals for which the 'adopted' tree is a habitat.	Use reference books to identify minibeasts found. Choose another habitat and research what animals live there.	Discuss that habitats are part of the environment. How are creatures adapted to their environment?	● Know that a habitat is a relatively small part of the environment within which plants and animals live. ● Can distinguish between an environment and a habitat.
LESSON 13	● To know that living things in an environment depend on each other.	Consider how a tree and the animals living in it depend on each other.		Discuss how living things, including humans, depend on each other.	● Know that living things in an environment depend on each other for such things as food and shelter.
LESSON 14	● To know that seasonal changes affect animals.	Consider how animals in different habitats are affected by the seasons. Discuss migration and hibernation.	Identify some creatures that hibernate. Find out where some birds migrate to.	Discuss and explain particular cases of seasonal changes or behaviour in animals.	● Can describe how some animals are affected by seasonal changes.
LESSON 15	● To know how to care for living things indoors. ● To create a habitat for small creatures.	Create a vivarium for snails. Observe how they move and what they eat.	Observe and record snail trails. Make a model of a snail on a leaf.	Discuss how snails should be cared for when being kept for observation.	● Can describe how to care for small creatures, such as snails, in a vivarium.
LESSON 16	● To know how to care for growing plants indoors.	Work in groups to create a tiny indoor garden.		Discuss how small plants should be cared for when being kept indoors.	● Can describe what needs to be done to care for plants indoors.

	OBJECTIVES	ACTIVITY 1	ACTIVITY 2	ACTIVITY 3
ASSESSMENT 17	● To assess the children's knowledge about the seasons. ● To assess whether the children know the names of some common minibeasts. ● To assess the children's knowledge and understanding about caring for living things.	Identify some of the features characteristic of each season.	Match pictures of some common minibeasts to labels.	Identify the things needed to make a vivarium for keeping snails.

LESSON 1

OBJECTIVE

● To know that the environment is the surroundings in which plants and animals live.

RESOURCES

Main teaching activity: The school grounds and the surrounding area.
Group activities: 1. Drawing and painting materials, paper. **2.** A display board, collage materials, scissors, adhesive, drawing and painting materials, paper.

Vocabulary

environment, habitat, sheltered, damp, warm, dark, sunny, clouds, windy, up, down, around

BACKGROUND

The environment consists of everything around us, indoors and outdoors, and children need to be made aware of this. They might begin by looking at their classroom and thinking about the area in which they work, which is a small part of the wider environment. Children may only be familiar with one or two aspects of the environment, such as school, home and the immediate surrounding area. It is useful, therefore, to visit different areas (such as woods, the seaside, a local park or a shopping centre) in order to give the children a wider experience, so that they can make comparisons.

Children very often do not realise that people have had a great impact on the environment, and that the buildings and other structures that we have made are as much a part of our environment as woods, fields, mountains and rivers. Even at Key Stage 1, they can start to be aware that they have a role in caring for the environment – for example, by always putting litter in bins provided (or taking it home), and keeping the classroom and cloakroom tidy and pleasant. It is important for the children to understand that they should not cause damage to trees or street furniture (for example), as this affects the environment for other people and other living things.

INTRODUCTION

Ask the children to look around the classroom. *What do you notice about the classroom environment? Is it too hot or too cold, or just right? Is it light enough for you to work comfortably? Can you find things when you need them? Do the displays, plants and collections make the room attractive?*

MAIN TEACHING ACTIVITY

Talk to the children about going out for a walk to look at the environment outside the school. Stress that the environment means everything that is all around us. Discuss the things they might look for. They need to look down at their feet and notice the different surfaces they walk on. They need to look around at bushes, flowers, walls, buildings and hedges. They need to see where shadows fall, and which places might be windy or sheltered from the wind. They need to look up and notice the trees and the sky. Remind them never to look directly at the Sun, as this can damage their eyes.

Walk around the school and look at the different areas and the conditions within them. Look for shady areas. *Why are they shady? What is making the shadows? Which places are sunny? Are there any windy places? Does litter collect in a particular corner? Where would you go to get out of the wind?* Look for different surfaces – for example, the playing field, playground, paths, pond, wildlife area and areas under trees where the grass is thin. Have a look at a tree that might be

suitable for the class to 'adopt' later (see Lesson 9, page 73). *Is it making shadows? Is anything growing underneath it?* Talk about the fact that the environment is all around us, and almost every area is home to some plants or animals. Turn over some damp leaves and wood. *Are there any woodlice?* (Make sure that you put anything you have moved back.) Look at the lichen on the path. Even though this is a hard, dry surface where people walk, something lives there and it is part of the environment.

GROUP ACTIVITIES

1. Ask each child to draw or paint a picture of their favourite area from the walk. Encourage them to put in as much detail as possible.
2. Make a large picture of the school's environment on a display board. This could be collaged or painted by small groups of children. Other children could then paint or make pictures of flowers, birds, animals, children playing and so on; these could be cut out and added to the big picture.

DIFFERENTIATION

1. More able children could write a sentence about their reasons for choosing a particular area, which could be mounted together with their picture.
2. All children can contribute at their own level to this activity.

ASSESSMENT

Ask the children to describe some features in the environment, indoors or outside. Ask: *What is the environment? What lives in it?* (The environment is all around us and is where plants and animals live.)

PLENARY

Reinforce the idea that the environment is all around us. Remind the children that plants and animals, including humans, live in the environment. Ask the children to say what they have seen. *Which was your favourite area? Was there an area that you didn't like? Why didn't you like it? What could be done to make it better? Could we do anything to make the classroom a better, more attractive environment?*

Talk about the tree that the class has looked at as being a habitat (that is, a particular 'home' area) within the environment for many small creatures, to whom it offers shelter and food. Talk about where the children live, play and go to school – this is their habitat, and is part of their environment.

OUTCOME

● Know that the environment is all around us, and that it is where plants and animals live.

LINKS

Unit 3, Lesson 9: observing seasonal changes in a tree.

LESSON 2

OBJECTIVES

● To know that there are simple features of the weather that can be observed.
● To use data collected to construct a pictogram or block graph.

RESOURCES

Main teaching activity: A large thermometer with a comparative scale (see below); a weather chart and symbols. A range of commercially produced weather charts are available, or you may prefer to make a simple one of your own. You may choose to have one that is changed daily, or one that can be used to record the weather over a week or a month. This lesson plan assumes that the chart used will be similar to (or an A3-sized copy of) photocopiable page 84.
Group activities: 1. Small notebooks for diaries, or paper for children to make their own. **2.** Reference books about weather in other parts of the world, particularly where conditions are extreme (as in deserts, the Arctic, rainforests and so on).
Plenary: A large outline for a pictogram or block graph.

BACKGROUND

The weather has a profound effect on people's lives. It affects what we wear, how we travel, how we do our work, and sometimes even the type of work that we do. The weather can affect how people feel and how they behave. The UK has a 'temperate' (that is, mild or moderate) climate. The Gulf Stream, bringing warm water from the tropics, moderates our temperature; and being an island, we have sufficient rainfall to keep the land green and fertile. The prevailing winds are from the west, so the western areas (such as Ireland, Wales, Cumbria and the Western Isles) tend to have a higher average rainfall than, for example, East Anglia. Because the UK has such a varied weather pattern, keeping a weather record can be fun: the weather is rarely the same two days running! However, we do get more settled periods of weather in the summer, so this may not be the best time of the year to carry out a weather survey if the objective is to look for changes.

Children may have seen reports on TV about floods and hurricanes in other parts of the world, and know that these are caused by extremes of weather. They may be aware that some parts of the world are always very hot or very cold.

Vocabulary

weather, sun/ sunny, rain/rainy, snow/snowy, frost/frosty, wet, dry, cold, warm, cloud/cloudy, fog/ foggy, drizzle, mist/misty, clear, symbols

INTRODUCTION

If possible, go outside and make first-hand observations of the weather. Talk about what the weather is like today. *Is it hot or cold? Is it wet or dry? Are there any clouds in the sky? Is there any wind?*

MAIN TEACHING ACTIVITY

Show all the children the weather chart and explain how it works. Discuss how often the chart needs to be changed. *How can we make sure that the record is fair? Do we need to record the weather at the same time each day?* Look at the symbols you are using and discuss what each one means (alternatively, the children could suggest symbols and make their own). Encourage the children to think again about what the weather is like today. Ask them to select the symbols that will best represent this weather.

Talk about what is meant by 'warm' or 'cold' weather. *How do we know it is warmer or colder than yesterday?* Present a large thermometer with a comparative scale: *cold, colder, warm, warmer, hot.* A large standard thermometer can be adapted by sticking a strip of paper or card down the side and writing on the appropriate words. Record the temperature word for today on the chart

Ask the children whether any of them have seen a weather forecast on television. *Why is it important to know what the weather is going to be like? Who might need to know?* The children might need to know if they were planning a picnic or a barbecue. Farmers need to know if they are planning to spray or harvest their crops. Fishermen and seafarers need to be warned of impending storms, and pilots need to know whether it will be safe to fly. *Who else might need to know and why?*

GROUP ACTIVITIES

1. The children can make and keep a weather diary to record the weather each day. They could use a small notebook or make their own booklet (about ten pages).
2. The children can use simple reference books to find out about weather in parts of the world that are very hot or very cold, or that have a lot of rain or no rain at all.

DIFFERENTIATION

1. Some children could use a photocopy of page 84 instead of making a weather diary; they could either cut and paste or redraw the appropriate symbols. More able children could read the temperature in °C (if you have a thermometer with a large enough scale) and add it to their diary each day.
2. The children could work in small mixed-ability groups and help each other. More able children could be encouraged to watch the weather forecast on television and report back each day. Some may be able to find the weather forecast in a newspaper.

ASSESSMENT

Ask the children to describe different types of weather. Look at their weather diaries. Note those children who are able to take information from the pictogram or block graph (see below).

PLENARY

This might take place at the end of the week, when there are several days' records to consider. Discuss what the weather has been like during the week. *How has it changed? How do we know? What has helped us to remember?* (The weather chart.) Help the children to transfer the information on the weather chart to a large pictogram or block graph. Ask: *Is it easier to find out now how many cloudy days we had in the week, or how many days it rained?* Encourage the children to use the graph to find out these things.

OUTCOMES

- Know that there are different types of weather.
- Can enter simple information on a chart.
- Can use the information from a chart to construct a pictogram or block graph.

LINKS

Maths: drawing block graphs.
Literacy: keeping a diary.
Geography: weather.

LESSON 3

Objective	● To measure rainfall over a period of time.
Resources	A watering can, a rain gauge (use a commercially produced one or make a simple one from an empty, clear plastic bottle – see illustration below), a measuring cylinder, a rain chart (or the weather chart from Lesson 2), felt-tipped pens.
Main activity	Discuss the fact that we have different amounts of rain on different days, and sometimes it is important to know how much rain has fallen. Use a watering can to demonstrate how a rain gauge collects the rain as it falls. Choose a suitable place to put the gauge outside. Make sure that it is firmly fixed so it cannot tip over. Make a chart to record the rainfall each day (or add this to the class weather chart).
Differentiation	Some children could mark the side of the rain gauge with a different-coloured felt pen for each day, and use this to note the days on which the most and least rain fell. Others may be able to measure the amount of rainfall in millilitres, using a measuring cylinder.
Assessment	Note those children who are able to measure the rainfall and transfer the information to their chart or the class chart. Note those who can take information from the chart at the end of the period.
Plenary	Find out on which days you had the most and the least rain. *How much rain has fallen altogether during the week?*
Outcomes	● Know how to use a simple rain gauge. ● Can enter information on a simple chart. ● Can retrieve information from a chart.

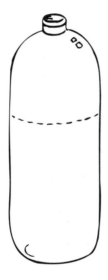 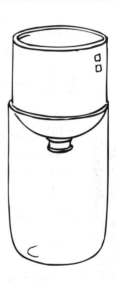

LESSON 4

Objective	● To make and use a simple wind meter to measure the strength and direction of the wind.
Resources	Strips cut from three or four different weights of plastic sheeting (carrier bags, freezer bags etc), several short pieces of dowel or cane (or large curtain rings), a simple compass.
Main activity	Tie three or four plastic strips (one of each weight) to the top of each short stick (or to each curtain ring). Go outside with the children and hold these wind meters up high. *How hard is the wind blowing? Which way is it blowing? Does it always blow in the same direction?*
Differentiation	More able children may be able to appreciate that the heavier-gauge plastic needs a stronger wind to make it blow, while the lighter gauge will move in a gentle breeze. Some children may be able to use a compass to find the direction in which the wind is blowing, while others may note that it is blowing (for example) towards the school gate or the big tree.
Assessment	During the plenary, note which children are able to say how we know which way the wind is blowing and understand that the heavier the 'streamer', the more wind is required to move it.
Plenary	Talk about other signs that tell us which way the wind is blowing, such as washing on a line, trees bending or smoke from a chimney.
Outcome	● Know that the strength and direction of the wind can be measured.

LESSON 5

OBJECTIVE

● To know how the environment changes as the year passes through the seasons (autumn).

RESOURCES

Main teaching activity: A picture of each of the four seasons, a camera, chalk, emulsion paint (optional), a large PE hoop, a small practice ball, a piece of wire or paper clip, a large yellow ball or balloon (if you use a balloon, it will need replacing as it gets old and deflates), crêpe paper in four seasonal colours.
Group activities: 1. Drawing materials, paper, thin card, adhesive. **2.** Photocopiable page 85, drawing materials.

PREPARATION

Divide a large hoop into four sections and wrap each section in different-coloured crêpe paper appropriate to each of the four seasons. Hang the hoop from the ceiling or other suitable place. Use a piece of wire or a paper clip to make a hook by which to attach the practice ball to the hoop. The practice ball represents the Earth, and the hoop its orbit. Hang the yellow ball in the centre of the hoop to represent the Sun. Make small labels for the months of the year and attach them to the hoop within the appropriate seasons. Using the hoop helps the children to appreciate that the seasons are cyclical and come round each year.

Vocabulary

spring, summer, autumn, winter, lighter, darker, longer, shorter, day length

BACKGROUND

The changing seasons affect our lives in many ways. However, these days, the traditional four seasons are becoming increasingly hard to distinguish. Climate changes have resulted in much milder, less 'seasonal' weather throughout the year, though the changes in trees and other plants still give a clear indication of the seasons. We notice changes in temperature and rainfall, but the change that has the greatest effect on us is probably that of the length of the day (that is, the number of daylight hours).

As the days lengthen in the spring, plants are stimulated into growth and many animals (such as birds and frogs) mate and prepare to raise their young. We have the seasons because of the tilt of the Earth's axis, not because we are nearer to the Sun at any particular time (the Earth's orbit around the Sun is slightly elliptical; those in the northern hemisphere are actually nearer to the Sun in the middle of January). Summer occurs in the northern hemisphere when the North Pole is tilted towards the Sun. The South Pole is obviously tilted away from the Sun at this time, so the southern hemisphere experiences winter. Six months later, halfway through the Earth's annual orbit of the Sun, the positions are reversed: the South Pole is tilted towards the Sun and the North Pole away from it, giving summer in the southern hemisphere and winter in the north. The change in day length is less noticeable in the tropics, but becomes greater the nearer to the poles you go. Few people live in the Antarctic, but the people living in the Arctic regions experience 24 hours of daylight in midsummer, while in midwinter the Sun does not rise at all.

Five- and six-year-old children will have had little experience of seasonal change that they can remember, so it is important to help them notice the changes that occur as each season comes round. It is helpful to go on the same walk, or visit the same areas in each season, so that the children can observe specific changes. Try to go at the same time of day if possible, especially if you choose to look at the shadows.

INTRODUCTION

Show the children a picture of each of the four seasons. Talk about what is in each picture and point out the differences between them. Ask them to name each season.

MAIN TEACHING ACTIVITY

Carry out this lesson in autumn. Ask the class: *Which season do you think we are in now? Which picture looks the most like how it is outside?* Go outside and look together for some of the things in the picture. Look at the colour of the leaves on the trees. *What is happening to the leaves?* Take some photographs. *Do any of the trees have fruits or berries?* Look for acorns, horse chestnuts, apples, blackberries and the seed heads of different plants. Ask the children to collect a few, so that they can set them in plant pots and watch them grow; but tell them not to collect many fruits or seeds, as the birds and small creatures will depend on them for food in the winter. Autumn is a good time to look for spider's webs, particularly if you go out on a misty morning when the dew clings to them like tiny diamonds. You may see flocks of birds gathering ready to fly off to warmer lands. *Why do they need to leave?* (Think about what they eat: many live on insects that are not available here in the winter, so they have to travel to where they can find food.)

Look at the shadows. *How long are they?* If you have a suitable surface, you could draw round a child's shadow with chalk and fill the shadow in with emulsion paint so that it lasts for a while.

When does it begin to get dark? Can you play outside until bedtime, or do you have to come in sooner? Is it light when you wake up in the morning? The children may not have noticed, so this could be a small homework task.

Back in the classroom, show the children the hoop and explain, very simply, that we have different seasons because the Earth travels around the Sun. Explain that each section of the hoop shows a different season. Add the photographs to the autumn section.

GROUP ACTIVITIES

1. Remind the children of some of the things they have seen. Ask each child to choose one of the things and draw a picture of it. Make sure that the children don't all choose the same thing to draw. Cut the pictures out and mount them on card; hang some of them from the autumn section of the hoop, and use the rest as a wall display.
2. Give each child a copy of photocopiable page 85 to complete. This sheet could be adapted for each season (see Lessons 6, 7 and 8) and used for comparison.

DIFFERENTIATION

1. All the children should be able to take part in this activity. Some children may be able to cut out and mount their own pictures, but others may need help with this.
2. All the children should be able to complete this sheet, though some may need help with reading.

ASSESSMENT

Ask the children to name the four seasons. Can they describe some of the changes they might find in autumn?

PLENARY

Talk about the things you have seen, and ask the children what else happens at this time of year. Some children may have birthdays that can be added to the hoop as they come round. Some children may celebrate Harvest Festival or Bonfire Night. Ask the children which season comes next. *What changes might we expect in that season?*

OUTCOME

● Can describe some changes associated with autumn.

LESSON 6

Objective	● To know how the environment changes as the year passes through the seasons (winter).
Resources	Autumn and winter pictures (or appropriate reference books), chalk, emulsion paint (optional), a camera, the 'seasons hoop' from Lesson 5.
Main activity	Remind the children of the autumn picture and what they saw. Look at the winter picture and discuss any changes. *What will you expect to see outside?* Go outside and revisit the places looked at in the autumn walk. *How have things changed?* If possible, draw a new shadow outline on top of the old one and paint it in a different colour. *How has the shadow changed?* Take photographs. Add new photographs to the seasons hoop. Take a photograph, outside, of the children dressed and ready to go home at the end of the school day (even though it will not come out). *What time does it get dark? Is it dark when you get up?*
Differentiation	Some children may not remember everything, so give them a specific area (eg a tree or flower bed) to look for. More able children could take some weather readings (see Lesson 2).
Assessment	During the Plenary, ask the children to describe some changes from autumn to winter.
Plenary	Talk about what you have seen. Look at the photographs taken in the autumn, and compare them with what the children have just seen. *How have things changed? What do you think has caused these changes?*
Outcome	● Can describe some changes associated with winter.

LESSON 7

Objective	● To know how the environment changes as the year passes through the seasons (spring).
Resources	Winter and spring pictures (or appropriate reference books), a camera, chalk, emulsion paint (optional), the 'seasons hoop'.
Main activity	Remind the children of the winter picture. Look at a spring picture and talk about the differences the children can see. Go out and revisit the places looked at in autumn and winter. *How have the places changed?* Take more photographs for the collection. Draw a new shadow outline. *Is it still dark when you get up in the morning and go to bed at night?* Add photographs to the spring section of the hoop.
Differentiation	Focus the attention of less able children on a specific area outside. More able children could measure the lengths of the three shadows and begin to think about the changes: *How have they changed? Why have they changed? Where might the next one be?* Take another 'home time' picture.
Assessment	During the Plenary, ask the children to describe some changes from winter to spring.
Plenary	Talk about what you have seen. Compare the photographs taken in spring and winter. Talk about how the hoop is filling up. *How many seasons are left? What will that season be like?*
Outcome	● Can describe some changes associated with spring.

LESSON 8

Objective	● To know how the environment changes as the year passes through the seasons (summer).
Resources	Pictures of all seasons (or appropriate reference books), a camera, chalk, emulsion paint (optional), a compass, the 'seasons hoop'.
Main activity	Remind the children about what they saw in the spring. Look at the spring picture and photographs, then look at the summer picture. Discuss the differences. Retrace the walk taken in previous seasons. Note changes and take photographs. Draw a new shadow outline; was the children's prediction from the last time correct? Add new photographs to the seasons hoop. Take another 'home time' picture.
Differentiation	More able children could make a block graph of the shadow lengths, and use a compass to find what direction the shadows lie in. Less able children might compare the changes to one specific area over the year.
Assessment	During the plenary, ask the children to describe some of the changes from spring to summer. Can they describe what will happen after that? Which season will it be?
Plenary	Look at the four season pictures and the photographs taken throughout the year. *What changes have taken place? What is going to happen next? Why have these changes taken place?*
Outcomes	● Can describe some changes associated with summer. ● Know that we have four seasons each year.

LESSON 9

OBJECTIVE

● To know that plants change according to the seasons.

RESOURCES

Main teaching activity: A tree in the locality, paper or books for diaries, a measuring tape, a camera (if possible), blank paper, fat wax crayons.
Group activities: Photocopiable page 86, simple reference materials about trees.

PREPARATION

Find a tree in the locality that will make a suitable subject for the children to observe in each season. You will need a deciduous and not an evergreen tree. If you can, choose a tree that changes dramatically through the year – for example, one that has very obvious blossom or fruits, or has brightly coloured leaves in the autumn.

Vocabulary

spring, summer, autumn, winter, seasons, change, grow, to flower (verb), die, tree, plant, bush, branches, leaves, flowers

BACKGROUND

Children often have very stereotypical ideas about what trees look like in the various seasons, and have never looked closely to make observations. Trees are flowering plants, and many of them are wind-pollinated. Wind-pollinated trees (such as the silver birch) often develop flowers before the leaves appear, so that the wind can carry the pollen through the bare branches to other trees. Many trees have relatively insignificant flowers, and the children will have to look closely to find them.

Trees are the biggest living things on the planet, and modern methods of dating have proved that some living trees are more than a thousand years old. In Britain, we have a rich heritage of very old trees – so much so that we tend to take them for granted. Because there are so many of them, they are often not protected; whereas in some countries that have far fewer ancient trees, they are all mapped and have rigorous protection orders on them.

Big, old oak trees are frequently hollow. This is not because they are beginning to die: it is part of the way in which the tree continues to thrive. The fact that the tree is hollow means that it is more pliable and can bend slightly with the wind, so there is less danger of it being blown over. The organic material from the core of the tree falls to the ground, and the nutrients it contains are recycled. This material provides food and habitats for many insects and other small creatures. Some hollow trees are nearly big enough for a whole class to stand inside – but for obvious reasons, this should not be attempted.

INTRODUCTION

Before leaving the classroom, remind the children of the need for sensitivity towards and care of all living things. Remind them that plants are living things. Recap on the fact that trees are flowering plants. Explain that the children are going to look closely at the tree and find out as many things about it as they can. Talk about the things they should look for: the shape and condition of the tree, the bark, any leaves, flowers or fruits. A good way of ensuring that they do note and discuss what they see is to tell them that each group is going to report back to the class and tell everyone what they have observed.

MAIN TEACHING ACTIVITY

Take the children outside to look at the tree that they are going to 'adopt'. Look at the chosen tree from a distance and ask the children what they notice. Go close up to the tree and make more observations. *What is the bark like? Is it rough or smooth? Are there leaves, flowers or fruits? What shape are they? Do they smell? What colour is the bark? Is the bark on the trunk a different colour from that on the branches? Is the trunk a different colour on one side from the other? Could that be because the wind and rain come mainly from one direction?* Encourage the children to measure the circumference

of the tree using a tape measure. They can take rubbings of the bark, including different bark areas (being careful not to damage any growth on the bark).

Take the children out to look closely at the tree in the spring, summer, autumn and winter. If possible, take photographs of the tree on every visit so that the changes can be compared in the classroom. The children should keep a 'tree diary' to record their observations over the year.

GROUP ACTIVITIES

1. Give each child a copy of photocopiable page 86 to complete for the appropriate season. Remind the children about what they saw when they were looking at the tree.
2. The children can work in small groups with reference materials to find out what type of tree the 'adopted' tree is and compare it with other types of tree – for example: *Do all trees lose their leaves? Are they all the same size?* Each group could report their findings back to the rest of the class.

DIFFERENTIATION

1. All the children can complete the sheet, but some may need help with writing the final sentence.
2. The children could work in small mixed-ability groups in order to communicate and help each other with their observations, then report back to the class. Some children may be able to use CD-ROMs to find out more about the type of tree chosen.

ASSESSMENT

Use the photocopiable sheet for assessment. When the children report back their findings, note whether they have observed a range of details (see the Introduction).

PLENARY

After each visit to the tree, talk to the children about what they have observed. After the first visit, draw their attention to the fact that they needed to make a record of their observations so that they will be able to make comparisons on future visits – for example, they will be able to compare times when the twigs were bare, had leaves, had flowers and so on.

OUTCOME

● Know that plants change according to the seasons.

LINKS

Unit 2, Lesson 6: know that plants have roots, stems, leaves and flowers.
Maths: measuring.
English: speaking and listening.

LESSON 10

OBJECTIVE

● To know the names of some common animals (minibeasts) in the local environment.

RESOURCES

Main teaching activity: A suitable outdoor environment (see Background); small, clear boxes for collecting minibeasts; pooters, hand lenses, binocular microscopes, soft brushes, trowels, a collection of simple reference books with minibeast pictures, Milton fluid.
Group activities: 1. Photocopiable page 87, scissors, adhesive. **2.** Modelling materials (treasury tags, stiff netting, sequins, play dough, clay, reclaimed materials, pipe cleaners and so on).

PREPARATION

Visit the area to be surveyed in advance.

BACKGROUND

Avoid doing this activity in the winter, when the children are unlikely to find any minibeasts. The school grounds, unless there is a specific wild area, are often rather poor in terms of the habitats and the numbers and variety of small creatures to be found. You may be able to find a corner in which to make a small log pile to encourage minibeasts; sometimes the bases of hedges or trees are useful places to look. If possible, take the children to a local park or area of waste ground where they are likely to find more of interest. Collecting boxes with magnifying lids are very useful, but beware of the very small bug boxes with magnifying lids: these are too small and contain too little air for minibeasts to be left in them for more than a minute or two. Well-washed clear plastic tubs (of the kind sometimes used for salads on supermarket delicatessen counters) are also useful. Make sure that any pooters you are using are complete with gauze over the end of one of the tubes, so that a woodlouse can't get sucked down an unsuspecting throat! Children should not swap pooters, and after use they should be soaked in a solution such as Milton fluid to disinfect them. If you are taking the class to an unfamiliar area, it is wise to go out and have a look round in advance so that you have some idea of what the children are likely to find and can point them in the right direction. If some small creatures are to be brought back to the classroom to be observed more closely, keep them for the shortest possible time and return them to their habitats as soon as possible.

Vocabulary

environment, common, woodlouse, spider, ant, bee, beetle, caterpillar, ladybird worm, snail, slug tally, magnifier, microscope, pooter, collecting box, minibeast

INTRODUCTION

Before going out, talk to the children about the fact that the minibeasts they are going to find are living things – and that they are delicate, can easily be damaged and must be handled gently and with great care. Show them the equipment and how to use it: digging with a trowel, sucking tiny creatures into a pooter, brushing larger ones (such as woodlice or beetles) into a collecting box. Let them practise by brushing tiny balls of rolled-up paper into their collecting boxes or sucking them into their pooters.

MAIN TEACHING ACTIVITY

Discuss with the children some of the things they might observe about the places where they find the creatures. *Is it dry or damp, light or dark?* Remind the children that if they lift stones and turn over rocks and logs, they should replace them carefully for the benefit of the creatures that live under them. Look in books at pictures of some of the minibeasts that the children may find. Ask the children to name them, or help them to learn the names.

Take the children out into the chosen area. Help them to choose suitable places in which to look for minibeasts. Check that they are collecting specimens in the correct manner. Help them to name the creatures they have found. Focus their attention on where the creatures have been found and the conditions in which they prefer to live. For example: *What kind of places do woodlice like? Do you find caterpillars and ladybirds in the same kind of places?* Remind the children again about handling living things carefully: how would they like it if a giant came along and popped them into a box? Question the children about the creatures they have found in order to focus their observations and help them to notice as many details as possible. After the children have looked closely at the specimens (using hand lenses), they should be returned to the places where they were found. You may want to bring a few minibeasts back to the classroom for closer observation (using binocular microscopes).

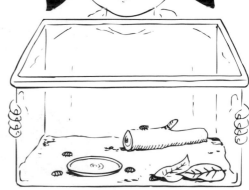

GROUP ACTIVITIES

1. Give each child a copy of photocopiable page 87. Ask the children to draw pictures of some of the things they have seen. They can then cut out the names of these things to label the pictures they have drawn. They do not have to fill every square.

2. The children, working individually, can make a simple model of a minibeast using reclaimed materials. For example: a spider, ladybird or ant could be made from an egg box and pipe cleaners; caterpillars could be made from

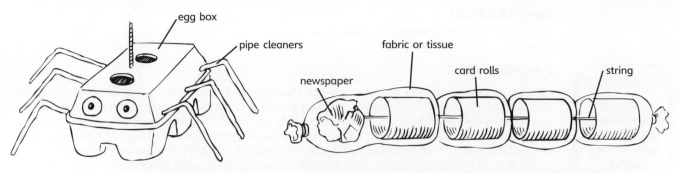

egg box

pipe cleaners

fabric or tissue

newspaper

card rolls

string

sections of cardboard roll, fastened together with treasury tags and covered in tissue or fabric (see illustration); bees and other flying insects could be made from cardboard rolls, with wings of stiff netting. They could add a few sequins for extra sparkle.

DIFFERENTIATION

1. Most children should be able to complete this activity. Some children may find creatures not named on the photocopiable sheet, such as a centipede. They could use simple reference books to find the names of these things.
2. All the children should be able to make a model according to their ability.

ASSESSMENT

Point to pictures of some familiar minibeasts in reference books, and ask the children to name them.

PLENARY

Discuss the number and range of minibeasts found, and the fact that they all live in the same environment. Ask the children whether they can remember the sort of place each creature was found in. *Why do they like to live there?* If, as sometimes happens, the number and range of creatures found is sparse, use pictures in reference books to identify and discuss some of the other creatures that live in the environment all around us.

OUTCOME

● Know the names of and can recognise some common animals (minibeasts) in the local environment.

LINKS

Art: model-making.

LESSON 11

Objective	● To know the names of some common animals (birds) in the local environment.
Resources	A bird table or hanging bird feeders that can be seen from the classroom window (see diagram opposite); a range of bird foods (bread, nuts, cheese, bacon rind and so on); notebooks or paper and clipboards; reference books about birds.
Main activity	Feed some birds and observe them. Encourage the children to learn to recognise and name the species that visit the table, and to keep a 'bird tally' to note the number of each type of bird that visits. Put out a range of foods and note what each type of bird eats. If only one type of food is put out, the range of birds attracted to the table will be narrower.
Differentiation	More able children may be able to find out more about the birds they have seen from secondary sources. Some children may be able to make a block graph or pictogram from the class tally chart (see Plenary).
Assessment	Note which children can answer the questions in the Plenary session and name some common birds.
Plenary	Talk about the birds seen on the bird table. Ask the children to add their individual bird tallies to a class tally chart. Ask: *How many different species have we observed? Which type of bird was the most frequent visitor to the table? Which type of food was the most popular?*
Outcome	● Can identify some common birds in the local environment.

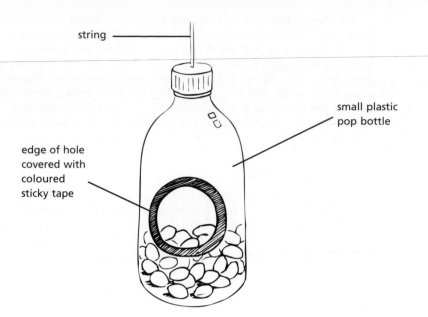

string

small plastic
pop bottle

edge of hole
covered with
coloured
sticky tape

Blue tits love this kind of feeder, because they can help themselves to a whole nut!

LESSON 12

OBJECTIVES

● To know that a habitat is a relatively small part of the environment and is the home of a particular plant or animal.

RESOURCES

Main teaching activity: The tree 'adopted' by the class and studied seasonally (see Lesson 9, page 73), a large square of white fabric, a long pole, hand lenses, a binocular microscope, minibeast collecting equipment (see Lesson 10, page 74).
Group activities: 1. Reference books on minibeasts. **2.** Reference books on wildlife habitats, photocopiable page 88.

(see Lesson 9, page 73)
(see Lesson 10, page 74)
photocopiable page 88.

BACKGROUND

Trees are the habitat and shelter of many animals and some plants, including birds, caterpillars, aphids (greenfly), spiders, gall wasps, squirrels, lichen, moss and fungi. The leaves of the tree will also be the food source for some of the creatures that live in it, and these creatures in turn will be the food of larger animals such as birds. Some species (such as birds) live and shelter in a range of trees; others are specific to a particular tree, such as the gall wasp (which causes the round galls on the twigs of oak trees). Choose an appropriate time of the year (the spring or the summer) for these activities, when the children are more likely to find a range of life in the tree.

Vocabulary

habitat, roost, environment, feed, depend, shelter, nest, burrow, adapted, lichen, moss, fungi, minibeast

INTRODUCTION

Talk to the children about the different places in which animals and plants live. We live in houses that give us warmth and shelter. If we have pets, they might live in a kennel, a hutch or a cage.

MAIN TEACHING ACTIVITY

Ask the children to think of some of the special places in which certain wild animals live – for example, fish live in rivers or seas, rabbits in fields and burrows. Explain that these are their habitats: the places they are adapted to live in. Discuss the fact that the tree the children have been studying is the habitat of many creatures. Can they think of any small animals or minibeasts that might live in a tree? Talk about the fact that animals live where they do because that is where their food source is and it provides the living conditions that they need. The birds living in a tree may eat the fruit, or the insects and other small creatures that live in the tree; caterpillars may eat the leaves, maggots may eat the fruit, and so on. Some minibeasts suck the sap out of the leaves for their food, causing the leaves to curl; others burrow into the bark. The tree offers shelter as well as food. Caterpillars may wrap the leaves around themselves when they become chrysalides to protect them while they are turning into butterflies.

Ask the children to stand round the tree. Ask: *What can you see? Are there any animals to be seen, or any sign that animals have been here? Can you see any holes nibbled in the leaves, any curled-up leaves or any bird droppings? Are there any lichens, mosses or fungi growing on the tree?* Place a large square of white fabric under the tree and gently beat the branches with a pole. Allow the children to make close observations of the animals that fall on to the sheet, using hand lenses. Can they identify any of them? Collect some carefully in bug boxes to take back to the classroom and examine under a binocular microscope. Remind the children that the minibeasts must not be kept in the boxes for too long and must be returned to their habitat, or else they will die.

GROUP ACTIVITIES

1. The children can work in pairs, using simple reference books to identify some of the things they have brought back to the classroom. They do not need to identify the particular variety of animal or plant: the generic name ('caterpillar', 'moss', 'beetle' and so on) is sufficient. Remind them again that they need to be very careful when handling animals.
2. The children can choose another habitat, such as the soil, a ditch, a pond or a rock pool, and use reference books to find out about and draw some of the creatures that live in it. They can use photocopiable page 88 for this work.

DIFFERENTIATION

Provide a range of reference books suitable for different abilities. More able children may be able to find out more about the creatures that they identify, using more demanding reference material. Less able children will need very simple, pictorial reference books.

ASSESSMENT

Ask the children to explain what 'habitat' means. Can they explain, for example, that woodlice or slugs live in dark, damp places, and that these places are their habitat – that is, the kind of place they live in?

PLENARY

Talk about a habitat as being a small part of an environment. Emphasise that a habitat is specific to a particular creature (or perhaps several creatures). Discuss ways in which creatures are adapted to their habitats. *Could animals live in a habitat that is different from their usual one? For example, could a fish live out of water or a woodlouse on a hot, dry path?*

OUTCOMES

● Know that a habitat is a small part of the environment within which plants and animals live.
● Can distinguish between an environment and a habitat.

LINKS

Literacy: using non-fiction materials to find information.

LESSON 13

Objective	● To know that living things in an environment depend on each other.
Resources	The list of creatures found in the tree in Lesson 12.
Main activity	Using the information gathered, can the children say which animals depend on the tree for food? *What eats the leaves? What eats the fruit?* Birds might eat the minibeasts that eat the leaves, or benefit the tree by eating the fruit and scattering the seeds.
Differentiation	Some children may only see very obvious relationships between animals (such as predator and prey), but more able children may begin to understand about food chains.
Assessment	During the plenary session, ask the children to describe some ways in which the creatures and plants that live in the tree depend on it or benefit it.
Plenary	Talk about the idea that all living things are dependent on other living things in some way. Discuss how humans are dependent on each other, and on other living things.
Outcomes	● Know that living things in an environment depend on each other for such things as food and shelter.

LESSON 14

OBJECTIVE

● To know that seasonal changes affect animals.

RESOURCES

Main teaching activity: Pictures or posters of animals in different seasons, videos of animals migrating or showing seasonal behaviour.
Group activities: 1. Photocopiable page 89, coloured pens or crayons, reference books on hibernation. **2.** Reference books on bird migration, a world map or globe.

Vocabulary

migrate, hibernate, nest, spawn, birth, hatch, plumage, fur, coat

BACKGROUND

Most animals, including humans, are affected by the changes in the seasons. Most people admit to feeling better when the Sun shines. Other animals may show more dramatic changes in appearance or behaviour. As the days lengthen and grow warmer in the spring, plants are stimulated into growth and provide a food source for newly hatched caterpillars. Birds advertise their desire for a mate by singing and displaying their plumage; they take advantage of the abundance of food to raise their families. Frogs and toads are stimulated to find a suitable pond for spawning, often travelling considerable distances to reach it. Other animals, such as sheep or deer, produce their young to coincide with the availability of food. During the summer and early autumn, most animals spend their time fattening themselves up to withstand the rigours of winter. During this time, some may change in appearance. Birds lose their baby down and assume their adult plumage; some adults may moult, losing the fine feathers they had in the spring before growing a new set. Tadpoles change shape completely, becoming frogs and leaving the confines of the pond. Caterpillars eat themselves to a standstill, then undergo a metamorphosis before emerging as moths and butterflies.

As winter approaches, the food source of many animals is depleted. Some overcome this by migrating to warmer climes: flocks of birds may be seen gathering, ready for the journey south. Other animals, unable to make such a journey, will 'winter out', or hibernate, living on the body fat that they acquired while food was abundant. The hedgehog is the classic example here; frogs also find a damp, dark spot, perhaps in the mud at the bottom of a pond, to sleep out the winter. Spiders, slugs and snails also hibernate. Some animals, such as squirrels, may keep to their nests on the very coldest days, but will venture out on brighter days to retrieve their hidden food store – they do not hibernate completely.

INTRODUCTION

Gather the children around you and ask them what they remember about the four seasons. *What difference do the seasons make to your lives?* Talk about the different clothes they wear. *When can you play outside until bedtime?* Some children may realise that certain foods (such as strawberries) are seasonal – however, this is not so obvious in these days of global supermarket supplies and technological farming.

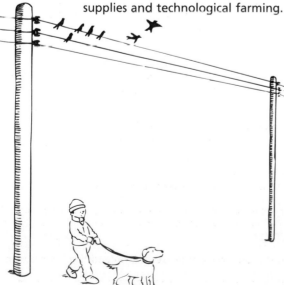

MAIN TEACHING ACTIVITY

Ask the children for their ideas about how animals adjust to the changes in the seasons. They don't have centrally heated homes to go to in the winter. They can't pop down to the supermarket for their food. *How do they manage?* Talk about how some birds migrate to warmer countries where there is still plenty of food for them. In the late summer or autumn, the children may see starlings gathering in huge flocks, often sitting on telephone lines or rooftops, ready to make the journey south together. Talk about how we can help the birds that stay here for the winter by putting food out. Talk about how other animals may adapt to the winter by hibernating (like hedgehogs), or by growing a thicker coat (like wild horses). Some children may have pets that grow a thicker coat in the winter.

How do the animals know it is spring? What happens to them? Many children will be familiar with tadpoles changing into frogs, but it may be a new idea to some. *What changes do you expect to see or hear in birds? Why are they wearing their brightest colours or singing their loudest songs?* (To attract and impress possible mates.) *Have some of the birds that went away for the winter returned?* Ask the children when they think would be the best time to go on a 'minibeast safari'. Discuss the fact that there are few flies, butterflies, ants, beetles, slugs or snails to be found in the winter, but lots in the summer. *Why do you think this is?*

If possible, watch a video showing how animals in other countries react to seasonal changes. Conditions are often much harsher than in Britain, and pictures of polar bears emerging from their snow holes with their cubs can be quite dramatic.

GROUP ACTIVITIES

1. Give each child a copy of photocopiable page 89. Ask them whether they can remember what 'hibernate' means. Encourage them to think carefully about each animal on the sheet and to colour just those that hibernate. This could be based on the previous discussion, or some children may want to use reference materials.
2. Ask the children, working in small groups, to use reference books to find out where some birds go to when they fly away for the winter. They can use a world map or globe to see how far the birds fly. Each group can report their findings back to the rest of the class.

DIFFERENTIATION

1. Some children may need help to read the photocopiable sheet, and some support in completing the final sentence. Very able children could use reference materials to find out about animals in other countries (such as bears, the Arctic fox and so on) that also hibernate.
2. The children could work in mixed-ability groups to help each other. Some groups may be able to find out whether any other creatures migrate (for example, butterflies).

ASSESSMENT

Use the photocopiable sheet to assess whether the children understand why some creatures hibernate. Ask: *What happens to birds in the spring?*

PLENARY

Ask the children to tell you how a particular animal changes in appearance and behaviour according to the seasons. Talk about the reasons for some of these changes.

OUTCOME

● Can describe how some animals are affected by seasonal changes.

LESSON 15

OBJECTIVES

● To know how to care for living things indoors.
● To create a habitat for small creatures.

RESOURCES

Main teaching activity: A plastic fish tank (or large plastic sweet jar) with a cover, a small amount of peat or compost, small stones or pieces of wood, twigs, a small lid from a jar, appropriate food materials, hand lenses.
Group activities: 1. Black paper, white chalk, reference books on snails.
2. Pictures of snails, clay or play dough, small cabbage leaves, empty snail shells.

PREPARATION

It is prudent to do a little reconnaissance before the lesson to make sure that snails can be found in the school grounds or nearby.

Vocabulary

live, living,
habitat,
vivarium, care,
shell, slime, trail

BACKGROUND

Keeping a few small creatures in the classroom for a short time can prove to be quite a focus of interest. It gives the children an opportunity to observe the creatures moving and feeding at close quarters, over a longer period than would be possible outside. Tadpoles are a classroom favourite – but remember that it is illegal to buy or sell frogspawn, or to take it from the wild. Some could be taken from a garden pond with the owner's permission. As a school staff, consider why you are keeping the frogspawn: does every class need to have some? What are your learning objectives? Do they ensure progression in the children's knowledge? If you do keep frogspawn, it needs to be in a cool position – not on the window sill in full sunlight. The tadpoles will need

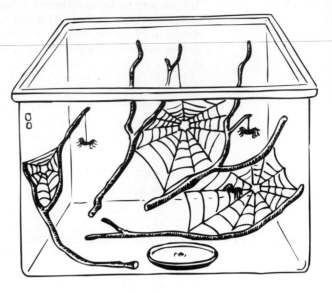

pondweed to feed on (watercress is quite a good alternative). As the tadpoles begin to develop legs, they will need extra protein to help their development. You may find that giving them a little flaked fish food is preferable to hanging small lumps of meat in the water, especially as using raw meat has obvious hygiene implications. The tadpoles will also need a rock or stone, so that they can climb out occasionally as they develop their legs. As soon as they become froglets, they will need to eat insects and should be returned to the pond from which they came.

A vivarium is equally fascinating, and can be made quite simply from a plastic fish tank or large plastic sweet jar. A variety of small creatures can be kept, but not all at the same time: they may eat each other! Snails, spiders or woodlice make suitable subjects, but none of them should be kept inside for more than a few days: you can, of course, change the population to keep the project going a little longer. Slugs and snails may dry out if they get too warm. Spiders need small insects to feed on – so unless you are prepared to become a fly-catcher, they should only be kept for a short time. You may be able to find a small parcel of spider eggs under a window sill or in the crack of an outhouse door. These will hatch if brought into the warm – but beware, there may be hundreds of babies! They will need water to drink soon after hatching, and should be released quite quickly.

Make sure that whatever container you use has a firmly fitting lid of some kind. You will need to make small holes in the lid to allow air to circulate. Be aware, however, that snails in particular are wonderful escape artists, and they can eat their way through your display books overnight!

INTRODUCTION

Look at some pictures of snails and talk about the conditions in which they like to live. *What do they eat?* Remind the children what they found out in Lesson 10.

MAIN TEACHING ACTIVITY

Working with the whole class, suggest that the children make a vivarium in which to keep some snails so that they can watch them closely for a few days. Ask some of the children to help you put a layer of damp peat or compost in the bottom of a plastic fish tank or sweet jar. Add a few stones or pieces of wood, so that the creatures will have somewhere to hide. Sink a small lid from a jar into the compost as a water dish. Place the vivarium somewhere cool, away from direct sunlight or any radiators.

Go out and find some snails to put in the vivarium. A small tank will accommodate up to ten snails, a sweet jar about five. When you have collected them, place them carefully in their new home. Give them some food such as lettuce, vegetable peelings or small pieces of fruit. Avoid putting too much in at any one time, and make sure that any food left over is removed each morning (snails will feed more at night) so that the vivarium stays fresh and clean. Ensure that the compost remains damp, but not wet – you may need to spray it occasionally. Keep the water dish topped up and fresh. Make sure the vivarium is snail-proof but allows air to circulate.

Watch how the snails move. You can see the ripples move along the snail's foot as it climbs the side of the vivarium. If the children use a hand lens, they may be able to see a snail's mouth. Ask: *What does a snail feel like as it crawls over your hand? Why can it pull its 'horns' in? Are all the snail shells the same colour? Do they all twist in the same direction?* Carry out a simple investigation to find out what a snail's favourite food is: put small amounts of different foods in the vivarium, and see which disappears first. Don't try too many at any one time; it is better to try just two or three different foods each time and make a list of favourites, then find out which is the favourite of these. The children may be surprised to discover that snails will eat paper – which is, of course, made from wood pulp. (Banknotes are made from cotton, but you may prefer not to feed your money to snails.)

GROUP ACTIVITIES

1. The children can place living snails on black paper and observe the slime trails. When these have dried, the children can go over them with white chalk to make a permanent record.
2. The children can make model snails as follows: roll out some clay on a small cabbage leaf to make a thin layer. Gently peel the leaf away, then bend the clay to make it look like a leaf. Mould a snail body from clay by pushing it gently into an empty snail shell. Damp the base of the snail and stick it to its leaf.

DIFFERENTIATION

1. More able children could use reference books to find out why snails leave a trail of slime.
2. All the children should be able to take part in this activity.

ASSESSMENT

During the Plenary session, ask the children to describe what they would need to create a small vivarium, and how they would do it.

PLENARY

Talk about what the children have found out. *What do snails eat? How did you look after them?* Make a list of all the things the children had to do. Discuss why it is important to return the snails into the environment when you have finished observing them.

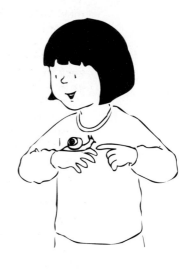

OUTCOME

● Can describe how to care for small creatures, such as snails, in a vivarium.

LINKS

Art: making 3-D models.

LESSON 16	Objective	● To know how to care for growing plants indoors.
	Resources	Plastic trays, such as those used for cat litter or school drawers; compost, small plastic mirrors, stones, grass seeds, twigs, lolly sticks, a small hand-held garden spray, small plants or cuttings.
	Main activity	The children work in groups, using the materials to design and make a model garden in a tray. They can use small mirrors for ponds, and use small stones to build walls, paths and rockeries. Garden seats can be made from lolly sticks, and trees from twigs. They can sow grass seeds and watch the lawn grow. Other small plants could be planted. The gardens will need daily care to keep the plants healthy (cutting the grass, removing dead flowers and leaves, spraying with water to keep fresh).
	Differentiation	All the children should be able to access this activity.
	Assessment	Note the children's responses during the Plenary session.
	Plenary	Discuss how the children made their gardens, and what they will need to do to help the plants grow and keep them healthy.
	Outcome	● Can describe what needs to be done to care for plants indoors.

ASSESSMENT

LESSON 17

OBJECTIVES
● To assess the children's knowledge about the seasons.
● To assess whether the children know the names of some common minibeasts.
● To assess the children's knowledge and understanding about caring for living things.

RESOURCES
Photocopiable pages 90, 91 and 92, pencils, drawing and colouring materials, scissors, adhesive.

INTRODUCTION
Assessment activity 1. Ask the whole class whether they know which season it is now. *How do you know? What are the signs? Are the trees bare or in leaf? Are there new shoots coming through? Are there birds building nests in parks or gardens? Are there baby lambs in the fields? Are the leaves changing colour? Are the hours of daylight getting longer or shorter?*
Assessment activity 2. Remind the class about the time they went out looking for minibeasts. *Can you remember any of the creatures you found?*
Assessment activity 3. Ask the class whether they remember setting up the vivarium to keep snails, and what things they needed. Say: *Ssh! Don't tell anybody, just remember it in your head, because we are going to fill in a sheet about it!*

ASSESSMENT ACTIVITY 1
Give each child a copy of page 90. Read out the sentences and make sure the children understand them. You may wish to put the names of the seasons up in the classroom, so that the children can choose and copy them if necessary. This activity is meant to sample the children's knowledge and understanding of some of the features of each season. Encourage them to think carefully about each season and draw things that show the differences between the seasons.
Answers
Mark the sheet to check that the children have identified the seasons correctly (1. spring, 2. summer, 3. autumn, 4. winter). Assess whether their pictures show something relevant to each season. You may need to ask some children to explain their pictures.
Looking for levels
Most children should be able to complete the sentences correctly and draw appropriate pictures. Less able children may not be able to draw pictures showing seasonal differences for all four seasons. More able children will be able to include several appropriate features in each picture.

ASSESSMENT ACTIVITY 2
Give each child a copy of page 91. Ask the children to complete it by choosing the correct word for each picture from the bottom of the sheet and writing it under the picture. Read through the list of words with the children before they begin.
Answers
1. snail, 2. ant, 3. woodlouse, 4. butterfly, 5. ladybird, 6. worm, 7. spider, 8. fly, 9. bee.
Looking for levels
Most children should be able to name six out of the nine creatures correctly. Less able children may have difficulty with all but the most familiar creatures, such as the snail, butterfly, ladybird, worm and spider. More able children should have no difficulty in naming all of the creatures.

ASSESSMENT ACTIVITY 3
Give each child a copy of page 92 and either drawing materials or scissors and adhesive, depending on how you want the children to complete the sheet. Identify the pictured items with the children. Read through the labels of the pictures before asking the children to choose the things needed to make a habitat for a snail. They can either draw the things needed or cut out the appropriate pictures and stick them inside the tank. They can complete the task by drawing a snail in its habitat.
Answers
The following should not be included in the picture: ice cream, chair, table, crisps.
Looking for levels
Most children should include food (green leaves), water, shelter (stone and/or log) and damp compost in their picture. Less able children may know that creatures need food and water, but may include inappropriate items such as crisps in their snail habitat. They may simply stick the objects in the tank without arranging them into a habitat picture. More able children will have no difficulty in distinguishing between the appropriate and inappropriate items.

My weather chart

Monday			
Tuesday			
Wednesday			
Thursday			
Friday			

Weather symbols to cut out and stick on chart – make several of each for class display, adjust sizes.

UNIT 3   THE ENVIRONMENT

The seasons

In _____

● we collected
these things

● the trees looked like this

● the weather was usually

UNIT 3   THE ENVIRONMENT

Our tree

This is our tree in_____

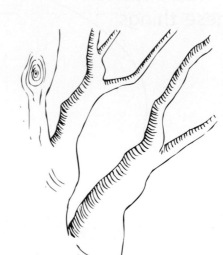
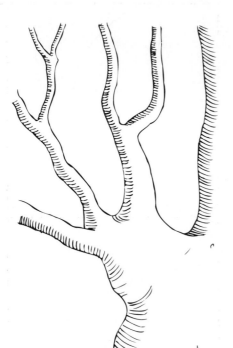

The tree measured _____cm round.

We found _____

_____

_____

_____ under the tree.

When we went out I saw...

Draw pictures to show what you saw.
Cut out the names to label your pictures.

✂

spider	ant	caterpillar	woodlouse	snail
ladybird	bee	beetle	worm	slug

Name

Habitats

The _____ is a habitat. These things live in it:

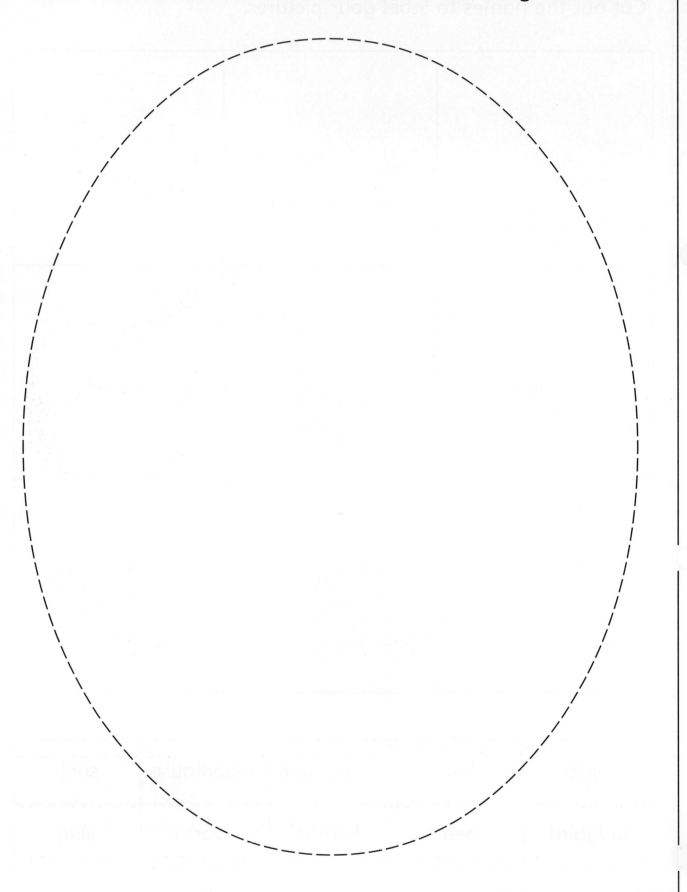

Name

Hibernation

Colour the animals that hibernate.

Animals hibernate because _____

_____

_____

Environments and living things

1. We see new shoots in the _____ .

2. The Sun is hottest in the _____ .

3. We collect acorns and conkers in the _____ .

4. Some trees have no leaves in the _____ .

Draw some of the things we see in:

spring	summer

autumn	winter

Environments and living things

Write the correct name under each picture. Use the list of names to help you.

| ant | butterfly | worm | bee | fly |
| spider | woodlouse | snail | ladybird | |

UNIT 3 THE ENVIRONMENT

Environments and living things

Name

Choose the things needed to make this tank into a habitat for a snail.

Cut out the things needed and stick them in the tank, or draw your own pictures of the things needed to make a habitat for a snail.

Name

UNIT 4

Properties of materials

	ORGANISATION (16 LESSONS)				
	OBJECTIVES	**MAIN ACTIVITY**	**GROUP ACTIVITIES**	**PLENARY**	**OUTCOMES**
LESSON 1	● To know that different materials have different properties.	Sorting materials into two groups, according to given criteria and then to their own criteria.	Sorting materials according to three given criteria. Name materials to match properties on cards.	Review names and properties of materials.	● Can name the properties of some common materials.
LESSON 2	● To be able to identify some common materials.	Match labels to samples of common materials.		Discuss the different forms that materials, especially plastics, can take.	● Can identify and name some common materials.
LESSON 3	● To know that the senses can be used to explore materials. ● To use the sense of touch to explore and identify materials.	Use a feely bag to describe or identify a hidden object.	Continue Main activity. Make a feely picture.	Review 'touch' vocabulary.	● Know that the sense of touch can help to identify materials.
LESSON 4	● To know that the senses can be used to explore materials. ● To be able to distinguish different materials by sound.	Experiment with percussion sounds. Guess a hidden material used to make a sound. Compare the sounds of different shakers and beaters.		Discuss why different materials make different sounds.	● Know that the sense of hearing can help to identify materials.
LESSON 5	● To know that the senses can be used to explore materials. ● To be able to observe closely and describe materials.	Describe a material in visual terms; other children try to identify it.		Review vocabulary. Discuss the importance of detailed observation, using all the senses.	● Know that the sense of sight can help to identify materials.
LESSON 6	● To know that some materials are magnetic, but most are not.	Predict whether various materials will be attracted to a magnet, then test.	Predict for a new set of objects, then test. Make a fridge magnet.	Establish that all the materials attracted to magnets are metals.	● Can distinguish between magnetic and non-magnetic materials. ● Can give examples of each.
LESSON 7	● To know that not all metals are magnetic.	Sort a collection of metal objects into 'magnetic' and 'not magnetic'.		Introduce the idea that only iron is magnetic.	● Know that all magnetic materials are metal, but that not all metals are magnetic.
LESSON 8	● To find out whether a magnet can work through things. ● To carry out a very simple investigation.	Investigate whether a magnet works through card and other materials.		Discuss how and why the relative thickness of the barrier alters the relative effect of the magnet.	● Can carry out a very simple investigation. ● Know that a magnet can work through other materials.

ORGANISATION (16 LESSONS)

	OBJECTIVES	MAIN ACTIVITY	GROUP ACTIVITIES	PLENARY	OUTCOMES
LESSON 9	● To know that a range of materials are used in our environment. ● To know that materials can be used in a variety of ways.	Walk around the school, inside and outside: identify materials and relate their uses to their properties.	Place labels on two photocopiable drawings of a school: outside and inside.	Children report back on findings. Compare materials used indoors to those used outdoors.	● Can recognise and name some familiar materials in their environment. ● Know that some have been used in a variety of ways.
LESSON 10	● To know that different objects can be made from the same material.	Sort a collection of objects according to type, then according to material.	Play 'Material dominoes' with objects. Say what materials some objects might be made from.	Discuss the usefulness and limitations of certain materials in different contexts.	● Know that different things can be made from the same material.
LESSON 11	● To know that an object can be made up of several materials.	Look at some everyday objects made from more than one material; identify what materials have been used and why.	Identify the materials used to make some composite objects. Suggest some unsuitable materials for these objects and explain why.	Review the work done, focusing on the properties of the materials.	● Know that some objects are made up of more than one material. ● Can identify some of these materials. ● Can explain, in simple terms, why different materials are used for different parts of an object.
LESSON 12	● To carry out a simple investigation with help. ● To know that some materials are waterproof and others are not.	Carry out an investigation to find out which material is best for keeping the rain out.	Test more materials and examine them closely. Sort them into sets: 'waterproof' and 'not waterproof'. Make an umbrella collage.	Review the investigation and discuss the reasons for choices of waterproof materials in real life.	● Can carry out a simple investigation with help. ● Understand the term 'waterproof'. ● Can draw a simple conclusion: that some materials are waterproof.
LESSON 13	● To know that some materials are changed in shape by forces.	Change the shape of play dough in a variety of ways. Consider the types of force used.	Make patterned clay tiles; consider the forces used. Make a torn paper collage; consider the forces used.	Review the work done and vocabulary used; consider other uses of force.	● Know that they can change the shape of some materials by using a force.
LESSON 14	● To know that some materials are changed in shape by forces.	Use a hammer and nails, a saw, and sandpaper on wood.		Consider the types of force used. Recap on vocabulary.	● Know that they can change the shape of some materials by using a force. ● Know that we use forces when we hammer and saw.
LESSON 15	● To know that some materials are changed in shape by forces.	Make biscuit dough and shape it into biscuits.		Consider the types of force used. Recap on ideas from previous two lessons.	● Know that they can change the shape of some materials by using a force.

	OBJECTIVES	ACTIVITY 1		ACTIVITY 2	
ASSESSMENT 16	● To know that different materials have different properties. ● To know about magnets.	State some simple properties of common materials and list some objects made from these materials.		Identify some things that are or are not attracted to a magnet.	

LESSON 1

OBJECTIVE

- To know that different materials have different properties.

RESOURCES

Main teaching activity: A collection of different materials: wood, rock, elastic, plastic (rigid, flexible, clear, coloured), glass (something like a paperweight that is not easily broken), fabric, Plasticine, paper, and so on; magnifiers.
Group activities: 1. Materials as for the Main teaching activity, A3-sized grids (see below), pencils. **2.** Cards from photocopiable page 113.

PREPARATION

Try to collect pieces or lumps of material that have not been made into a recognisable object; this will help the children to concentrate on the properties of the material rather than the properties of the object. Most fabrics these days are mixtures of several different fibres, but try to find a fabric made from a single type of fibre (such as wool or cotton). Make a set of 24 properties cards for each group from photocopiable page 113; mount them on thick card and laminate them for durability. Prepare copies of a suitable properties grid (see below).

BACKGROUND

Vocabulary

stretchy, bendy, clear, see-through, transparent, opaque, flexible, rigid, mould, hard, material, rough, smooth, waterproof

Make sure the children realise that the term 'material' does not just mean 'fabric'. These days, many synthetic materials are very convincing and may be difficult for children to sort from natural materials. Some materials have several useful properties. Wood is used for its strength and its insulating properties, and because it is relatively easy to cut and shape. Metal is strong, can be shaped and moulded, and conducts electricity. See the Vocabulary list for the main properties that children would be expected to identify at this stage.

Children need to be given experience of the ways in which some materials change. For example, water can be changed into ice, chocolate can be melted and then allowed to harden again. Some materials, such as dough and clay, change profoundly when they are heated. Later, children will learn that some changes in materials are reversible and some are not.

Beware! 'rough' and 'smooth' are often used as criteria for sorting, but these are usually properties of the objects rather than the material. A metal file is rough because it has been made so, not because metal is naturally rough. Natural rocks are rough, but a pebble has been worn until it is smooth.

INTRODUCTION

Ask the class to look at and handle the collection of materials.

MAIN TEACHING ACTIVITY

Working with the whole class, pass the materials around. Can the children name any of them? Ask: *What do they look like? What do they feel like?* See how many words the children can think of to describe them. Make a list on the board or flip chart. Introduce any appropriate words that the children have not suggested. Words such as 'flexible', 'transparent' and 'opaque' may be new to the children; each time you use such a word, add a definition to

help the children's understanding. Encourage them to use a magnifier to examine the materials closely.

Hold up each material in turn and ask the children to suggest ways of sorting the materials into two sets according to their properties. To begin with, suggest criteria such as 'hard' or 'soft', 'flexible' or 'rigid', 'transparent' or 'opaque'. Then allow the children to sort with their own criteria; ask them to give reasons for these. Encourage them to use any new vocabulary introduced earlier, and to suggest labels for their sets using correct scientific language. Write labels for the sets according to the children's suggestions.

GROUP ACTIVITIES

1. Give each pair (or group of three) an A3-sized copy of a grid like the one below, and ask them to sort the materials into the appropriate columns. The children may need help with reading the words initially.

Flexible	Rigid	Opaque	Transparent	Hard	Soft

2. Give each group of four a set of 24 properties cards (see page 113). Go through the set, making sure that the children can read and understand each card. Place the cards face-down on the table. The children take turns to pick up a card and read it out. If they can name a material that matches the property on the card, they can keep the card. If not, they return it face-down to the bottom of the pile. Each material can only be used once. When the cards run out, the player with the most cards wins.

DIFFERENTIATION

1. Less able children could be given a grid with four rather than six columns, and fewer materials to sort.
2. Children may need some adult support the first time they play the game. You may wish to put them into mixed-ability groups so that they can help each other.

ASSESSMENT

Check that when the children are sorting the materials, they are able to identify some of their simple properties.

PLENARY

Return to the collection of materials and discuss the properties of each with the children. Ask them to name the materials. Encourage them to use the new vocabulary introduced during the lesson. Name a property (such as 'opaque'), and ask the children to choose a material with that property.

OUTCOME

● Can name the properties of some common materials.

LINKS

Maths: sorting into sets.

LESSON 2

Objective	● To be able to identify some common materials.
Resources	Samples of wood, glass, paper, metal, rock, plastics; labels with names of the materials.
Main activity	Gather the children around you, look at the collection of materials and ask the children to name those they know. Make sure they name the material and not the object. Ask them to match labels to the materials they can identify. Tell them the names of any they are unable to identify, and attach the appropriate labels.
Differentiation	Less able children may need help with reading the labels. Offer more able children more than one example of each material (such as foam plastic, polythene and rigid plastic; balsa wood and oak).
Assessment	During the Plenary session, hold up the materials and ask the children to identify them.
Plenary	Discuss the fact that some materials can occur in different forms, especially made or manufactured materials. Talk about the variety of ways in which plastics are used: hard containers, bags, windows, CDs, clothing etc.
Outcome	● Can identify and name some common materials.

LESSON 3

OBJECTIVES
● To know that the senses can be used to explore materials.
● To use the sense of touch to explore and identify materials.

RESOURCES
Main teaching activity: A collection of materials that feel different, such as a small wooden block, plastics (a piece of synthetic sponge, a section from a squeezy bottle, a piece of a carrier bag), metal, fabric, glass (a paperweight), paper, cork, wax; feely bags. Make sure that there are no sharp edges on which children could hurt themselves.
Group activities: 1. Enough sets of equipment, as listed for Main teaching activity, for one set per group. **2.** Large sheets of paper, a variety of collage materials of different textures (sawdust, bottle tops, cotton wool, fabric, sand and so on), adhesive, scissors.

Vocabulary

stretchy, bendy, flexible, rigid, mould, hard, material, rough, smooth, cold, warm, natural, made, manufactured

BACKGROUND
It is important to use pieces or lumps of materials rather than objects at this stage, because children often find it difficult to distinguish between the object, the actual properties of the material, and its attributes. Young children only need to be able to name some simple properties of a small range of common materials, but it is important for us to be clear about the differences between the intrinsic properties of materials and their attributes (what properties can be given to them in the manufacturing process). For example, all plastics are waterproof and have a relatively low melting point. These are properties of the material. But plastics can be made rigid or flexible; transparent, translucent or opaque. These are attributes of the manufactured products. Wood is strong, it floats and it insulates; these are properties. It can be made rough or smooth, flat or curved, dyed or polished; these are attributes.

INTRODUCTION

Working with the whole class, look at a range of materials and talk about what they might feel like. Tell the children that they are going to use their sense of touch to identify these materials. Encourage them to feel the materials and think of words to describe them. Introduce any new words you think relevant.

MAIN TEACHING ACTIVITY

Use a feely bag or box in which to hide the materials, so that the children can only explore them by touch. It is important that they have seen and felt the materials before these are put in the feely bag. At first, put a single material in the bag and ask a child to try and describe it using the sense of touch alone. Ask: *What does it feel like?* Encourage them to use any words they can think of, but help them to focus on words that describe the properties of the materials (see Background). Ask the class to guess what material is in the bag. Take the material out to check the answer.

Next, put two materials in the bag. Name one of the materials and ask a child to find that one in the bag. You will not have the time (or stamina!) to let every child in the class have a turn in this way; but the activity can be continued by groups (see below) so that every child will eventually have a turn. As a general rule of hygiene, make sure that the children wash their hands after playing the game.

GROUP ACTIVITIES

1. Continue from the Main teaching activity, using one feely bag for each group. One child describes what he or she can feel, and the other children in the group try to guess what material it is. Encourage the children to use the vocabulary introduced in the Main teaching activity.

2. Groups of four can make feely pictures. Using a large sheet of paper, they should 'take a pencil for a walk' to create a random pattern, then fill in each area with a different collage material (see Resources). Encourage the children to describe the materials they are using in terms of what they feel like. Alternatively, you could stick several large sheets of paper together and have six to eight children at a time making a class feely picture (to cover a display board).

DIFFERENTIATION

1. More able children could try to describe two fairly similar materials (such as paper and sheet plastic) and distinguish between them. Less able children will need help to use the correct vocabulary. They may well need reminding not to tell the other children what is in the bag!
2. This activity is accessible to all the children.

ASSESSMENT

Do the children understand that their sense of touch is helping them to identify the materials? Are they able to use some of the vocabulary appropriately?

PLENARY

Have another look at the materials the children have been working with. Remind them that they have used their sense of touch to help them describe and identify the materials. Hold up some of the materials and ask: *What 'touch' words can we use about this material?*

OUTCOME

● Know that the sense of touch can help to identify materials.

LINKS

Unit 1, Lesson 3: how our senses make us aware of the surroundings.

LESSON 4

Objectives	● To know that the senses can be used to explore materials. ● To be able to distinguish different materials by sound.
Resources	Samples of materials (Plasticine, wood, metal, plastic sheet, rigid plastic, paper, dough etc); percussion instruments, beaters made from various materials, a large cloth or cardboard screen, empty plastic pots with lids.
Main activity	Bang materials on the table, rub them together, crush them or drop them on to a hard floor. Let the children choose a material to drop or bang and listen to carefully. Hide materials behind a screen and ask the children to guess the materials from the sounds. Make shakers from small plastic pots, fill with different materials and compare the sounds. Use different beaters with percussion instruments and compare the effects.
Differentiation	Be sensitive to the fact that some children may have difficulty in hearing some sounds.
Assessment	During the Main activity, note those children who are able to identify the materials.
Plenary	Talk about why materials make different sounds, for example hard materials tend to make louder or harsher sounds than softer materials.
Outcome	● Know that the sense of hearing can help to identify materials.

LESSON 5

Objectives	● To know that the senses can be used to explore materials. ● To be able to observe and describe materials visually.
Resources	A collection of different materials (as for Lesson 3).
Main activity	Lay out the collection of materials where the children can see them. Take turns to describe a material, without touching or naming it. The others try to guess which material is being described. Let the children name some uses of the material as part of their description, for example 'Sometimes it is used for windows' (glass).
Differentiation	With less able children, restrict the number of materials. With more able children, introduce materials with similar visual properties where the differences may be more subtle.
Assessment	During the Main activity, note those children who can describe or identify materials.
Plenary	List the vocabulary used to describe the materials. Talk about how observations need to be careful and detailed. Discuss how our observations can be further enhanced if we can use all of the senses.
Outcome	● Know that the sense of sight can help to identify materials.

LESSON 6

OBJECTIVE

● To know that some materials are magnetic, but most are not.

RESOURCES

Main teaching activity: Good magnets of different shapes and sizes; a collection of materials such as small pieces of wood, plastic (a piece of synthetic sponge, a section from a squeezy bottle, a piece from a carrier bag), metal (a paper clip, a nut, a washer), fabric, paper, cork, wax, string; set rings for sorting. The samples of materials should be small enough to be picked up by the magnet if they are magnetic. Remove any non-magnetic metal samples at this stage. Plain metal discs are useful for this activity, since the object cannot be confused with the material.
Group activities: 1. Photocopiable page 114, more samples of some different materials, magnets. **2.** Magnetic tape, card, scissors, adhesive, felt-tipped pens or crayons, collage materials.

Vocabulary

magnet, magnetic, attract, attraction, repel, repulsion, pick up, stick to, metal, non-metal

BACKGROUND

Most children will probably already have some experience with magnets. They may have a collection of fridge magnets at home. Some of them may have noticed the magnetic catches on cupboard doors.

Make sure that any magnets you use are reasonably strong. Bar magnets are available from most educational suppliers. Old audio speakers (often available from car boot sales) can be a source of really strong magnets that would otherwise be expensive to buy. Magnets should always be stored properly in order to help them remain magnetic for as long as possible. Store ceramic bar magnets in pairs in the box they were supplied in. Store other magnets complete with a keeper. Magnets will lose their strength if dropped continually, though plastic-coated ceramic magnets (which have iron particles baked into the clay) are a little more resilient.

Children should be warned about the dangers of putting strong magnets next to equipment such as tape recorders, computers or television sets, which may be damaged by the magnetic field. At this stage, it is not necessary to mention 'magnetic fields' to the children: this is far too abstract a concept. They may discover during their play that 'the red ends push away' or 'don't stick', but learning about north and south poles and like poles repelling comes later. It is important that, at first, the children encounter only metals that are magnetic. This allows them to develop the concept that only metal is magnetic. The next stage is for them to discover that not even all metals are attracted to a magnet: it is only those that contain iron. Other metals, such as aluminium, tin, copper or gold are not magnetic unless they are mixed with iron. For example, aluminium soft drinks cans are not magnetic, but steel ones (which contain iron) are. **Never** use loose iron filings with the children – they make a terrible mess, are almost impossible to clean off magnets, and are toxic if ingested in any quantity. There is also a danger of children rubbing them into their eyes.

INTRODUCTION

Show the class the range of magnets. Ask: *Do you know what these are? What do they do?* Find out what the children already know about magnets. Do they understand the terms 'repel' and 'attract'? Reinforce these, giving definitions.

MAIN TEACHING ACTIVITY

Tell the children that some of the magnets in the collection are stronger than others. Ask: *What do we mean by a 'strong' magnet?* Demonstrate that a stronger magnet will pick up more or heavier objects than a weaker one. Talk about the importance of keeping the magnets well away from TVs, tape recorders or computers, because of the damage they can do.

Go through the names of the materials in the collection, and ask the children to predict which of these materials will be attracted to a magnet. *Why do you think that?* Make a 'yes' and 'no' list on the board. Ask the children to test their predictions by taking turns to try one of the materials and putting it into the correct set ring. Ask: *Do you know what all the materials in the 'yes' set are made from?* Reinforce the fact that they are all made of metal.

GROUP ACTIVITIES

1. Ask the children to look at a new set of objects and predict which ones will be attracted to a magnet. They can then sort the objects using a magnet and record their findings on a copy of photocopiable page 114.
2. The children can make a simple fridge magnet by sticking magnetic tape to the back of a small picture card. The picture could be drawn and coloured in, cut from a commercial card, or collaged with sequins and other attractive scraps.

DIFFERENTIATION

1. Children who have not experienced magnets before will need time to play with the magnets and discover that they 'stick' to things.
2. Encourage more able children to design their own game using magnets.

ASSESSMENT

Use the photocopiable sheets to check that the children can sort magnetic from non-magnetic materials. Do they know that all the magnetic materials are metals?

PLENARY

Talk about the things that were attracted to the magnet, and the materials from which they were made. Make the generalisation that all the things attracted to the magnets were made of metal. Reinforce any new vocabulary.

OUTCOMES

● Can distinguish between magnetic and non-magnetic materials.
● Can give examples of each.

LINKS

Maths: sorting.

LESSON 7

Objective	● To know that not all metals are magnetic.
Resources	A collection of coins, or a set of discs of different metals (named if possible). Check the 'copper' coins that you use: the composition of the metal used for these coins has changed. Newer coins contain more steel, and are therefore magnetic; older coins are not.
Main activity	Sort the metals and coins into 'magnetic' and 'not magnetic'.
Differentiation	More able children could find out the names of some of the metals using a named set of samples.
Assessment	Observe and question the children as they do the Main activity. Can they tell you that all materials attracted to a magnet are metal, but not all metals are magnetic?
Plenary	Discuss why not all metals are magnetic. Introduce the idea that some metals contain a special metal called iron, and that this is attracted to the magnet.
Outcome	● Know that all magnetic materials are metal, but that not all metals are magnetic.

LESSON 8

Objectives	• To find out whether a magnet can work through things. • To carry out a very simple investigation.
Resources	Fairly strong magnets, paper clips, sheets of card.
Main activity	Ask the children (working in pairs) to put a paper clip on top of a piece of card, then to hold a magnet underneath and see whether they can move the paper clip. How many sheets of card can they add before the paper clip fails to move? Does the magnet work through a table or a chair seat?
Differentiation	More able children could test two or three magnets to see whether they all work through the same number of sheets. Less able children could draw a simple road map and take the 'car' (paper clip) along the road to the garage.
Assessment	Observe and note which children are able to carry out this investigation. During the Plenary session, note which children could say why the magnet appeared to stop working (too many layers).
Plenary	Discuss why the magnet stopped working when there were too many layers, and why some worked through more layers than others. Remind them that the card is not magnetic: the magnet is working through it.
Outcomes	• Can carry out a very simple investigation. • Know that a magnet can work through other materials.

LESSON 9

OBJECTIVES
• To know that a range of materials are used in our environment.
• To know that materials can be used in a variety of ways.

RESOURCES
Main teaching activity: The environment within and around the school.
Group activities: 1. Photocopiable page 115, scissors, adhesive. **2.** Photocopiable page 116, scissors, adhesive.

Vocabulary

metal, glass, plastic, brick, clay, wood, wax, paper, stone, concrete, tarmac, same, different

BACKGROUND
Plastics, these days, can be made to mimic or replace most materials, and their use is constantly increasing. Children will be very familiar with plastic bags, toys and cups, but may find some other forms more difficult to distinguish from the material they are replacing (for example, a plastic table-top and a wooden one). Plastics are now widely used in buildings, replacing the traditional materials: roof tiles, pipes, windows, doors and even paint are now often plastic. For this reason, there may be some confusion if you ask children about the materials used to build a house. An old cottage may still have wooden window frames, a thatched roof and metal pipes, but a modern dwelling is likely to have a very high plastic content. The surface finish of some materials may also be confusing –

for example, metals may be plastic-coated; high-gloss paint may hide wood or metal. Some materials, such as concrete and tarmac, are aggregates or composites. Concrete is often made to look like natural stone, as in paving slabs and garden ornaments.

INTRODUCTION
Tell the children that they are going on a 'materials walkabout'. Explain that they are looking for the materials from which things are made, and also looking for examples of different things made from the same material.

MAIN TEACHING ACTIVITY

Before going out, mention some of the materials that the children might find and help them to identify examples around the classroom. Talk about the fact that they might see the same material used in a variety of ways. Name one or two of the objects they are likely to find outside (such as railings, benches or litter bins), and discuss the materials they are made from. Draw their attention to some of the properties of these materials. Discuss why they have been used in the manufacture of those particular objects.

Walk round the school, first inside and then outside. Help the children to focus on various objects and the materials from which they are made. Encourage them to link the properties of the materials with the objects, and to compare and contrast some materials. For example, railings, lampposts and chair legs are made of metal for strength, but chair seats would be very uncomfortable if they too were made of metal. A metal door would be strong, but far too heavy to open and close. Talk about materials, such as concrete, that have been made from a mixture of other materials. Ask them how many examples of the same material they can find being used to make different objects, such as wooden doors and chairs.

GROUP ACTIVITIES

1. Give each child a copy of page 115. Ask the children to cut out the labels and stick them in the appropriate boxes to label the picture.
2. Give each child a copy of page 116. Ask the children to cut out the labels and stick them in the appropriate boxes to label the picture.

DIFFERENTIATION

1. Less able children may need help with reading the labels. More able children may be able to add some properties of the materials to their labels.
2. More able children could look for and label mixed materials (such as concrete or tarmac) in the picture. They could make additions to the picture, such as a metal letter-box cover.

ASSESSMENT

Use the photocopiable sheets to check whether the children are naming familiar materials correctly.

PLENARY

Encourage children to report back to the whole class about their findings. Talk about the materials that were found both inside and outside, and the properties that make them suitable for both localities. Ask: *Why do you think both doors and pencils are made of wood? Is it because wood is both strong and easy to cut and shape? Were any materials only indoors or outdoors? Why might this be? Would tarmac be a sensible type of flooring for the classroom? Was any particular material found more often than the others?* Reinforce the new vocabulary learned.

OUTCOMES

● Can recognise and name some familiar materials in their environment.
● Know that some have been used in a variety of ways.

LINKS

English: labelling.

LESSON 10

OBJECTIVE
● To know that different objects can be made from the same material.

RESOURCES
Main teaching activity: A collection of similar objects made from different materials (two or three examples of each object), such as toy cars (wooden, plastic and metal), bricks (wooden and plastic), cups (paper, plastic and pottery), spoons (metal, plastic and wood) and bowls (paper, plastic, pottery and wood).
Group activities: 1. A collection as above. **2.** Photocopiable page 117, pencils.
Plenary: Pictures of other objects made from the same materials as the objects in the collection.

BACKGROUND
As children become more familiar with different materials, they will appreciate that some have more than one useful property and are therefore suitable for a range of purposes. For example, metal can be shaped (when heated) into bowls, cups or jewellery; but it is also strong, and so can be used to make furniture, ships or bridges. Both of these properties make it ideal for making tools to work other materials. Wood is warm to the touch, is strong, can be shaped and joined, and is pleasing to look at, so it is ideal for use in building and furniture-making. Always encourage the children to think about why a particular material has been chosen to make an object.

Vocabulary

same, different, materials, wood, plastic, metal, paper, clay, objects, strong, pliable, shaped, joined

INTRODUCTION
Gather the children around you and look at the collection of objects. Ask the children to name the objects and say what they are used for.

MAIN TEACHING ACTIVITY
Sort the collection into sets according to the object: all the cups, all the spoons and so on. When the collection has been sorted, look at each set and ask the children to name the material from which each object has been made. Explain that pottery objects are made from clay. Now ask the children to re-sort the objects according to the material from which they are made. Discuss why different materials might be used to make each object. For example, plastic cutlery is very useful for parties, because it is safe and saves lots of washing-up; but it is not really strong enough for everyday use, so metal is better. Wooden bowls look nice and are good for keeping fruit in; but they would burn if put in the oven, so they are not suitable for cooking.

GROUP ACTIVITIES
1. Groups of three can play 'Material dominoes'. One child chooses an object from the collection and places it on the table. The next child chooses a different object made from the same material. The third child chooses a similar object made from a different material, and they go on alternating – for example: wooden fork, wooden bowl, metal bowl, metal knife, plastic knife, plastic cup.
2. Give each child a copy of page 117. Ask the children to write the names of the materials from which the object could be made in the space opposite each picture. They can use the words at the bottom of the page to help them.

DIFFERENTIATION
1. Some children may still need help with identifying the materials rather than the objects. More able children could be given objects where the material is not so obvious (such as painted wood or metal) and asked to name the materials.
2. All the children should be able to do this activity. More able children may be more inventive in their choice of materials for some objects and include materials not on the list. They should be asked to justify their choices.

ASSESSMENT

Observe the children playing the dominoes game, and use the photocopiable sheet to check their understanding.

PLENARY

Choose a few objects from the collection that are made of the same material. Review the properties of that material, and talk about which property has made it suitable for each object. Discuss the limitations of the material – for example, wooden or plastic bowls would burn or melt if heated. Pottery plates are easily broken, but paper plates are weak and can only be used once. Use pictures to stimulate discussion about other uses of the materials in the collection: buildings, bridges, cars and so on.

OUTCOME

● Know that different things can be made from the same material.

LESSON 11

OBJECTIVE

● To know that an object can be made up of several materials.

RESOURCES

Main teaching activity: A collection of objects made up of two or three (fairly evident) materials, such as a shoe, a trainer, a Wellington boot, a pencil, a pencil case, an umbrella, a chair, scissors (with plastic handles), a plastic pencil sharpener, a torch.
Group activities: 1. Photocopiable page 118, pencils, the objects listed on page 118.
2. The objects listed on page 118.

BACKGROUND

Many objects are made from more than one material because no single material is the most suitable for every aspect or function of the object. The materials from which composite objects are made are chosen largely for their properties, but also for their price, availability and appeal. For example, wood makes a pencil strong and more comfortable to hold. The lead alone would break easily, be messy to use and be difficult to hold. (The 'lead' in a pencil is really graphite.) Scissors need metal blades to cut efficiently, but may have plastic handles for more comfortable and secure handling. It is not always easy to identify the individual materials that go to make up an object; in particular, plastics can be made to mimic a wide range of other materials. Plastics have also taken over many of the roles of more traditional materials such as wood. A wooden item has to be cut, shaped and finished individually, whereas many plastic objects can be produced from the same mould with little finishing required. It is therefore much less labour-intensive and much less time-consuming to make objects from plastic. Plastic is a manufactured material, but it is chemically derived from oil – a natural substance that has formed from the decomposed bodies of sea creatures that died several millennia ago.

INTRODUCTION

Working with the whole class, recap on some familiar materials and remind the children what they look and feel like. Choose a familiar object made from one material. Discuss the material, its properties, and why that particular material has been used for that particular object.

MAIN TEACHING ACTIVITY

Introduce an object that has been made from two or three materials and ask the children to identify them. Can they say why the different materials have been chosen? You may need to help them identify the properties that have made these materials suitable. Invite the children to handle and explore several simple objects made from more than one material. Identify and discuss the materials that have been used. Encourage the children to describe these materials and to relate their uses to their properties. For example, the outside of a Wellington boot is made from plastic and plastic is waterproof – ideal for splashing through the puddles on a rainy day! The insole is usually cotton, which is warm and makes the boot more comfortable to wear.

If a writing pencil is one of the objects discussed, the children should be made aware that the 'lead' is actually a natural material called graphite (though it is usually called 'lead'). As well as making the pencil stronger and more comfortable to hold, the wood is easy to shape and cut to the correct length in the pencil factory. The children could compare a plain wooden pencil and a painted one. *Why do you think the pencil has been painted? Does it make it easier to hold or to write with, or does it just make the pencil look more attractive?*

GROUP ACTIVITIES

1. The children can complete page 118 by ticking the appropriate boxes. It will be helpful to provide the corresponding objects for them to handle. They could work individually, or in groups of about four with one child (or an adult helper) filling in a group sheet.
2. Working in groups of about four and using the same objects as in Group activity 1, the children suggest materials that could not sensibly be used for each particular object and explain why. For example, a paper shoe would get soggy when wet and fall to pieces – and it would not wear very well even if you could keep it dry. This activity could be purely oral, or the children could record in their own way.

DIFFERENTIATION

1. Less able children could be given fewer, very familiar objects made of no more than two materials – for example, a plastic pencil sharpener or scissors with plastic handles. You may need to adapt the photocopiable sheet to make it more appropriate for some children. Others may need a set of labels listing the materials from which the objects are made. More complex objects and more subtle differences between materials can be introduced to extend more able children.
2. Some groups may need adult support throughout, while other groups will be able to report their ideas back to the whole class at the end of the activity.

ASSESSMENT

Can the children identify the materials in some objects made from more than one material? Can they say why some of these materials have been chosen?

PLENARY

Discuss some of the objects and identify the various materials from which they have been made. Talk about why particular materials have been used. Reinforce the properties of the materials – for example, that some are easily shaped, some are strong and some are soft and pliable. Encourage the children who have done Group activity 2 to report back on some of their 'strange' objects.

OUTCOMES

- Know that some objects are made up of more than one material.
- Can identify some of these materials.
- Can explain, in simple terms, why different materials are used for different parts of an object.

LESSON 12

OBJECTIVES

● To carry out a simple investigation with help.
● To know that some materials are waterproof and others are not.

RESOURCES

Main teaching activity: 'Happiness (John's got great big waterproof boots on)' by AA Milne (from *When We Were Very Young*, Mammoth); an umbrella, sheet plastic (a piece of a carrier or plastic bag), paper, a metal lid (not sharp) or small metal tray, a piece of cotton or woollen fabric, a see-through plastic container, elastic bands, a small watering can, a tray, water, a small plastic teddy bear, an ordinary teddy bear.
Group activities: 1. More samples of waterproof and non-waterproof materials, a magnifier, a water trough, scissors, adhesive, art paper. **2.** Photocopiable page 119, material samples, scissors, adhesive.

PREPARATION

Cheap and cheerful containers can be made from cut-off plastic drinks bottles. Turn the top upside-down to make a funnel. Bind the edges with sticky tape to cover any sharp edges.

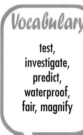

Vocabulary

test, investigate, predict, waterproof, fair, magnify

BACKGROUND

Children at this stage will need lots of help with planning and carrying out an investigation. Nevertheless, they need to be encouraged to contribute their ideas about how an investigation could be done. They should also be encouraged to think about what the results might be. It may be a fairly wild guess – in some cases, based on a favourite colour or because a material feels nice. A scientific prediction is usually based on past experience or an observable pattern, and most young children have limited experience on which to draw at this stage. Always ask children to give you a reason for their prediction.

Children will be able to tell you whether a test is not fair long before they are able to plan a fair test. Some may spontaneously volunteer the information; but for most, careful questioning will be needed. *Was it fair that we started from different places? Does it matter if one piece is much bigger than the other? How much water should we put on each one?* Questions such as these will help children to start thinking about the need for tests to be fair if the results are to be valid. It is also important for them to think about what they have found out and draw some kind of conclusion.

Fabrics may be made from natural materials such as wool, cotton or silk, but many these days are synthetic or a mixture of different fibres. Unless you have the label to hand, it is often impossible to identify what the mixture is. However, the emphasis of this lesson is on carrying out an investigation and on the property of being waterproof, so identifying the exact type of each fabric is less important.

INTRODUCTION

The poem 'Happiness' by AA Milne would be a good stimulus at the start of this lesson. Working with the whole class, present an ordinary teddy bear. Say that Teddy needs a new roof on his house, a raincoat, a hat or an umbrella, and you need to find the best material from which to make it. Remind the children what they found out in Lesson 11 about waterproof materials. Look at an umbrella and ask: *How do we know it is waterproof?* (It stops the rain from coming through.)

MAIN TEACHING ACTIVITY

Show the children a selection of materials and ask which they think would be best for making an umbrella. Ask them to give reasons for their choices. Draw their attention to the holes between the threads in a woven fabric, and ask what they think might happen if you poured water over that material. Ask them for ideas about how they could find out which materials are waterproof. Have the container and other apparatus on the table, so that the children may pick up some clues. Suggest that the test needs to be the same for each material, and ask how that could be done. Look for suggestions such as using pieces of material of the same size and using the same amount of water. If these ideas are not forthcoming, questions such as: *Do you think it will be fair if we pour more water over that one?* may elicit answers.

One way of carrying out this investigation is to put the small plastic bear in the bottom of a clear container, then place the material to be tested over the top and hold it in place with an elastic band. (Explain that the real Teddy would be too big for the container.) Stand the container in a tray, or work outside if the weather permits, and pour water from a small watering can over the container and material. *If the little bear stays dry, then the material is waterproof; if it gets wet, oh dear!* Children may come up with ideas on how to carry out the test, or you may have to tell them. Ask the children to predict which materials will be waterproof and which will not. Sort them into two sets. Carry out the test on each set and re-sort as necessary. Try not to give the impression that the children were 'wrong' if their prediction proved to be false: emphasise the fact that what happened was different from what they expected.

GROUP ACTIVITIES

1. Pairs or groups of three can explore more waterproof and non-waterproof materials, using a water trough (inside or outside). They can look at the materials through a magnifier. Draw their attention to the holes between the threads in woven fabrics. They could use a baby bath or washing-up bowl if a water trough is not available. After testing, they can sort the materials and stick small pieces of them onto sheets marked 'waterproof' and 'not waterproof' as a record.
2. Give each child a copy of photocopiable page 119. Help the children to choose a suitable waterproof material for the umbrella and collage it onto the picture.

DIFFERENTIATION

1. Less able children may need to be told what to do, but they may be able to make suggestions or choose from the available equipment. Encourage them to make predictions even though they may be unable to give reasons for them – any prediction, even one without a stated reason, is testable. More able children will be able to predict and give valid reasons for their predictions without help. They will be able to say when a test is not fair.
2. All the children should be able to do this activity.

ASSESSMENT

Note whether the children understand the term 'waterproof'. Can they identify waterproof materials at the end of their investigation? Which children can make a simple prediction and understand when a test is not fair?

PLENARY

Help the children to understand what they have found out. Remind them what they thought would happen. Talk about how they did the test and what happened. *How did we keep the test fair? Why was the result different from what you expected? Was it because the material you chose was not waterproof when you tested it? Which of the materials would be best for making a raincoat, hat or umbrella? Which other properties need to be considered as well as being waterproof? Metal is waterproof, but why wouldn't it make a good coat? What would it be useful for?* (Maybe a roof, a car or a mug to keep water in.)

OUTCOMES

- Can carry out a simple investigation with help.
- Understand the term 'waterproof'.
- Can draw a simple conclusion: that some materials are waterproof.

LESSON 13

OBJECTIVE

● To know that some materials are changed in shape by forces.

RESOURCES

Main teaching activity: Play dough (see recipe on page 110), rolling pins, cutters, safe knives.
Group activities: 1. Clay, rolling pins. **2.** A selection of papers to be torn for collage work, adhesive, spreaders.

Vocabulary

squeeze, squash, push, pull, roll, press, hammer, saw, cut, tear

BACKGROUND

Most forces are basically a push or a pull. Children will be familiar with the fact that they can change the shape of a material or object by such actions as banging, pressing, squashing and rolling (which are all types of push). They will also know that stretching and tearing (which are types of pull) will cause materials to change their shape. They need to be made aware that the above are all types of forces, and that the use of a force is necessary to cause a change in shape. Always use the correct vocabulary with the children, and provide definitions. For example: *Use a little more force to flatten your play dough – push it harder.* Be careful of using words such as 'pressure' in the context of changing the shape of materials. It has a different, precise scientific meaning which the children will learn about later. They should simply be taught that they are using a force to change the shape of things.

For Lesson 14, the children should be taught how to use tools correctly, safely and sensibly. Small junior hacksaws are quite safe for them to use, provided that they have been shown how to hold the wood in a vice and the wood is soft and easy to cut. Beware of bags of offcuts of wood, which are often too hard, thick and splintery.

INTRODUCTION

Remind the children that they have been learning about materials. Say that pushes and pulls can change the shape of things. For example: flattening dough is a push, tearing paper is a pull.

MAIN TEACHING ACTIVITY

Work with the whole class initially. Show the children a piece of play dough and ask them how many ways they can think of to change its shape. Encourage them to use appropriate vocabulary such as 'roll', 'push', 'press', 'squash', 'pinch', 'pull' and 'cut'. Discuss the fact that we are using a force every time we change the shape of the play dough. Ask them as you change the shape of the play dough: *Is this a push or a pull?*

Sit the children at their tables and give them each a ball of play dough. Ask them to reshape their dough in as many ways as they can, into pancakes, sausages, worms and so on. Encourage them to cut the play dough with safe knives and cutters, make pancakes with rolling pins, and press their fingers into it to make patterns. Can they say whether they are using a pull or a push force on their play dough? Can they get it back into the ball shape they started with?

Reinforce the vocabulary used earlier.

GROUP ACTIVITIES

1. The children could work either individually or in pairs. Ask them to roll out some clay to make a tile, and then to push smaller pieces of clay into the tile to make a pattern. They should make sure that the base tile is not too thin, or they will end up with something that is full of holes and looks more like lace than a tile when they push their pieces into it! Talk about the fact that they are changing the shape of both the actual tile and the little pieces of clay being pushed into it. If possible, the patterned tiles could be glazed and fired.

2. Individuals or groups could tear paper to make a collage. This could be an abstract design or a picture showing something being pushed or pulled (such as a tug of war). Remind the children that they are using a force to change the shape of their paper by tearing it, and are pushing the small pieces onto the glue. *Do you need more force to tear several layers at once?*

DIFFERENTIATION

1. Although this activity is accessible to all, some children may need extra help to relate what they are doing to the idea of using a force to change the shape of an object. You may need to explain that rolling clay with a rolling pin and pressing other pieces of clay into it are examples of pushes.

2. This activity should be accessible to all the children.

ASSESSMENT

Do the children understand that when they change the shape of a material, they are using a force? Are they able to name these forces as pushes and pulls?

PLENARY

Ask the children to show some of the tiles they have made to the whole class. Ask them what sort of force they used to make them. See how many of the words they practised earlier they can remember. Can they think of any other activity where forces are used to change the shape of things (for example, squeezing the sponge in the bath to get the water out, cutting up their dinner, folding a piece of paper)? Look at the collaged pictures made by the children, and discuss how they used a (pulling) force to tear the paper.

OUTCOMES

● Know that they can change the shape of some materials by using a force.

LINKS

Unit 6, Lesson 4: using forces to shape pastry.

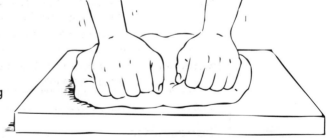

Play dough recipe
2 cups plain flour
2 tsbp cooking oil
2 cups water
1 cup salt
2 tsp cream of tartar
a few drops of food colouring

Mix all the ingredients together in a large saucepan and cook over a medium heat, stirring all the time, until the mixture leaves the sides of the saucepan. Turn onto a board and knead the dough until smooth.

Play dough is a good material to use, as it is often softer than Plasticine and less messy than modelling clay. It will keep for a very long time in an airtight tin; in fact, it usually gets unacceptably grubby before it becomes hard and crumbly!

LESSON 14

Objective	● To know that some materials are changed in shape by forces.
Resources	Small, light hammers; blocks of wood (balsa is ideal), nails, sandpaper, a junior hacksaw, a workbench with a vice; coloured wools, ribbons and threads.
Main activity	Working in groups, the children can use sandpaper to smooth and round the edges of a block of wood, hammer some nails into the wood and decorate the block by winding coloured wool, ribbon and thread around and between the nails. They can take turns to place another block of wood in a vice and saw it in half.
Differentiation	Children can be taught to hammer and saw safely at this stage, especially using balsa wood; but some may need closer supervision.
Assessment	Talk to the children while they are working to find out whether they understand that they are using a force to change the shape of the wood.
Plenary	Relate the hammering, sawing and sandpapering of the wood to forces (pushes and pulls). Recap on vocabulary learned and practised.
Outcomes	● Know that they can change the shape of some materials by using a force. ● Know that we use forces when we hammer and saw.

LESSON 15

Objective	● To know that some materials are changed in shape by forces.
Resources	Biscuit ingredients, rolling pins, bowls, biscuit cutters, baking trays, an oven, the recipe below.
Main activity	Working in groups of four, the children can make the biscuit dough, roll it out, cut biscuits and decorate them – using, practising and reinforcing all the forces vocabulary and ideas learned in Lesson 13.
Differentiation	Some children will need extra support to link what they are doing to the ideas in Lesson 13.
Assessment	Talk to the children as they are rolling and shaping their biscuits to find out whether they understand that they are using a force to change the shape of the dough.
Plenary	Discuss what the children have been doing and relate this to other work on changing shapes by using a force. Ask them to identify actions and forces that they used with the play dough and are using again here.
Outcomes	● Know that they can change the shape of some materials by using a force.

Biscuit recipe
150g plain flour
25g cornflour
125g butter
50g sugar

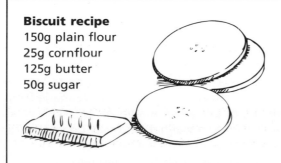

Mix the dry ingredients together in a bowl. Knead the butter into them until a soft dough is obtained. This is quite a sticky procedure, but each child in the group could have a turn. Divide the mixture into four, one piece for each child. Roll out and cut into shapes. Place on a greased baking sheet and bake at 180°C (350°F, Gas Mark 3) until light gold in colour.

ASSESSMENT

LESSON 16

OBJECTIVES
- To know that different materials have different properties.
- To know about magnets.

RESOURCES
Photocopiable pages 120 and 121, pencils, colouring materials.

INTRODUCTION
Ask the children: *Can anyone remember some of the properties of some of the materials we have looked at? What are the special words we have used?* (Strong, waterproof, transparent, hard, soft, flexible, rigid, magnetic and so on.)

ASSESSMENT ACTIVITY 1
Give the children a copy each of page 120. Read through the text together and make sure they understand it. Some children may need to have the sentences read to them again as they work through them. Ask the children to finish each sentence and then make a list of other things made from the same material. Some children may prefer to draw picture lists rather than make a written list.

Answers
Accept answers that show understanding even if they do not make proper sentences.
1. '...we can see through it' or '...it is transparent'. The list could include: vase, bowl, tumbler, dish, bottle, fish tank, greenhouse, conservatory and so on.
2. '...it is strong or rigid' or '...it is not too heavy'. The list could include: chairs, tables, fences, gates, wooden spoon, chopping board and so on.
3. '...it is waterproof'. The list could include: bucket, spade, cups, saucers, bowls, lunchboxes, carrier bags and so on.
4. '...it is strong' or '...it can be sharpened to a point'. The list could include: tools, spoon, bucket, car, nails, screws, letterbox and so on.

Looking for levels
Most children should be able to identify a correct property for three materials, and to list at least three other objects made from the same material. Less able children may only be able to identify a correct property for one or two materials, and to name one or two other objects made from the same material. They may provide their lists in pictorial form (and some may need to explain their pictures). More able children will identify at least one property for each material, and list more than three other objects.

ASSESSMENT ACTIVITY 2
Give the children a copy each of page 121. Ask whether there are any pictures they do not recognise. Name the objects shown. Read through the sheet with the children. Ask them to colour in things that will be attracted to a magnet, and to put a cross through things that will not be attracted. Ask them to answer the questions on the sheet.

Answers
The things attracted to a magnet are: paper clip, drawing pin, nail, paper fastener, scissors. All the things attracted to a magnet are made from metal. In a house, there may be magnetic catches on some cupboard doors; most fridges have a magnetic catch, and may have fridge magnets on the door; a magnet could also be used for picking up dropped pins or retrieving other metal objects from awkward places.

Looking for levels
Most children will identify at least four objects that are attracted to a magnet. All the children should know that things attracted to a magnet are made from metal. The children should identify one use of a magnet in a house. Less able children may identify only two objects that are attracted to a magnet, and may be unable to identify a practical use for a magnet in the house. More able children will identify all the objects, and should be able to suggest two or three practical uses for a magnet.

Properties card game

strong	opaque
hard	stretchy
flexible	rigid
soft	transparent

Photocopy this page three times to make a set of 24 cards. Cut them up, mount them on thick card and laminate them for durability.

Name

Magnets

● These things are attracted to a magnet:

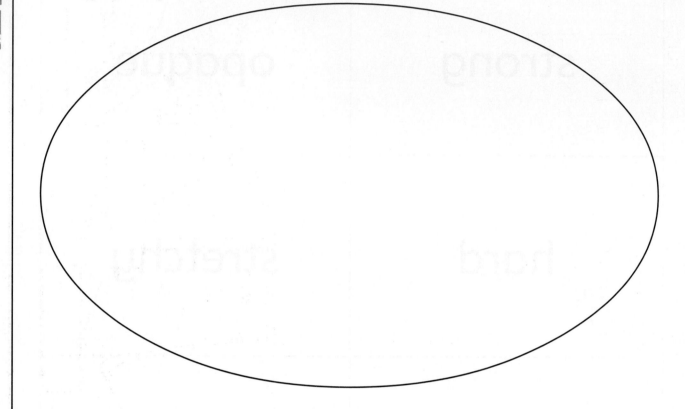

● These things are not attracted to a magnet:

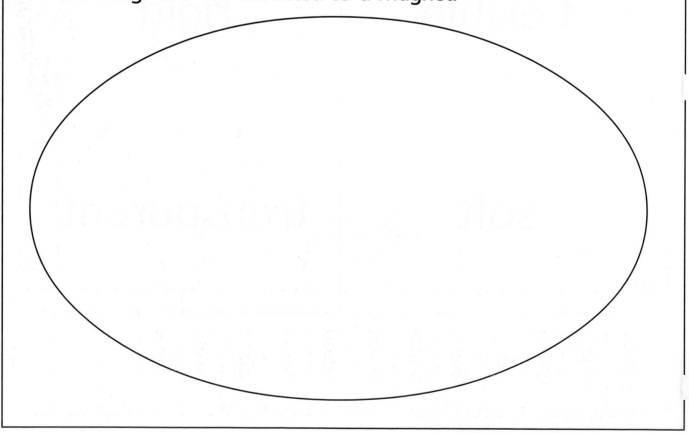

Name

Materials in the classroom

Cut out the labels and stick them in the correct places on the picture.

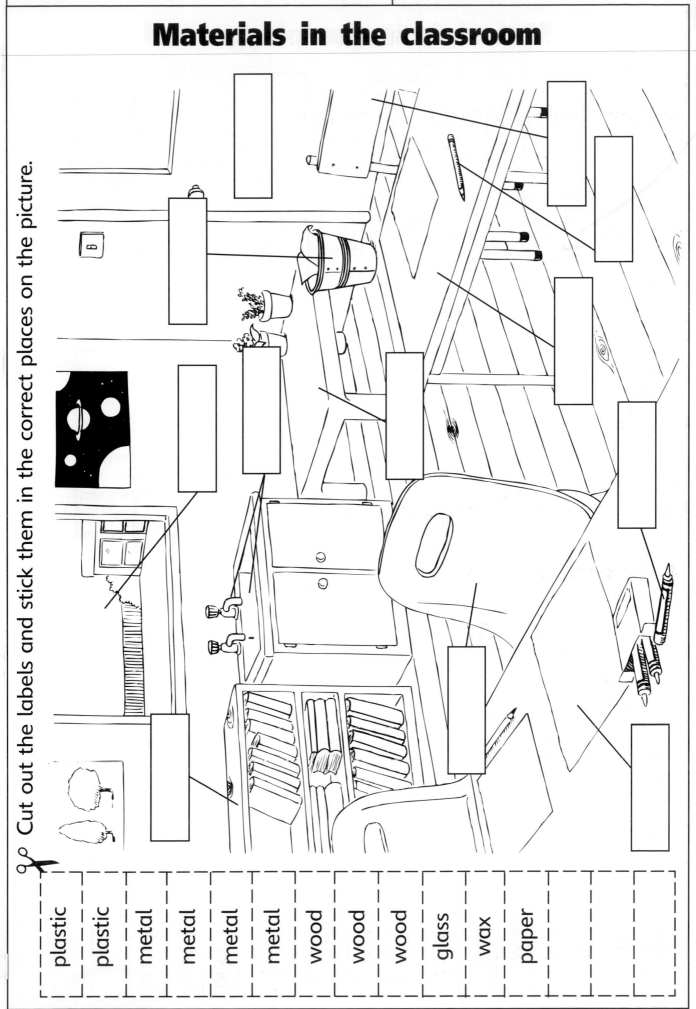

plastic

plastic

metal

metal

metal

metal

wood

wood

wood

glass

wax

paper

Name

Materials in the playground

Cut out the labels and stick them in the correct places on the picture.

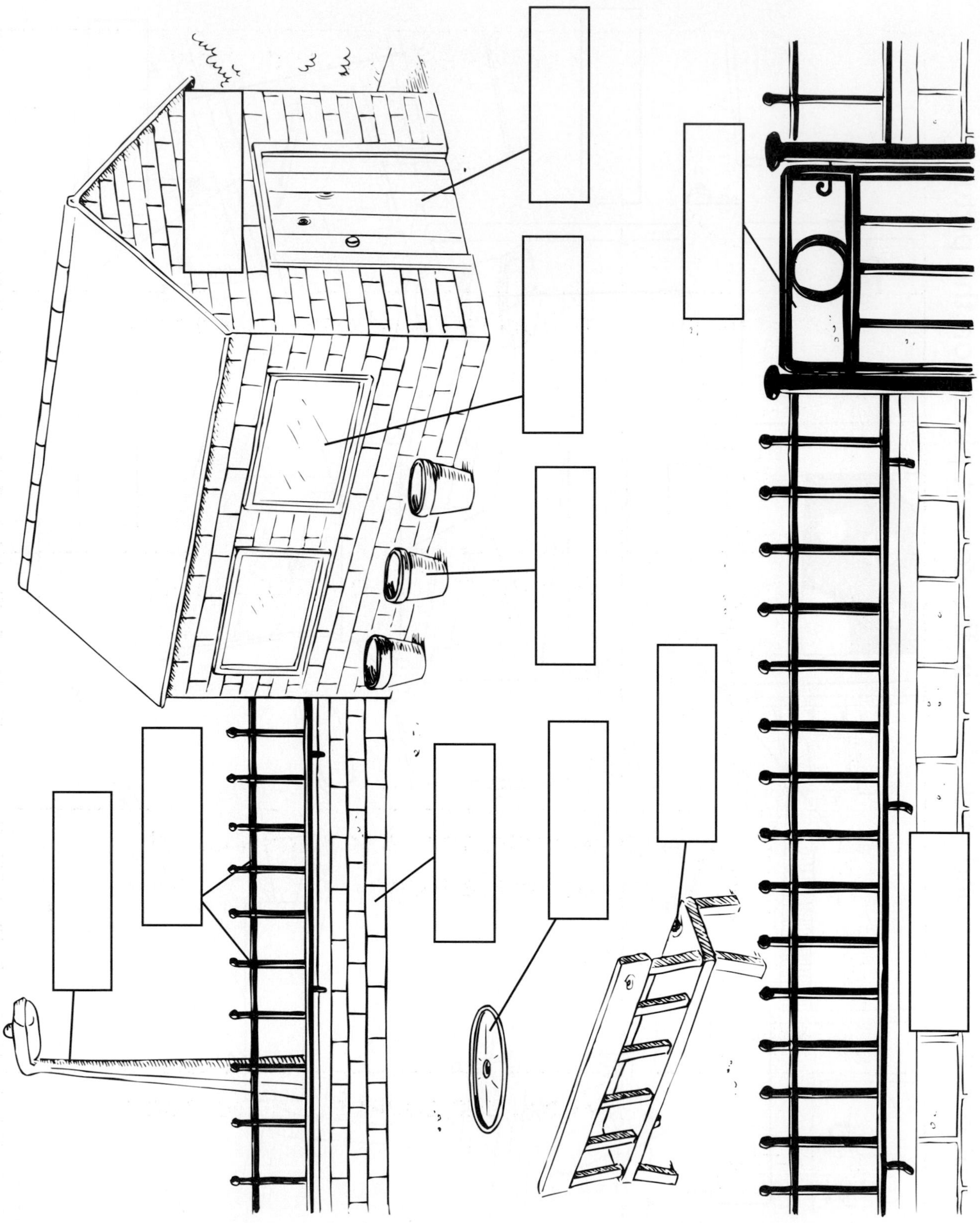

glass

glass

glass

metal

metal

metal

plastic

plastic

plastic

wood

wood

wood

brick (clay)

brick (clay)

brick (clay)

It could be made from...

	A bowl could be made from:
	A bucket could be made from:
	A mug could be made from:
	A knife, fork and spoon could be made from:
	A toy car could be made from:

Choose from these words:
wood metal glass paper fabric stone clay plastic

Name

What is it made from?

Put a tick against the materials each object is made from.

	plastic	wood	metal	cotton	glass	graphite	leather	fabric

Teddy's umbrella

Cover Teddy's umbrella with waterproof material.

Properties of materials

1. Windows are made of glass because _____

_____

These things are also made of glass:

2. Doors are made of wood because_____

_____

These things are also made of wood:

3. Umbrellas are made of plastic because_____

_____

These things are also made of plastic:

4. Knives and forks are made of metal because_____

_____

These things are also made of metal:

Properties of materials

Which of these things are attracted to a magnet?

Colour in the ones that are. Cross out the ones that are not.

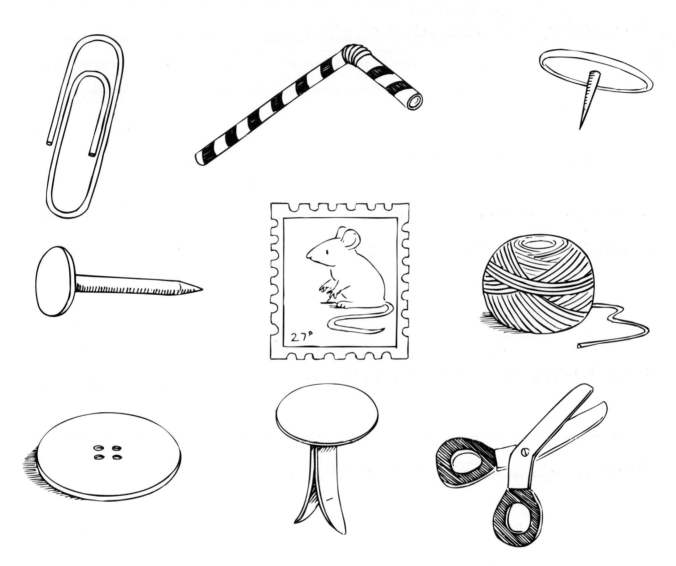

What are the things that are attracted to a magnet made from?

_____

Where might you find or use a magnet in a house?

_____

_____

Using and misusing electricity

ORGANISATION (5 LESSONS)

	OBJECTIVES	MAIN ACTIVITY	GROUP ACTIVITIES	PLENARY	OUTCOMES
LESSON 1	● To know that many appliances need electricity to make them work.	Look at a mains electrical appliance. Discuss how it is turned on and off. List other mains appliances.	Sort pictures of electrical appliances from other household objects. Identify the electrical appliances on a drawing of a house.	Work through both photocopiable group activities. Discuss the purposes of various household appliances.	● Can recognise a range of household electrical appliances. ● Can identify the purposes of a range of household appliances.
LESSON 2	● To know that electricity is obtained from the mains or from batteries (cells).	Sort electrical appliances into mains-operated and battery-operated.	Play card games to test knowledge of electrical appliances.	Discuss the usefulness of batteries and how some batteries can be recharged.	● Can distinguish between appliances that use batteries and ones that have to be plugged into the mains.
LESSON 3	● To know that electricity can be dangerous and must be treated with extreme care.	Write a list of rules for the safe use of electricity.	Make a poster to illustrate one of the rules. Play a board game to reinforce safety knowledge.	Discuss the usefulness of electricity, particularly for lighting.	● Understand that electricity can be dangerous. ● Know some rules for keeping safe when using electricity.
LESSON 4	● To plan and carry out a simple investigation with help.	Investigate a range of batteries to see which lasts the longest.	Use reference books to find out about situations where torches are used.	Review the investigation and the group work.	● Can plan and carry out a simple investigation in a group, with adult help.

	OBJECTIVES	ACTIVITY 1	ACTIVITY 2
ASSESSMENT 5	● To assess whether the children know what appliances need electricity to make them work. ● To assess whether the children know the dangers of electricity.	Draw a flex and plug on things that need electricity to make them work.	Sort statements into sets of 'dangerous' and 'safe' actions.

LESSON 1

OBJECTIVE
● To know that many appliances need electricity to make them work.

RESOURCES
Main teaching activity: A table lamp, computer or other mains electrical appliance.
Group activities: 1. Photocopiable page 130, A4 paper, scissors, adhesive. **2.** An A3-sized copy of page 131, colouring materials.
Plenary: Enlarged copy of page 130, Blu-tack.

BACKGROUND
Our mains electricity is mostly generated in power stations linked to the National Grid, and is brought into our homes via a system of cables that are either buried underground or carried overland by pylons. A small amount of electricity, in certain regions, is generated by

> **Vocabulary**
>
> electricity,
> electric,
> appliance, mains,
> plug, flex, socket,
> dangerous,
> shock, generated

water or wind power. At this stage, children need to know that electricity can be dangerous. Whenever you are working on the concept of electricity with children, always reinforce the potential hazards. Make it clear that the children should never play with mains appliances or touch the sockets. Very young children should not be allowed to plug anything into the mains themselves. Your local electricity company may have materials (including videos) about the dangers of misusing electricity and of playing near pylons and sub-stations. If you use such materials, check their suitability for the children in your class.

INTRODUCTION

Ask the class: *What do you know about electricity?* This gives the children a chance to voice their ideas, and gives you an opportunity to discover whether they have any misconceptions (such as the idea that electricity leaks, like water, out of the end of a wire that is attached to a battery).

MAIN TEACHING ACTIVITY

Ask the children to look around the classroom. *Can you see anything that needs electricity to make it work?* Have a table lamp, computer or other mains electrical appliance switched off and unplugged. Show the children the plug and flex, and ask whether they know the names of these parts of an appliance. *What has to be done to make something that uses electricity work?* (It has to be plugged in and switched on.) Explain and use the words 'appliance', 'plug', 'flex', 'electric', 'electricity', 'socket' and 'mains'. Reinforce the children's awareness that electricity can be dangerous, that very young children should never plug things in for themselves, and that mains electricity can give a very dangerous and painful electric shock. What we call 'mains electricity' is electricity that is generated (or made) in a power station and comes along wires to our homes and schools.

Plug the appliance in and switch it on. Talk about the fact that it is using electricity from the mains, and that it doesn't work when it is not plugged in. Switch the classroom lights on and off and explain that they, too, use mains electricity; but they do not have to be plugged in every time, like lamps and computers, because they have more permanent connections.

Can the children think of anything at home that uses mains electricity, has a flex and a plug, and has to be plugged into a socket to make it work? List their suggestions on the board. Can they think of anything that is used in the garden (such as a lawnmower)?

GROUP ACTIVITIES

1. Give each child a copy of page 130 and a sheet of A4 paper. Ask the children (working individually) to divide the blank sheet into columns labelled 'Yes' and 'No', then cut out the pictures, sort them according to whether or not they use electricity, and stick them into the correct columns on the sheet. Ask the children to think, and talk to each other, about what the things in the 'Yes' column are used for.
2. Give each child, pair, or group of three an A3-sized copy of photocopiable page 131. Ask them to find all the things in the picture that use electricity and colour them in.

DIFFERENTIATION

1. Less able children may need the support of working in mixed-ability pairs instead of individually. More able children may be able to write the purpose of one or two of the electrical appliances on the back of the sheet.
2. Most of the children should be able to do this activity successfully. Some may mistake the gas cooker for an electric one.

ASSESSMENT

Ask the children to name two or three appliances that use mains electricity. Ask them to describe what needs to be done to make these appliances work.

PLENARY

Have an A3 sheet pinned up, divided into 'Yes' and 'No' columns. Go through the collection of pictures from page 130, and ask the children to indicate whether each one should be put in the 'Yes' or the 'No' column. Stick the pictures in the correct columns. Ask all the children to check their own sheets. Look together at the picture on page 131. Ask the children to name the appliances and to say what each one is used for.

OUTCOMES

- Can recognise a range of household electrical appliances.
- Can identify the purposes of a range of household appliances.

LINKS

Unit 7, Lesson 2: understand that light can come from many sources.

LESSON 2

OBJECTIVE

- To know that electricity is obtained from the mains or from batteries (cells).

RESOURCES

Main teaching activity: A battery; a collection of appliances that use mains electricity only or batteries only (such as a torch, a table lamp, a kettle, a toaster, a personal stereo and a mobile phone); pictures of things that use mains electricity and of things that use batteries. Make sure that all the electrical appliances that use mains electricity have their flex with them, and that any appliance (such as a mobile phone) that uses rechargeable batteries have their charger flex and plug with them.
Group activities: 1 and 2. Sets of picture cards from page 132, mounted on stiff card and laminated, and copies of photocopiable page 132.

PREPARATION

Make sets of cards from page 132: cut out and colour the pictures, then mount them on card and laminate them (or cover them with sticky-backed plastic) for durability. Make base boards from the whole page in a similar way. You will need a base board and set of cards for each child.

Vocabulary

batteries, mains, electricity, electric, appliance, mains, plug, flex, socket, dangerous, shock

BACKGROUND

Some electrical appliances work on quite a low voltage, and can therefore be operated using batteries that provide a low-voltage supply. Other equipment may require a higher voltage in order to work, and thus may have to be connected to the mains supply. Some, such as portable radios, have been designed so that they can work on either batteries or mains. In some cases (such as mobile phones), the batteries are an integral part of the appliance and can be recharged using mains electricity via a transformer. A transformer converts mains electricity, which is usually 230–240V in Britain, to the lower voltage required by the equipment. Strictly speaking, the smallest batteries that we use should be called 'cells'; a battery is a collection of individual cells in a case (for example, a 6V battery may consist of four 1.5V cells). However, it is common usage to call them all batteries. Children do not need to know the above at this stage – but sometimes curious, able children do ask difficult questions!

Rechargeable batteries should not be used in situations where the children have direct access to them. In certain circumstances they can discharge all their energy at once, creating a great deal of heat. Children could receive a nasty burn if this happens. All batteries contain caustic substances, and should never be taken apart.

INTRODUCTION

Remind the class about the dangers of electricity and of putting anything into a mains socket. Talk to the children about what they did and what they learned in Lesson 1. Ask them whether they can remember and name some of the appliances that they identified as using mains electricity.

MAIN TEACHING ACTIVITY

Show the children a battery (cell). Discuss what it is. Warn the children of the danger of trying to take a battery apart: the contents are very harmful. Ask: *Can you think of anything that just uses batteries to make it work, and doesn't have to be plugged into the mains?* Show the collection of electrical appliances to the children and ask whether they can identify any of these. Name the items and talk about what they are used for. Now ask the children to sort the collection into things that need to be plugged into the mains and things that use batteries. If some children say 'Both' for such items as a radio, put these between the sets and discuss this with the children. Ask them whether they can suggest any more things that use batteries or mains electricity.

GROUP ACTIVITIES

1. Play 'Electricity Lotto'. Each child will need a copy of page 132 (the base board) with a corresponding set of cards. Explain the rules of the game to the children, and sort them into groups of four or six. The cards are shuffled and placed face-down on the table. The children take turns to pick up a card. If they can name the appliance and say whether it uses the mains, batteries or either, they can put the card over the corresponding picture on their base board. If they cannot say, the card is returned to the bottom of the pack. The first child to cover every picture on his or her base board is the winner. Encourage them to talk about the pictures as they pick them up: can they explain what each appliance does?
2. Play 'Appliance Snap'. Sort the children into groups of four, with a set of cards per child. After saying 'Snap', a child has to say whether the appliance uses batteries or the mains before he or she can claim the pile of cards.

DIFFERENTIATION

1. This activity should be accessible to all the children, though the less able may need some support.
2. It is a good idea to have an adult present the first time the children play the 'Snap' game, to make sure that they all understand the rules without arguing.

ASSESSMENT

Ask the children to explain where they might find a supply of electricity. (Mains sockets or batteries.) Can they name some appliances that use the mains supply and some that use batteries?

PLENARY

Ask the children why they think batteries are useful. (They allow things to be used more flexibly; they make things more portable; some appliances can be used where there is no mains supply available.) *Where might there be no mains supply?* You could listen to the radio in the garden, use a cordless drill in the shed, or use a mobile phone in the street. *Why would it be inconvenient to have to connect these devices to the mains supply every time you used them?* Explain the difference between an ordinary battery and a rechargeable one: an ordinary battery has to be thrown away when it no longer works, but a rechargeable one can be plugged in to a charging unit which in turn is plugged into the mains. It can then be re-used.

OUTCOME

● Can distinguish between appliances that use batteries and ones that have to be plugged into the mains.

LESSON 3

OBJECTIVE

- To know that electricity can be dangerous and must be treated with extreme care.

RESOURCES

Main teaching activity: A large sheet of white paper, a large felt-tipped pen.
Group activities: 1. Drawing and painting materials, large sheets of art paper.
2. 'Snakes and ladders' gameboards (see Preparation), dice, shakers, counters.

PREPARATION

Make one A3-sized copy of page 133 per group. Colour it in, mount it on thick card and laminate it (or cover it with sticky-backed plastic) for durability.

Vocabulary

dangers, dangerous, care, shock, pylon, sub-station

BACKGROUND

Electricity can be fun and exciting, but can also be very dangerous. Working with batteries up to 6V is quite safe, and children can have a great deal of fun experimenting with these in circuits. Rechargeable batteries should not be used where the children have direct access to them, and batteries should never be taken apart. Some children may be curious about what the 'V' on a battery stands for – it is 'volts'. The voltage (or difference in electrical potential between the two terminals) determines the 'push' given to the electricity in the circuit. The higher the voltage, the greater the 'push'. Electricity pylons may carry 30 000V, and are therefore extremely dangerous. Electricity sub-stations may carry even higher voltages, and should be avoided. Most batteries are between 1.5 and 9V.

Other electrical units that you may encounter (the children do not need to know these at this stage) are ohms and amps. Amps (A) measure the current or flow of electricity. An electrical current will flow very easily through some materials. Other materials are more resistant, and this resistance is measured in ohms (Ω).

Your local electricity company may have useful materials (including videos) about the dangers of misusing electricity, including the dangers of playing near pylons and sub-stations. Some of these may not be suitable for very young children, so do check them first.

INTRODUCTION

Talk to the children about the things they have learned from their work on electricity. Discuss some of their ideas about the dangers of electricity. *What silly or dangerous things might some people do?*

MAIN TEACHING ACTIVITY

Working with the whole class, devise a set of rules to keep people safe from the dangers of electricity. Ask the children for suggestions and make a list on the board or flip chart. Help the children to think of any important aspects they may have missed. Discuss the list and decide on the order of priority. *Is everything on this list sensible? Do you want to make any changes?* Make a new list with the most important rules at the top.

GROUP ACTIVITIES

1. The children can make a poster to illustrate one of the rules, working individually or in pairs. Help them to decide which rule they are going to illustrate, so that there is a variety of posters for a class display.
2. Groups of four can play 'Electricity snakes and ladders', using a gameboard copied from page 133 (see Preparation).

DIFFERENTIATION

1. This activity is accessible to all.
2. Some children may need help in reading the instructions for the board game. This could

be overcome by the children working in mixed-ability groups and helping each other with the reading. Some groups will need initial adult support while playing the game.

ASSESSMENT

During the Plenary session, ask the children to describe some of the dangers associated with electricity. Can they tell you some of the rules for keeping safe?

PLENARY

Talk to the children about the dangers of electricity, and remind them of the rules they drew up for its safe use. Now talk about how useful electricity is, and list some of the things it helps us to do. For example, we can use electricity to keep us warm, to make toast or to boil a kettle. Mention the fact that hospitals rely on electricity to run the machines that save lives and help people to get better. Discuss the importance of electric light, and how difficult we would find it to manage without electricity these days. If you are doing this activity in the winter, try to save it for late in the afternoon when it is getting dark. Switch off all the classroom lights and tell the children: *Now get on with your work!* What would the children miss most if there were no electricity?

OUTCOMES

- Understand that electricity can be dangerous.
- Know some rules for keeping safe when using electricity.

LESSON 4

OBJECTIVE

- To plan and carry out a simple investigation with help.

RESOURCES

Main teaching activity: Pictures of miners or pot-holers with torches on their hats; several torches, a range of different torch batteries, a timer with an alarm, an A3-sized copy of photocopiable page 134.
Group activity: Reference books with information about other contexts in which electric torches are used.

PREPARATION

Obtain several torches that are of the same size and type and use batteries of the same voltage. Choose a selection of batteries of the same voltage – for example, an ordinary cheap one and two different 'long-lasting' ones. Each battery and torch needs to be colour-coded, so that the children can record which battery is in which torch.

Vocabulary

investigate, test, plan, last longest, fair, unfair, torch

BACKGROUND

Children are not expected to have an understanding of fair testing until well into Key Stage 2; but they need to be given opportunities to discuss and participate in simple tests from an early stage in order to develop their skills and begin to understand the concepts. Very often, children will be ready to understand when a test is not fair long before they can identify and manipulate variables in order to conduct a fair test. It is a good idea to talk to them about how to make a test fair, and to ask questions that highlight unfairness. *If we turn the torches on at different times, will that be fair? If the batteries are all in different kinds of torches, will all the batteries be getting the same chance?*

INTRODUCTION

Remind the children how useful electric light is, and how difficult they found it to work when it was getting dark and the lights were turned out. Talk about how miners wear torches on the front of their hats when they go down a mine. Show the children some pictures of this and/or of other uses of electric torches.

MAIN TEACHING ACTIVITY

Children at this age should be given opportunities to plan and carry out a simple investigation with help. Ask the class: *Can you think of anywhere or any situation where torches would be really useful? What about putting out the rubbish on a winter's night? Walking home with Mum or Dad when you have been round to a friend's house in the evening? Reading under the bedclothes?* Show the children the torches and the batteries. Tell them that they are going to do an investigation to find out which battery will last the longest.

Read the information on the battery packets with the children, pointing out that some packets say the batteries will last an especially long time. Ask them: *Which one do you think will last the longest? Why? What will you need to do to find out? Can you think of a good way to make the test fair?* Ask further questions such as: *Do you think, if we are*

using different batteries, then all the torches should be the same to make it fair? Would it be fair if we turned the torches on and off at different times? How often do you think we need to check the torches to see if the batteries are still working? (A sensible answer would be: 'Every half hour or hour.') *Do you think you need to record anything while you are doing the investigation?* (They may suggest that each look at the torches should be recorded with its time.)

Help the children to set up the activity and leave the torches shining. A rota of children should look at the torches during the day and record whether they are still bright, recording on a class record sheet (an A3 copy of page 134). You might find it useful to set a timer to ring each hour to remind you that it is time to check. If any (or all) of the torches are still shining at the end of the day, ask the children: *What do we need to do now to keep the test fair and carry on tomorrow?* (Turn all of the torches off at the same time, then turn them all on again together the next day.)

GROUP ACTIVITY

Working as individuals, in pairs or in groups of three, the children can use reference books to find out what kind of people use torches in their work. (Miners, divers, firefighters, police and so on.) How many different examples can they find? Ask them to make a list. (If they are working individually, a lot of reference material will be needed.)

DIFFERENTIATION

Some children may need help with reading the information in the reference books and making their list. Some children might record their list pictorially.

ASSESSMENT

Note which children show an understanding of when a test is not fair, and which children are aware of the importance of making regular observations and recording them.

PLENARY

Ask the children which of the batteries lasted the longest. *How do you know?* Discuss the record sheet and what it shows. *Did the one you thought would last the longest actually last the longest? Are the claims on the packet true?* Remind them of how they did the test and how they made it fair: that the different batteries all had to go into the same type of torch, and that the torches had to be switched on and off at the same times. Discuss the usefulness of torches, and when and where they are used.

OUTCOME

● Can plan and carry out a simple investigation in a group, with adult help.

LINKS

Maths: measuring time.

LESSON 5

OBJECTIVES

● To assess whether the children know what appliances need electricity to make them work.
● To assess whether the children know the dangers of electricity.

RESOURCES

Photocopiable pages 135 and 136, pencils, scissors, adhesive.

INTRODUCTION

Ask the children to tell you something they have learned about electricity in this unit. Can they remember some of the special words that go with electricity? (Appliance, mains, plug, socket, flex and so on.)

ASSESSMENT ACTIVITY 1

Give each child a copy of photocopiable page 135. Go through the pictures with the children to make sure they recognise each one. Ask them to draw a lead (or flex) and plug on all the things that need mains electricity to make them work.

Answers

A lead and plug should be drawn on the table lamp, washing machine, TV, computer, toaster, iron and vacuum cleaner.

Looking for levels

Most children should be able to identify and draw a lead and plug on at least five of the electrical items. Some children will identify and draw a plug and flex on all the correct appliances. Less able children may only manage two or three, and may draw a lead and plug on inappropriate items, such as the kettle.

ASSESSMENT ACTIVITY 2

Give each child a copy of photocopiable page 136, scissors and adhesive. Ask the children to put their finger under each instruction as you read through them together. Some children may need further help with reading as they work through the sheet. Ask the children to cut out the instructions and stick each one into the correct box: 'dangerous' or 'safe'.

Answers

Dangerous: 1, 3, 6, 8.
Safe: 2, 4, 5, 7.

Looking for levels

Most children will place six out of the eight statements into the correct boxes. More able children will place all of the statements correctly. Less able children may only achieve two or three.

Name

Using electricity

Electricity at home

● Colour in the things that use electricity.

Name

Matching game cards

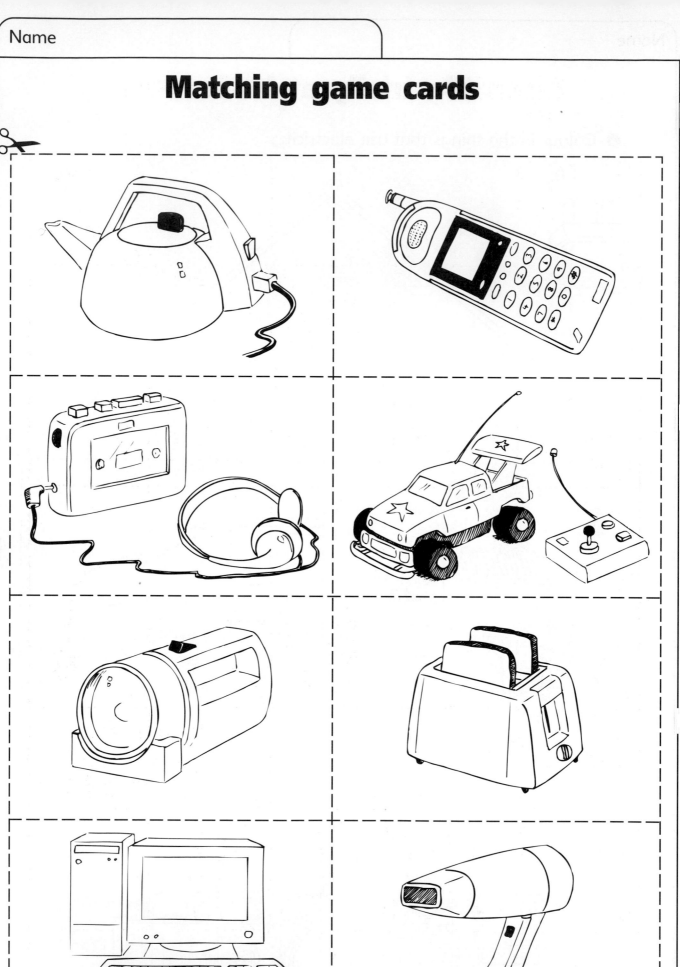

Electricity snakes and ladders

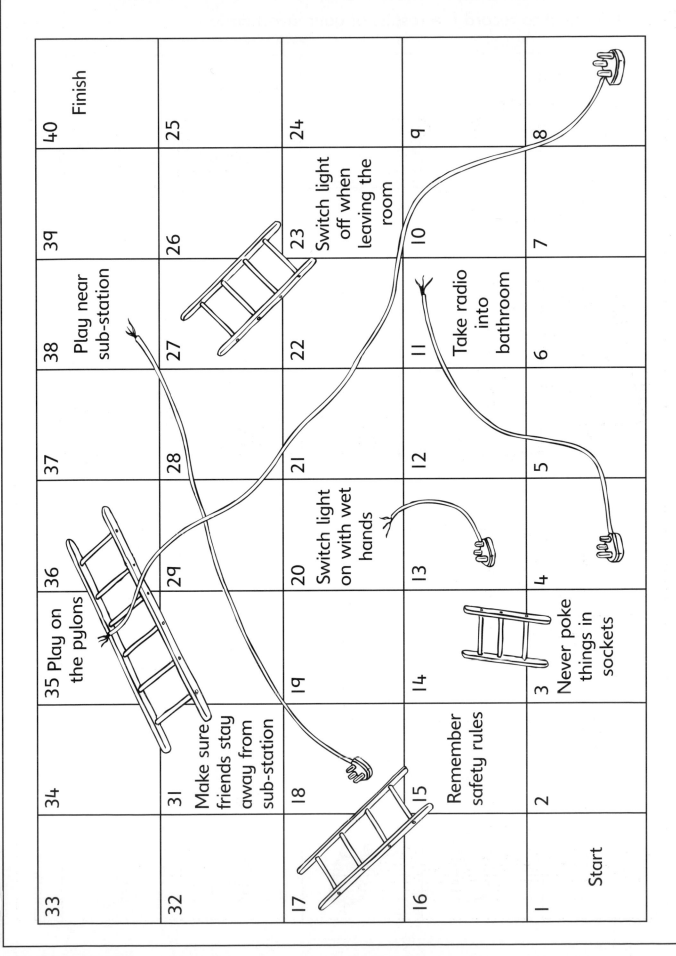

33	34	35 Play on the pylons	36	37	38 Play near sub-station	39	40 Finish
32	31 Make sure friends stay away from sub-station	30	29	28	27	26	25
17	18	19	20 Switch light on with wet hands	21	22	23 Switch light off when leaving the room	24
16	15 Remember safety rules	14	13	12	11 Take radio into bathroom	10	9
1 Start	2	3 Never poke things in sockets	4	5	6	7	8

Record sheet

Use this sheet to record the results of your investigation.

Battery	Time (hours)									
	1	2	3	4	5	6	7	8	9	10
1										
2										
3										
4										

Colour in a square for each hour that the battery lasts.

Using and misusing electricity

Draw a lead and plug on all the things that need mains electricity to make them work.

Using and misusing electricity

dangerous

safe

Cut out these instructions and stick each one into the correct box.

✂

1	2	3	4
Poke something into a socket.	Allow grown-ups to plug things in for you.	Play near a sub-station.	Never play with electrical things near water.
5	6	7	8
Never go near a railway line.	Climb on pylons.	Never play near sub-stations.	Take a battery to pieces.

Introducing forces

ORGANISATION (9 LESSONS)

	OBJECTIVES	MAIN ACTIVITY	GROUP ACTIVITIES	PLENARY	OUTCOMES
LESSON 1	● To know that there are different kinds of movement. ● To collect data from observations and use a simple record sheet.	Carry out and identify different kinds of movement when playing. Keep a tally chart of movements.	Create individual 'movement' pictures of themselves. Make a block graph from the information on the tally chart.	Extract information from the block graphs. Name movements seen on a video of themselves.	● Can recognise and name different kinds of movement. ● Can use a simple recording sheet to collect data.
LESSON 2	● To know that forces help us to move our bodies. ● To begin to identify the forces involved.	In a gymnastics lesson, identify some of the forces involved in travelling (as pushes or pulls).	Groups devise a short sequence of movements using pushes and pulls.	Demonstrate some movements and sequences. Name the forces and body parts used.	● Know that forces help us to move our bodies. ● Can name some of the forces involved.
LESSON 3	● To know that forces, such as pushes and pulls, can move objects and change their direction. ● To begin to understand cause and effect.	Use small apparatus to experience how forces cause things to move and change direction.	Pairs pull on a skipping rope and throw soft balls at each other. Discuss the forces being used.	Review the activities. Discuss the effects of increasing degrees of force.	● Can describe the pushes and pulls involved in moving an object or changing its direction. ● Begin to understand cause and effect (eg that the harder the push, the further and faster an object will move). ● Can explain the potential dangers of some moving objects.
LESSON 4	● To know that forces such as pushes, pulls and twists can change the shape of objects.	Change the shape of play dough, describing the forces used (pulling, pushing, twisting).		Review the activity and vocabulary.	● Know that they can use forces (pushes, pulls and twists) to change the shape of objects.
LESSON 5	● To experience the downward force of gravity. ● To know that objects always fall down towards the Earth.	Drop a range of objects. Establish that they all fall down. Discuss whether any objects can 'fall' upwards.	Make a marble run and observe how it works. Pour water onto a water wheel and observe how it works.	Identify gravity as the force that makes everything fall downwards.	● Know that objects always fall downwards because of a force called gravity.
LESSON 6	● To consider the wind as a force. ● To know that wind is moving air. ● To know that the wind can make things move.	Blow bubbles outside on a windy day and watch them being blown by the wind. Discuss the appearance of the bubbles.	Make ribbon streamers and consider how they blow in the wind. Make and fly carrier bag kites.	Review the observations made and the vocabulary used.	● Can describe how the wind makes things move. ● Know that the wind is moving air. ● Know that the wind can make things move.
LESSON 7	● To know that the wind is air that pushes on things in the environment and makes them move. ● To know that the wind can exert a push on their bodies.	Go on a 'windy day walk' to observe how the wind blows trees, umbrellas and themselves.		Discuss how the wind's force is a push that can make things move.	● Can describe how the wind pushes on and moves things in the environment. ● Can talk about the feel of the wind pushing on them.

ORGANISATION (9 LESSONS)

	OBJECTIVES	MAIN ACTIVITY	GROUP ACTIVITIES	PLENARY	OUTCOMES
LESSON 8	● To experience the upward push (force) of water. ● To know that water pushes upwards on objects.	Push floating objects down in a tank of water and feel the water pushing up.	Fill floating cups with water until they sink; discuss what is happening. Write about what happened in the main activity and why.	Review the activities, using appropriate vocabulary to discuss the forces involved.	● Know that water pushes upwards on objects, and that this push is a force. ● Know that a force is needed to push a floating object down into water and that when the force is removed, the object floats again.

	OBJECTIVES	ACTIVITY 1	ACTIVITY 2
ASSESSMENT 9	● To know that pushes and pulls are forces. ● To know that forces can make things move.	Name forces by labelling pictures 'Push' or 'Pull'.	Paired practical activity with partner: move small apparatus and name forces used.

LESSON 1

OBJECTIVES

- To know that there are different kinds of movement.
- To collect data from observations and use a simple record sheet.

RESOURCES

Main teaching activity: Space for the children to move about in (for example, a playground, the park, an adventure playground), photocopiable page 150, pencils, clipboards (one per group of six), a video camera (if possible).
Group activities: 1. Drawing materials, plain A4 paper, scissors (sharp enough to cut fabric), adhesive; collage, painting or printing materials. **2.** Large squared paper, colouring materials.

Vocabulary

move, movement, jump, skip, hop, run, roll, climb, walk, balance, crawl, travel, body, tally, graph

BACKGROUND

'Forces and motion' is among the most difficult areas of the science curriculum for us to teach and for young children to grasp, because it is so abstract. At this stage, children should be given the opportunity to experience forces and identify them in simple terms. We cannot see a force, only its effect – for example, the resulting change in movement when a shopping trolley is pushed or when a wheeled toy is pulled. Forces are therefore often described in terms of the effect they have. Forces can start something moving (a push or pull), make it stop (a stone hitting the ground), make it slow down (friction from a rough surface or a car brake), make it go faster (a push or pull) or make it change direction (hitting a ball with a bat).

Identifying the various ways in which we move our bodies is a good way of introducing young children to forces. Friction helps us to walk; gravity brings us back to the ground when we jump. In this first lesson, children will identify the various ways in which they move their bodies; in the second lesson, they will begin to relate some of these movements to the forces involved.

INTRODUCTION

Sort the children into groups of six, each group with a clipboard, a copy of page 150 and a pencil.

MAIN TEACHING ACTIVITY

Tell the children that they are going to move about the playground in as many different ways as they can think of. Ask them: *How many ways of moving can you think of?* (Run, hop, skip, jump, walk on hands and feet, and so on.) *Think about which parts of your body you are using.* Tell them to find a new way of moving every time you call 'Change'.

Now say that four members of each group are going to move while the other two watch and record their movements on the tally chart. The four children moving should move as individuals, and choose the ways they are going to move for themselves. One of the 'talliers' calls out the different movements of the members of the group, and the other marks the tally chart accordingly. Give all the children a chance to move and to record the movements of their group. If possible, make a video of the children moving about.

GROUP ACTIVITIES

1. Each child can draw or collage a 'movement' picture of him or herself (on A4 paper). These pictures can be cut out and stuck to a background to make a class picture. The children can label their pictures with the type of movement each one shows. The pictures can be made more vivid by allowing the children to add fabric for their clothes, wool for their hair and so on.
2. Using the information from the tally chart, each group can make a block graph of their movements.

DIFFERENTIATION

1. All the children should be able to do this activity.
2. Some children may need help in counting the marks on their tally charts and transferring the information to a block graph. They may make a block graph of two or three movements only (such as 'hop', 'skip' and 'run').

ASSESSMENT

Observe the children as they move and record. Can they name the ways in which they are moving? Are they able to enter their data on the recording sheet? Note which children are able to transfer the information from their tally chart to a block graph.

PLENARY

Talk to the whole class about their work. How many kinds of movement did they identify? *Look at your graphs: which movement did you see the most often? Which did you see the least often?* If you have been able to video the session, show the video to the class and encourage them to name all the different kinds of movement they can see. Remind them of the work they did (Unit 1, Lesson 4, page 18) when they were learning about themselves, the ways in which their bodies could move and the names of the body parts they were using.

OUTCOMES

● Can recognise and name different kinds of movement.
● Can use a simple recording sheet to collect data.

LINKS

Unit 1, Lesson 7: moving in different ways, identifying the body parts used.
Unit 2, Lesson 4: observing and describing how various animals move.
Maths: making graphs and charts.

LESSON 2

OBJECTIVES

● To know that forces help us to move our bodies.
● To begin to identify the forces involved.

Vocabulary

move, travel, push, pull, twist, force

RESOURCES

Main teaching activity: The hall, large PE apparatus (benches, mats, wall bars, ladders, crossbars and so on).
Group activity: Space to move around in.

BACKGROUND

The forces involved when children are moving their bodies are usually muscular pushes and pulls, friction and gravity. At this early stage, it is usually sufficient for children to focus on the pushes and pulls and know that these are forces. To walk, you push against the ground with each foot in turn. To jump, you push with both feet; gravity pulls you back to the ground. An extension for more able children is to think about the part that friction plays in movement. It is the friction between a body part and a surface that allows us to move in a controlled way. Where there is less friction, movement is harder to control (for example, walking on a slippery surface or skating on ice). Children need to be helped to distinguish between a pull and a push as they move their bodies. Gymnastics sessions are a good way of doing this – for example, pulling themselves along a bench just using their arms, or pushing themselves up off the floor (in as many ways as possible) using different parts of the body.

INTRODUCTION

If your 'hall time' is limited, you may prefer to spread this lesson over two sessions. Talk to the whole class about what they learned in Lesson 1. Ask them to remember all the ways in which they were moving.

MAIN TEACHING ACTIVITY

Introduce the children to the idea that they were using forces to move their bodies in Lesson 1. Ask a child to run across the hall while the others watch. *What is Jane doing with her feet?* (Pushing against the floor.) Tell the children that a push is a force that can help them to move their bodies. Ask another child to move along a bench, lying flat and just using his or her arms. Ask the children what is happening. *What force is being used to move along the bench?* Encourage the children to use the words *pull, push, pulling, pushing* and *force*. Ask them to think about whether they would use a push or a pull force to move on the large apparatus. *What part of your body would you use?*

GROUP ACTIVITY

Groups of about four children can devise a short sequence of movements using pushes and pulls, then practise the sequence and be ready to show it to the whole class, describing each movement and saying whether the force being used is a push or a pull. This is a good opportunity to remind the children about safety: emphasise that the pushes and pulls in their sequence of movements should be gentle and safe, and that pushing or pulling other people too roughly can hurt them.

DIFFERENTIATION

Some children may be ready to consider the role of friction in movement – for example, the friction between our feet and the floor enables us to walk or run.

ASSESSMENT

Observe the children during the lesson. Ask them to name the forces (as 'push' or 'pull') and the body parts they are using.

PLENARY

At the end of the lesson, talk to the whole class and discuss what they have done. Ask some children to demonstrate some of the movements they have practised on the apparatus. *What part of the body did you use? Can you name the force that you were using?* Give the groups (or some of them) the opportunity to show their sequences of movements, naming the forces involved and the parts of the body they have used. More able groups should be able to talk about how the friction between a surface and the various parts of the body enable them to move.

OUTCOMES

● Know that forces help us to move our bodies.
● Can name some of the forces involved.

LINKS

Unit 1, Lesson 1: locating and naming the main external parts of the body.
Unit 1, Lesson 7: moving in different ways, identifying the body parts used.

LESSON 3

OBJECTIVES

● To know that forces, such as pushes and pulls, can move objects and change their direction.
● To begin to understand cause and effect.

RESOURCES

Main teaching activity: A collection of small apparatus (large and small soft balls, bats, skittles, hoops, bean bags and so on).
Group activities: 1. Skipping ropes. **2.** Balls or beanbags.

Vocabulary

pull, push, change direction, start, stop, move, speed up, slow down, change shape, twist, roll, flatten, cut

BACKGROUND

Children should be helped to develop the appropriate language to describe moving things. They need to realise that a throw is a type of push, as is hitting something with a bat or rolling it along the ground. Hitting a moving ball with a bat is a push force that changes the direction of the ball – in the case of young children, usually in a completely different direction from that intended! They should begin to appreciate that the amount of force (whether a push or pull) they apply will affect the way in which the object moves: a harder throw (push force) will make a ball or beanbag go faster and further. In Lesson 4, make sure they realise that a twist is a type of force (a push and a pull combined).

INTRODUCTION

Remind the class that they were using forces when they were moving their bodies. Tell them that they are going to find out more about forces in this lesson, using small apparatus. The children could work in pairs.

MAIN TEACHING ACTIVITY

Go through the various available activities with the whole class – for example, throwing large and small balls to each other, batting balls to each other, throwing balls or beanbags into hoops, knocking skittles over by rolling balls at them. Ask some children to demonstrate each activity to the class. Remind them of the forces work that they did in the previous two lessons. *Can anyone remember the names of the forces we were using to move our bodies?* Remind them that these forces were called 'pushes' and 'pulls'.

Tell the children that they are going to work on the various activities, and that you would like them to notice the forces that they are using to move each piece of apparatus. Ask them to really think hard about what is happening – for example, when they are batting a ball to each other. Talk about the forces that are acting in this situation. Batting a ball is a push; hitting the ball back is another push that changes the direction of the ball. *What happens when you bounce a ball?* (You are pushing it against the floor.) *What happens when you bounce it harder?* (You are pushing it harder, so it bounces higher.) Allow the children time to work in pairs on each of the above activities before going on to the Group activities below.

GROUP ACTIVITIES

1. Ask the children, in pairs, to pull gently on either end of a taut skipping rope so that they can feel the pull on the rope. They can take turns to pull a little harder, so that they can feel the force increasing. Ask them: *What is your friend doing when you are pulling? Are you both pulling in the same direction? What happens if you both stop pulling? What happens if one stops pulling before the other?* Remind the children that they are feeling a force, not playing tug-of-war, and that they must pull safely and gently. However, if you do have a safe, soft, grassy area, it could be fun to arrange teams of several children and have a tug-of-war.

2. Ask the children, in pairs, to throw a ball or beanbag gently at each other's bodies. Ask: *Can you feel it push on your body? Might it hurt if it was thrown really hard? Can you think of any other moving objects that might be dangerous?* (A moving swing, traffic, a cricket or golf ball.) *Why are they dangerous?* (Because they can push on the body with a very strong force.) Discuss with the children the need for care and for playing safely.

DIFFERENTIATION

1. Some children using the skipping rope may be ready to recognise that if two people pull with equal force there is no movement, but as soon as one pulls harder than the other, they both move (one backwards and one forwards).
2. All the children should be able to take part in this activity.

ASSESSMENT

During the paired work, ask the children to explain what they are doing and to name the forces they have used on a specific piece of small apparatus.

PLENARY

Gather the children together and ask some of them to go through the activities again, describing what they are doing and naming the forces involved. *Are these the same forces that we use to move our bodies?* (Yes.) Talk about the fact that if you throw something harder, using a greater force, you cause it to go further and faster.

OUTCOMES

● Can describe the pushes and pulls involved in moving an object or changing its direction.
● Can begin to understand cause and effect (for example, that the harder the push, the further and faster an object will move).
● Can explain the potential dangers from some moving objects.

LESSON 4

Objective	● To know that forces such as pushes, pulls and twists can change the shape of objects.
Resources	Ingredients for cheese straws (see recipe below), pastry boards, rolling pins, safe knives, pastry brushes, baking trays, access to an oven.
Main activity	Working in groups of four, the children make some cheese pastry dough. As they are doing this, draw their attention to the forces they are using (eg pushing the ingredients through their fingers to make a crumbling mixture, pushing the dough with their hands to knead it). They should roll the pastry out, cut it into strips and twist them. Ask the children to name the forces they are using to change the shape of the dough. *What are you doing, what forces are you using?* Encourage the children to use words such as 'pulling', 'pushing' and 'twisting'. Bake the straws.
Differentiation	All the children should be able to take part in this activity.
Assessment	While the children are working, note those who can tell you what forces they are using to shape the pastry.
Plenary	Talk to the children about what they have been doing. Look at the finished straws. Have fun eating the straws! Ask some of the children to describe how they changed the shape of their pastry, and to say what forces they were using.
Outcome	● Know that they can use forces (pushes, pulls and twists) to change the shape of objects.

CHEESE STRAWS RECIPE

(Makes about 24 straws)
125g flour
50g butter or margarine
50g cheese, finely grated
1 egg, beaten
1 level tsp mustard powder
a pinch of salt

Put the flour, mustard and salt together in a bowl. Add the butter or margarine and rub (push and pull) together until the mixture resembles fine breadcrumbs. Add the cheese and mix thoroughly with a knife. Add the beaten egg, and mix in well, keeping a little back to brush the finished straws with. Turn out onto a floured surface and knead (push and pull) lightly until just smooth. Take a quarter of the mixture each. Roll out (push and pull) to between 0.5cm and 1cm thickness. Cut (push) into long strips. Hold both ends of each strip and twist it into a spiral. Place on a greased baking tray and brush with the remaining egg. Bake in the oven at 180°C (350°F, Gas Mark 4) for 12–15 minutes until golden brown.

LESSON 5

OBJECTIVES
● To experience the downward force of gravity.
● To know that objects always fall down towards the Earth.

RESOURCES

Main teaching activity: A collection of objects that are safe to drop, such as balls, cotton reels, paper and feathers.
Group activities: 1. A marble run made from a construction kit or found materials (see figures on page 145), marbles. **2.** A water tray, containers for pouring, a water wheel.

BACKGROUND

The concept of gravity is very difficult and abstract – but it is a force that has a major and constant effect on our lives. At this stage, children are not expected to understand gravity in newtonian terms; but they need to experience the effect of gravity and know that all objects fall downwards and not upwards. Gravity is the attraction between any two objects that results from their having mass: the more massive the object, the greater the gravitational pull. Because it is the biggest object we have direct contact with, the Earth's gravitational pull is the one that dominates our lives. The force of gravity pulls all objects down towards the centre of the Earth. All objects, in the absence of air resistance or friction, accelerate downwards at the same rate. In practice, there is always air resistance; but if two objects such as a golf ball and a screwed-up ball of paper of the same size are dropped, they will fall at the same rate. If the piece of paper is flattened out, the increased air resistance will cause it to fall more slowly. This is how parachutes work.

INTRODUCTION

Ask the whole class to stand up, then to jump as high as they can. *What happens?* (They all come back down to Earth.) *Does anyone carry on going upwards?*

MAIN TEACHING ACTIVITY

Show the children the collection of objects. Ask them what will happen if the objects are dropped. (They will fall to the floor.) *Do things always fall to the floor when they are dropped? What about a piece of paper and a feather?* Let some children come out and drop the various objects in the collection while the others watch. *What happens? Can you think of anything that falls upwards?* Some children may suggest things such as gas-filled balloons and kites. Explain that the special gas in helium balloons makes them float, because it is lighter than air. Without that gas it would fall like an ordinary balloon. Also explain that the wind may carry a kite into the sky, but if the wind stops the kite falls. Say that the force that causes things to fall down towards the Earth is called 'gravity'.

GROUP ACTIVITIES

1. Make a marble run, using a construction kit or found materials (see illustration), and ask the children to roll marbles down it. *What happens? Do they all roll downwards? Can you change your marble run to make the marble go less fast?* (Make the slopes less steep.)
2. Ask the children to pour water from one container to another above a water tray. *What happens? Does it always pour downwards? Can you make it pour upwards? If you use the water to turn a water wheel, does the water go upwards then?* Let them try this and observe that the water falls, making the water wheel turn; the water does not flow upwards (though it may splash upwards before falling again).

DIFFERENTIATION

1. Some children may be able to devise their own marble run, using found materials.
2. All the children should be able to take part in this activity.

ASSESSMENT

In the Plenary session, establish whether the children realise that everything falls to the Earth. Do they know that this is caused by a force called 'gravity'?

PLENARY

Talk to the children about what they have been doing. *Did everything you tried fall to the ground? Why? Could you make the water fall upwards? Why not? What is the force called that makes everything fall to the ground?* (Gravity.) It would be fun to finish the session by singing 'This is the way we jump (hop, skip) up and down... all fall down' to the tune of 'Here we go round the mulberry bush'.

OUTCOME

● Know that objects always fall downwards because of a force called gravity.

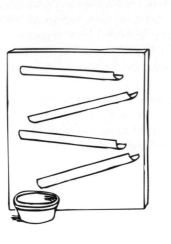
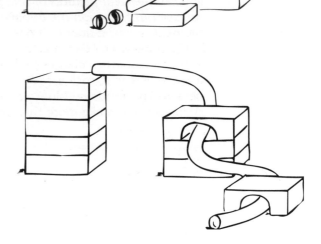

Do not make the slope of the channels any steeper than 10°.

LESSON 6

OBJECTIVES

- To consider the wind as a force.
- To know that wind is moving air.
- To know that the wind can make things move.

RESOURCES

Main teaching activity: The playground; bubble mixture pots (one per group of four), bubble wands (one or two per group). If you wish to make a record of this activity, you will need paper, paint and circular objects (cotton reels or card tube ends) for printing.
Group activities: 1. Ribbon, scissors. **2.** Light plastic carrier bags, string.

Vocabulary
air, wind, blow, force, move, push, bubbles, burst, float, reflection, shiny, colourful, rainbow, transparent

BACKGROUND

Force is an abstract concept, and is therefore difficult for children to understand. The wind blowing on objects and moving them is a good example of a visible effect of a force. On a windy day, you can feel the push of the air as you battle against the wind. Washing blowing on a line, trees bending or flags flapping are common examples of the effects of the wind. In some regions, the power of the wind is harnessed to generate electricity and the large turbines can be seen on the skyline. People have used the force of the wind for centuries to push their sailing boats along and to turn their windmills. You may have a windmill near you that is open to visitors.

INTRODUCTION

Introduce the lesson by talking to the whole class about the wind. *Mrs Mopple's Washing Line* by Anita Hewitt (Picture Puffin) or the poem 'The Wind' by Robert Louis Stevenson (in *A Child's Garden of Verse*, Puffin) would be a good initial stimulus for this lesson. Choose a day when there is some wind (but not too much), so that the children can watch the bubbles blowing about for a reasonable length of time before they burst.

MAIN TEACHING ACTIVITY

Ask the children where the air is. (All around us.) *Can you see it? How do we know it is there?* Some children may say that we need it to breathe, or that they can see it moving things. Ask the children what the wind is. (Moving air.) *Can you see it? Can you see what it does?* Talk to them about washing or flags flapping in the wind. *Can you feel it when the wind is blowing?*

Take the children out into the playground and organise them into groups of about four. Ask each group to take turns to blow bubbles and watch what happens to them in the wind. Encourage them to describe what is happening and what the bubbles look like. Use the vocabulary listed on page 145, defining such words as 'reflection' *(this means that you can see clear pictures of things in the bubbles)* and 'transparent' *(this means that you can see right through the bubbles)* each time you use them. Ask questions such as: *What is happening to the bubbles? Why are they moving about? What is making them move? Can you see the wind? Can you feel it?*

If you wish, the children could make a circular print to represent their bubble and write a few words in it, such as: 'My bubbles blew away in the wind', 'My bubble danced because the wind was blowing' or 'The wind blew my bubble up into the sky'. Some children could make more than one print and caption.

GROUP ACTIVITIES

1. Each child can make a streamer from ribbon, then go out, hold it up and watch it blow in the wind. Talk about what is happening. Discuss the fact that the wind is blowing (pushing) the streamer. Ask: *Is everyone's streamer blowing in the same direction? Why?*
2. Each child can make a carrier bag kite by tying a length of string to one handle of the carrier bag, then running in the wind to see how it flies. Make sure they understand that the force of the wind is making their bags lift. **Beware!** Make sure the children know that it is dangerous to put plastic bags over their heads.

DIFFERENTIATION

Both Group activities are accessible to all the children.

ASSESSMENT

Note the children who are able to describe what is happening to their bubbles or streamer, and who understand that the wind is moving air. Also note those who understand that the wind is pushing on things and making them move.

PLENARY

Talk to the children about what they have been doing. Ask them what was happening to their bubbles and streamers. *What was moving them? What was the wind doing to move things?* (Pushing on them.) *What is the wind?* (Moving air.) Practise some of the vocabulary. *Does anyone know what some of the long words we have been using, such as 'transparent' and 'reflection', mean?*

OUTCOMES

- Can describe how the wind makes things move.
- Know that the wind is moving air.
- Know that the wind can make things move.

LINKS

Unit 3, Lesson 2: measuring wind strength and direction.

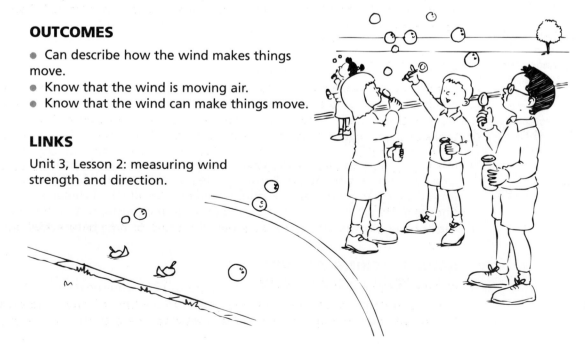

LESSON 7

Objectives	● To know that the wind is moving air that pushes on things in the environment and makes them move. ● To know that the wind can exert a push on their bodies.
Resources	An area containing trees and bushes, and perhaps tall grass; a fairly exposed area; an old umbrella, a windy day.
Main activity	Carry out a 'windy day walk' to observe how the wind blows through trees and bushes and moves them. Let the children stand in an open area to feel the push of the wind on their bodies. Open the umbrella and let the children take turns to feel the air pushing it.
Differentiation	This activity is accessible to all the children.
Assessment	During the Plenary, note those children who understand that the force of the wind is pushing on things and moving them.
Plenary	Talk to the children about what was happening to the trees, bushes and grass. *What was pushing on you? Could you feel the wind on your bodies?* Talk about the wind being moving air that pushes on things and makes them move.
Outcomes	● Can describe how the wind pushes on and moves things in the environment. ● Can talk about the feel of the wind pushing on them.

LESSON 8

OBJECTIVES

● To experience the upward push (force) of water.
● To know that water pushes upwards on objects.

RESOURCES

Main teaching activity: A plastic tank or water tray (deep enough to cover the largest object being used), and two or three objects of different sizes that float (for example, a cork, a beach ball, a piece of balsa wood) per group. One of the following stories: *The Cow Who Fell In the Canal* by Phyllis Krasilovsky (Little Mammoth), the Noah's Ark story from the Bible, *Norah's Ark* by Ann and Reg Cartwright (Red Fox), Chapter 6 of *The House at Pooh Corner* by AA Milne (Methuen).
Group activities: 1. Objects (such as plastic cups and containers) that float when they are empty, but sink when they are filled with water; tanks, water trays. **2.** Paper, pencils, colouring materials.

Vocabulary

float, sink, push, force, underwater, surface

BACKGROUND

The scientific explanation of what happens when objects float and sink is very complex, and it is not expected that children will begin to understand it until Key Stage 3. At Key Stage 1, they should be given opportunities to explore floating and sinking – mostly in terms of predicting and testing whether a range of objects will float or sink. They can also experience and describe what is happening when they try to push objects that float down into water: they can feel the water pushing back, and understand that this is a force.

INTRODUCTION

Read one of the suggested stories about boats and floating to the children as a stimulus for this lesson.

MAIN TEACHING ACTIVITY

Working with the whole class, put a large ball into a tank of water and ask the children to tell you what it is doing (floating). *What would you need to do if you wanted to make the ball sink?* (Push down on the ball.) *What would you need to do to keep the ball underwater? What would happen if you let go?* Divide the children in groups of four together with a set of equipment. Invite them to try out the various objects. While they are doing this, ask them such questions as: *What can you feel? What is happening to the ball? Why won't the object stay down in the water? What happens when you let go? Why? Can you feel the water pushing? What is that push?* (A force.) Ask the children to think very carefully as they try the different objects. *Do you have to push just as hard on each one to get it to go under the water? Do they all bob up again and float?*

GROUP ACTIVITIES

1. Ask the children to put some empty cups and containers on the water surface. Ask: *What will happen as they are filled with water?* Let the children try it. *Why do they float when they are empty and sink when they are full?* (The push down when they are empty is too small, but when they are full the push down is bigger than the push up from the water in the tank.)

2. Ask the children to write about what happened in the Main teaching activity when they tried to push the ball under the water. They should try to write down their ideas about why the ball popped up again. Remember that at this stage, the children's explanations do not have to be scientifically correct.

DIFFERENTIATION

1. Some children may still be at the experiential stage and need help to describe what is happening. More able children may begin to understand and explain what is happening.
2. Less able children could present their work in the form of pictures.

ASSESSMENT

Note which children understand that the water is pushing up, and that this upward push is a force. Can some children say that when they are pushing down a cup or filling it with water, the downward push (force) is bigger than the upward force, and that is why the cup goes under the water?

PLENARY

Talking to the whole class, ask the children to describe what was happening in the Main teaching activity. Encourage them to use the words 'push', 'force', 'float' and 'sink' in their explanations. Ask whether all the objects needed the same force to push them under the water. *Can anyone say why the objects bob up again when you stop pushing?* (Because the objects float and a force is needed to push them down – when that force is removed, they float again.) Ask the children why they think the empty containers floated and the full ones sank. Help them understand that heavier things experience a greater downward force, and that the air in the empty containers made them lighter than the full ones.

OUTCOMES

● Know that water pushes upwards on objects, and that this push is a for[...]
● Know that a force is needed to push a floating object down into water [...]
the force is removed, the object floats again.

LESSON 9

OBJECTIVES

● To know that pushes and pulls are forces.
● To know that forces can make things move.

RESOURCES

Activity 1. Photocopiable page 151, pencils. **Activity 2.** Medium-sized or large balls, skipping ropes.

INTRODUCTION

It would be fun to start this assessment lesson by telling the traditional story of 'The Enormous Turnip'. Remind the children that a pull is a force, and ask whether they can name any other forces.

ASSESSMENT ACTIVITY 1

Give each child a copy of photocopiable page 151. Ask them to look carefully at the pictures and write 'push' or 'pull' as appropriate under each one.

Answers

Push: 1, 3, 4, 7, 8.
Pull: 2, 5, 6, 9.

Looking for levels

Most children will label six of the pictures correctly. More able children will label them all correctly. Less able children may complete two or three pictures successfully. Some children may be able to label them all correctly if given help with reading the instructions: they may understand the science, even though they have difficulty in reading the words.

ASSESSMENT ACTIVITY 2

Ask the children to work in pairs. Give each pair a medium-sized or large ball. Ask them to pass the ball back and forth to each other by throwing and catching it, bouncing it and then rolling it. After each exercise, ask: *What force are you using to move the ball?* Give each pair a skipping rope and ask them to play a gentle 'tug-of-war'. Ask: *What force are you using?*

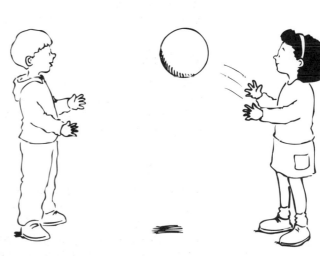

Answers

Throwing, bouncing, rolling are all pushes. Catching and tug-of-war are pulls.

Looking for levels

Most children will identify throwing, bouncing and rolling as push forces and tug-of-war as a pull force. More able children will also identify catching as a pull force. Less able children may have difficulty in relating the movements to the forces involved because of the abstract nature of forces.

Movement tally

Tick every time you see someone:

running	walking	jumping	hopping
✔	✔	✔	✔
total	total	total	total

skipping	waving	climbing	swinging
✔	✔	✔	✔
total	total	total	total

Introducing forces

Write **push** or **pull** under each picture.

1 _____

2 _____

3 _____

4 _____

5 _____

6 _____

7 _____

8 _____

9 _____

Sources of light and sound

ORGANISATION (19 LESSONS)

	OBJECTIVES	MAIN ACTIVITY	GROUP ACTIVITIES	PLENARY	OUTCOMES
LESSON 1	● To know that light is needed for us to see things. ● To carry out a simple investigation.	Look at an object in a 'dark box': the more light is admitted, the more clearly the object can be seen.	Put different-coloured objects in the box to see which shows up best. Write about what they have found out.	Try seeing in a dark room. Review the 'dark box' investigation.	● Know that light is needed for us to see things. ● Can carry out a simple investigation with help.
LESSON 2	● To know that there are many sources of light.	Look at a collection of light sources. Look at light sources inside and outside the school. Discuss fire.	Sort light sources on cards into 'families'. Make a large class picture showing light sources.	Discuss the purposes of different light sources.	● Understand that light can come from many sources.
LESSON 3	● To know that light sources vary in brightness. ● To carry out a simple investigation.	Test a number of different torches and rank them in order of brightness.		Review the investigation and results.	● Know that light sources vary in brightness. ● Can carry out a simple investigation with help.
LESSON 4	● To know that objects with shiny surfaces can only be seen in the presence of light.	Look at shiny and dull objects in a 'dark box'. Which are easiest to see in poor light?	Use shiny materials to make a collage mobile. Draw or paint a picture of someone wearing reflective clothing.	Relate the investigation to the uses of reflective clothing.	● Know that light is needed even to see shiny things. ● Know that some shiny things, such as reflective armbands, can help us to be seen more easily when there is only a little light.
LESSON 5	● To know how to keep safe with or near light sources.	Discuss the dangers associated with some light sources. Role-play keeping safe at a birthday party.	Draw up a set of rules for keeping safe at a birthday party. Design a poster about the dangers of looking at the Sun.	Review the safe use of various light sources.	● Know some of the dangers associated with some light sources.
LESSON 6	● To know about the dangers associated with bonfires and fireworks. ● To know how to call the emergency services.	Think about keeping safe at a bonfire or firework party. Role-play calling the emergency services, giving name and address.		Review the dangers of fire and fireworks.	● Know how to avoid accidents at a bonfire or fireworks party. ● Know how to call the emergency services. ● Know their own address.
LESSON 7	● To know that there are many different sources of sound in the school.	Go on a 'sound walk' around the school. Think about the sources of the sounds heard.	Make a zigzag book of sounds heard. Mark the sounds heard at each location on a simple map of the school.	Review and compare the findings of different groups.	● Know that there are different sources of sound in the school. ● Can offer some explanation for sounds they hear.
LESSON 8	● To know that there are many different sources of sound in the locality.	Go on a 'sound walk' in the local environment. Think about the sources of the sounds heard.		Review and compare the findings of different groups.	● Know that there are different sources of sound in the locality. ● Can offer some explanation for sounds they hear.
LESSON 9	● To identify some objects that make sounds.	Collect pictures of objects that make sounds. Consider the types of sound made and their purposes.		Discuss the purposes of sounds made by objects.	● Can identify some objects that make sounds. ● Can explain the purposes of some of the sounds.

ORGANISATION (19 LESSONS)

	OBJECTIVES	MAIN ACTIVITY	GROUP ACTIVITIES	PLENARY	OUTCOMES
LESSON 10	● To know how we make sounds with our voices. ● To conduct a simple investigation.	Investigate how we can alter the vocal sounds we make by modifying the use of the mouth, tongue and nose.	Use voices to make sound effects to accompany a story; record it on cassette. Several children stand behind a screen; the others try to guess who is speaking.	Discuss how the groups made the sound effects. Practise tongue twisters and animal sounds.	● Know that they can change the sounds they make with their voice.
LESSON 11	● To know that there are different ways of making sounds.	Sort musical instruments and materials according to how a sound can be made with them.	Sort pictures of instruments according to how they are played. Use percussion, voices and materials to make sound effects for stories.	Perform stories with sound effects.	Know that there are different ways of making sounds.
LESSON 12	● To make a simple musical instrument.	Make and play a simple shaker and an elastic band guitar.		Discuss why the shakers and guitars make different sounds.	● Can make a simple musical instrument.
LESSON 13	● To know that a 'noise' is often an unpleasant sound. ● To know that loud noises can be harmful.	Discuss what sounds are pleasant or unpleasant. Discuss dangers of very loud sounds, and ways of protecting the ear.	Make a set of rules for a quiet school. Sort sounds into 'horrible' and 'pleasant'.	Review the ideas discussed.	● Know that not all sounds are pleasant. ● Know that some loud noises can be harmful.
LESSON 14	● To know that we hear with our ears, but that we can alter the amount of sound entering our ears. ● To be able to carry out a simple investigation and record the results.	Discuss how to carry out a simple investigation to find the best material for making ear defenders.	Investigate which material is best for stopping sound entering our ears.	Review the investigation and results.	● Know that we hear sounds with our ears, but that we can alter the amount of sound entering our ears. ● Can carry out a simple investigation and make a simple record.
LESSON 15	● To investigate how we know from which direction sounds are coming.	Ask a blindfolded child to say which direction a sound is coming from. Repeat with the child using movable ear trumpets.		Discuss binaural hearing and its importance for various animals.	● Know how our ears help us to locate sounds. ● Can carry out a simple investigation with help.
LESSON 16	● Io know that loud sounds can be heard over a greater distance than quiet sounds. ● To carry out a simple investigation.	Investigate how 'loud', 'quiet' and 'inaudible' sounds change with distance.	Draw and write about sounds made to be heard at a distance. Investigate the audibility of spoken messages at different distances.	Review the Main teaching activity.	● Know that loud sounds can be heard over a greater distance than quiet ones. ● Can carry out a simple investigation.
LESSON 17	● To know that sounds get fainter as they travel away from a source.	Walk away from a 'standard sound' and stop when it becomes inaudible. Try in reverse.	Research how people send messages over a distance.	Discuss how and why the volume of a sound changes with distance.	● Know that sounds get fainter as they travel away from a source.
LESSON 18	● To know that our hearing helps to keep us safe.	Discuss warning sounds including crossings, bells, sirens. Go outdoors to demonstrate the role of hearing in road safety.	Find out about animals that use warning sounds. Practise crossing the road in a role-play situation.	Review warning sounds, road safety and contacting the emergency services.	● Know that our sense of hearing helps to keep us safe.

	OBJECTIVES	ACTIVITY 1		ACTIVITY 2	
ASSESSMENT 19	● To know that there are many sources of light. ● To know there are many sources of sound.	Identify sources of light from pictures. Name more light sources.		Draw pictures of the sources of sounds that might be heard in various locations. Name other sound sources.	

LESSON 1

OBJECTIVES

● To know that light is needed for us to see things.
● To carry out a simple investigation.

RESOURCES

Main teaching activity: A cardboard box, masking tape, a craft knife, greaseproof paper, scissors, cloth, a small object (see Preparation); a copy of *A Dark, Dark Tale* by Ruth Brown (Andersen Press) or *The Park In the Dark* by Martin Waddell and Barbara Firth (Walker Books).
Group activities: 1. The 'dark box' (see Preparation); several similar objects (such as counting bears) in different colours. **2.** Writing materials, paper.

Vocabulary

light, dark, see, eyes, dim, bright, shadow, cave, reflect

BACKGROUND

Objects can only be seen because light is reflected from them. Many young children believe that light comes out of their eyes, enabling them to see. Some children will never have experienced complete darkness, especially if they live in a town or city. Streetlights mean that there is almost always some ambient light that allows things to be seen, if only very dimly. Draping some very heavy fabric over a table can make a dark place for the children to experience.

PREPARATION

Make a 'dark box' from a fairly large cardboard box (a photocopier paper box would do, but a slightly bigger and longer one would be better). Paint it black inside, and make two 'peep-holes' (the size of a pencil) in one end. Use some masking tape to cover one of the holes (you will need this in Lesson 4). Cut a long slit (about 2cm wide) in the top of the box to form a 'window' and cover this with greaseproof paper or some other translucent material. Cover the window with a piece of cloth or card that will exclude all light (see illustration on page 155). Place a small object near the back of the box. If you are working in bright light, you may find it helpful to have a cloth that is big enough to cover the child's head as he or she looks through the peep-hole (as you would with an old-fashioned camera).

INTRODUCTION

Read out a story such as *A Dark, Dark Tale* by Ruth Brown (Andersen Press) or *The Park In the Dark* by Martin Waddell and Barbara Firth (Walker Books).

MAIN TEACHING ACTIVITY

Work with a group and talk about dark places the children may have been in. Some of them may have visited caves, have been out very late at night, or even have a dark corner somewhere in their home. *What could you see in that place? Could you see anything at all? Were there lots of dark shadows? Could you see any colours?* Ask the children for ideas about why they could not see very well. Remember that at this stage we are not looking for scientifically correct answers, but for the children to express their own ideas.

Invite a child to look in the 'dark box'. Make sure the cover is over the box, excluding all light. *Can you see anything?* Gently fold back the cover a little way. *Can you see anything now?* Fold the cover back a little more. *What can you see now?* Carry on, asking the child to describe what he or she can see at each stage, until the cover is completely removed. At first the children should see nothing at all; then they may see the object, but the colours will not be clear. They should see the object best when the cover has been completely removed.

GROUP ACTIVITIES

1. Groups of three or four children can investigate putting similar, different-coloured objects (such as counting bears) in the box to find out which colour shows up best. *How far does the cover have to be folded back before you can see what colour it is?* Pale colours, such as white or yellow, will show up before darker colours.

2. The children can write individually about what they have found out. Encourage them to write down their ideas about how we can see things.

DIFFERENTIATION

1. Some children may be able to decide for themselves how they will carry out the investigation. Others will need some help to decide whether they will put the objects in one at a time and measure how far back the cover needs to go or put them all in a row across the box and say when they can see the first one. (Either method is valid.)
2. Some children may need help to write down their ideas. They may find it easier to record their ideas on cassette.

ASSESSMENT

Ask the children to describe what they could see in the 'dark box'. Can they explain the difference between what they could see when the box was covered and when it was uncovered? Do they know that we need light to be able to see anything?

PLENARY

If possible, close the classroom curtains and switch off the lights. *Can you still see things clearly?* Switch the lights back on and talk about the difference this makes to our ability to see things. *What has made the difference?* Help the children to understand that our eyes can only see things when there is light available. Ask them to describe what they could see in the 'dark box'. *Why couldn't you see anything at first?* Ask some of the children who carried out the investigation to describe what they did. *Which colour was the easiest to see? Was the test you carried out fair? Did you put all the objects in the same place? Did you measure anything?*

OUTCOMES

● Know that light is needed for us to see things.
● Can carry out a simple investigation with help.

LINKS

Unit 1, Lesson 3: the human senses.
Literacy: writing a report.

LESSON 2

OBJECTIVE

● To know that there are many sources of light.

RESOURCES

Main teaching activity: A collection of light sources (candles, torches, lanterns, table lamps and so on); pictures or posters of the Sun, bonfires, fireworks and neon advertising displays.
Group activities: 1. Cards from photocopiable page 176 (see Preparation). **2.** Drawing, painting or collage materials, paper.

BACKGROUND

Many light sources contain glass, and children need to be aware that it is necessary to take care when near them. If you have an oil lamp in your collection, make sure that it is completely empty of any oil. Children can become quite intrigued by 'old-fashioned' forms of lighting. They have probably never known an environment without electricity, and find it difficult to imagine light not being available at the touch of a switch. Working by gaslight or candle-light was relatively difficult. This is one reason why people often used to get up with at and go to bed when it became dark.

The Sun is our main source of light. The Moon, although it gives us light at night, does not have any light of its own and only shines because it reflects light from the Sun. Stars (which are similar to our Sun) do shine with their own light, but they are so far away that this has a fairly minimal effect.

PREPARATION

Use a copy of page 176 to make a set of cards that can be used to play a 'Happy Families' type of game. Colour the pictures, mount them on stiff card and cover them with sticky-backed plastic to make a permanent resource. The same cards could be used to play 'Snap' or (if you make base boards) 'Lotto'.

INTRODUCTION

Ask the children what gives us light during the day. Remind them that they should never look directly at the Sun, even through sunglasses.

MAIN TEACHING ACTIVITY

Have the children sitting comfortably on the carpet. Ask them: *What happens when the Sun has set at night? Where do we get light from then? We might get light from the Moon if we are outside, but what about inside?* Look at some light sources from the collection. Look first at sources that are more familiar to the children, such as torches or table lamps. *When might we use such things?* We might need a torch to find our way along a dark path. Some children might go camping and use torches to find their way across the campsite at night. Table lamps are often used for decoration, or they might have one by their bed. *What do we have to do to make electric lights work?* Remind them about switches, and look for the switch on a lamp that you have. Remind the children about the dangers of misusing electricity, and that they should always ask a grown-up to help them plug things in.

How did people light their homes before we had electricity? Look at any lanterns, oil lamps or candles you may have, and talk about how they work. The children may have had experience of a power cut; how did they cope with the lack of electricity? You may have some specialist lights in your collection, such as a miner's hand-held lamp or helmet lamp. Remind them of what they learned in Unit 5, Lesson 5 (see page 127) about miners and pot-holers using lamps when they go underground.

Walk around the school and look for lights inside the school. Note where they are placed. *Why has that light been put in that particular place?* Look for lights on stairs or in dark corridors. *Are all the lights the same shape?* Now look for lights outside the school. *Do you have security lights that come on as soon as it gets dark? Why do we need streetlights? Why do we need traffic lights? Why are some road signs illuminated? How do they help to keep us safe?*

Back in the classroom, think about what else would give us light. Look at some of the pictures you have of bonfires or camp-fires. *How is this light different from the electric lights we are used to?* It is not as controllable or as bright; and although electric lights will get hot, they will not get as hot as a bonfire. *Could we carry a bonfire around with us, to light our way like a torch?* People used to carry small fires around in the form of candles or flaming torches. *What do we use candles for these days?* Most children will have had candles on their birthday cakes, and some may use them in religious festivals. Some people just like burning candles, particularly scented ones. Take this opportunity to remind the children about the dangers of playing with matches and fire and the need to keep safe. They should never have a bonfire or use fireworks unless a grown-up is present.

GROUP ACTIVITIES

1. The children play 'Happy Families' in groups of four, using the prepared cards. Each child is dealt a 'family name' card. This will tell them which type of light source they are collecting. They then take it in turns to take a card from the picture pile. If the card is in their 'family', they keep it; if not, they put it at the bottom of the pile. It would be helpful to have an adult working with the children the first time they play the game.
2. The children make a class picture showing various light sources. This could be either a daytime or a night-time picture. It could be a representation of a house (with the front

wall removed to show the interior), garden, garage and street. The house could contain ceiling lights, wall lights, table lamps, a standard lamp, a fireplace and a TV. The garage could contain a car, a torch and a fluorescent light. In the garden, you could have a bonfire and a barbecue with the Sun shining (or the Moon and stars). Finish the picture off with a streetlight. Give the children pieces of paper approximately the size required for the item that they are drawing or collaging.

DIFFERENTIATION

1. Some children may simply sort the cards into 'families'. More able children could make up their own games using the cards.
2. All the children should be able to contribute to this activity.

ASSESSMENT

Ask the children to name two or three different sources of light. Ask them to choose an item from the collection and describe where and how it would be used.

PLENARY

Ask the children to name some of the different types of light they saw on their walk and describe their purpose. Talk about the different ways in which we use lights: for working, reading and travelling; for decoration, information and safety.

OUTCOME

● Understand that light can come from many sources.

LINKS

Unit 5: uses, sources and dangers of electricity.
Unit 8: the Sun and the Moon; day and night.

LESSON 3	Objectives	● To know that light sources vary in brightness. ● To carry out a simple investigation.
	Resources	A collection of three or four different torches; a dark corner or a dark space under a table.
	Main activity	The children carry out a simple test to find out which torch is brightest: shining each torch in turn onto white paper with simple words written on it. Which torch helps them read best? Can they rank the torches in order of brightness? Discuss the need to shine the torches from the same distance to make it fair.
	Differentiation	Some children may understand that shining the torches from different distances will not be fair. Less able children will need help to realise this.
	Assessment	Observe the children as they carry out their test. Note which children try to keep their test fair. During the Plenary session, note which children can explain their findings.
	Plenary	Ask groups to report back what they have found. Did the results change as time went on because of the batteries running down?
	Outcomes	● Know that light sources vary in brightness. ● Can carry out a simple investigation with help.

LESSON 4

OBJECTIVE

● To know that objects with shiny surfaces can only be seen in the presence of light.

RESOURCES

Main teaching activity: A collection of shiny objects (such as a tablespoon, a teaspoon, plastic mirrors, scissors, saucepans and lids, silver foil, crumpled silver foil, holographic paper, coloured foil, reflective armbands), comparable dull objects (wooden spoon, paper etc); the 'dark box' and cover from Lesson 1, a torch; pictures of a crossing patrol, or of emergency services people in uniforms with reflective strips.
Group activities: 1. Shiny and dull papers or materials, glitter, adhesive, spreaders, thick paper. **2.** Reflective strips or silver foil paper.

Vocabulary

reflect, reflective strips, shine, shiny, dull, light

BACKGROUND

Year 1 children will have explored shiny (reflective) things in Reception. Some children may still have misconceptions about how we see things, and think that shiny things shine with their own light. All objects reflect light, but dull objects scatter light in all directions. Shiny things reflect light more directly, which appears to make them shine. If the object is very smooth, like a mirror, it may allow us to see reflected images. If there is no light, then no light can be reflected and we cannot see the object at all.

INTRODUCTION

Gather the class together on the carpet. Ask the children to look at the collection of shiny objects and tell you what they have in common. The children should be able to tell you that they are all shiny.

MAIN TEACHING ACTIVITY

Working with a group, choose one of the shiny objects and compare it with a similar dull object – for example, a tablespoon and a wooden spoon. Ask the children to describe some similarities and differences. Both spoons have a handle at one end and a bowl shape for picking things up at the other end. A metal spoon is smoother, shinier and thinner than a wooden spoon. The spoons are different colours. The metal spoon feels colder than the wooden one.

Ask the children to vote on which spoon they might see if it was really, really dark. Note on the board who voted for the metal spoon, who voted for the wooden spoon, and who thought they would see both or neither. Ask the children for their ideas about how they could find out. Remind them of the investigation they did with the 'dark box' in Lesson 1, and explain that they can use the same box to test these objects.

Put the two objects in the box and make sure it is well covered. Ask the children to take turns to look and see whether they can see anything through the peep-hole. Look at the predictions the children made and ask whether anyone wants to change their mind. Ask the children to think back to Lesson 1 and tell you why they cannot see anything. Remove the cover from the second peep-hole and ask them to look again. *Are you beginning to see the objects?* Shine a torch through the second peep-hole and ask them to look again. *What has made the difference? Can you see the objects better because of the light?* Ask the children whether they think there is anything in the collection that they would be able to see in the dark. *What about the reflective armbands?* Put these in the box and find out whether they can be seen in the dark, or whether you still need some light. These should shine quite brightly even at low light levels, but will still not be visible in complete darkness.

Discuss why people wear armbands. *Where might the light come from to make them shine?* Talk about how street lights and car headlamps provide the light so that the armbands shine, helping to make them visible in near-darkness. Talk about people such as a crossing patrol, firefighters, paramedics or police officers who wear reflective strips on their uniforms, so that they can be seen more easily at night. Refer to pictures if possible.

Reinforce the finding from Lesson 1 that we can only see things when some light is present, even if they are shiny. Leave the 'dark box' on display for the next day or two, so that the children can look again and carry out their own investigation.

GROUP ACTIVITIES

1. The children can work in groups of three or four, or as individuals, to make a shiny collage mobile (for example, showing icicles or raindrops). Give them a mixture of shiny and dull materials from which they have to choose the shiny ones. The mobiles can be hung where they will catch the light.

2. The children can draw or paint a picture of a child, firefighter, crossing patrol, paramedic or police officer wearing reflective strips on his or her clothing. They can stick small strips of reflective material (or of silver foil) in appropriate places on the picture.

DIFFERENTIATION

1. Less able children may not be able to sort the materials into shiny and dull.

2. All the children should be able to do this activity.

ASSESSMENT

Can the children say what we need in order to be able to see things, even if they are shiny? Can they describe how some shiny things help us to be seen more easily when there is not much light? Observe them choosing the materials for their collage: do they know which are the shiny materials?

PLENARY

Look at the mobiles the children have made, and talk about how shiny they are. Watch how they change if you move them in the light. Ask the children: *Could we see them if they were in the dark box?* Talk about why the emergency services have shiny (reflective) strips on their uniforms.

OUTCOMES

● Know that light is needed even to see shiny things.

● Know that some shiny things, such as reflective armbands, can help us to be seen more easily when there is only a little light.

LINKS

Art: making mobiles.

LESSON 5

OBJECTIVE

● To know how to keep safe with or near light sources.

RESOURCES

Main teaching activity: A collection of light sources (as for Lesson 2); paper napkins, streamers, paper hats, paper cups and plates, a small table, an empty matchbox, candles, a 'pretend cake' (see Preparation).

Group activities: 1 and 2. Paper, drawing and painting materials.

BACKGROUND

Vocabulary

safe, burn, bright, emergency, emergency services, light sources, heat

Small children do not appreciate that looking at a very strong light can damage their sight. The light-sensitive cells in the retina at the back of the eye can be damaged, and they cannot be repaired. Children should be told never to look at the Sun, even through sunglasses or other 'safe' materials such as smoked glass. Binoculars can be very useful for looking at the night sky, but must never be used for looking at the Sun: they will concentrate the Sun's rays directly into the eye, causing irreparable damage. You may have a child who gains access to a laser pointer and plays at making the red dot appear on the faces of classmates. This, too, is extremely dangerous and should be discouraged.

Many light sources produce heat, and it is often the heat that constitutes the greater danger as far as children are concerned. The Sun, candles, bonfires and fireworks are obvious sources of heat; but even a lightbulb can get very hot after it has been on for a short time and remain hot for some time after being switched off. Mains electricity is always a hazard, and children should always be taught to treat any equipment using this source of energy with respect.

PREPARATION

Make a 'pretend cake' from a small, round biscuit tin. Punch the required number of holes in the top with a hammer and nail. Paint the tin white. Put a cake frill round the tin and poke plastic candle holders into the holes on the top. Add the candles.

INTRODUCTION

Remind the class about some of the light sources they encountered in Lesson 2, showing them the same collection of objects.

MAIN TEACHING ACTIVITY

Talk about the light sources that the children use. We all use the Sun during the day. Remind the children that they should never look directly at the Sun. *What lights do you use at home?* (Living room, bedroom, kitchen and so on.) These lights are usually quite safe as long as the children switch them on and off sensibly. *Do you ever use a torch?* These again are usually quite safe, but the children should be warned against shining any torch directly into another's eyes: a bright torch can cause temporary loss of vision. *Are there lights that tell you when equipment is switched on?* (The little red light on the television, kettle or washing machine.) Talk about how these lights help to keep us safe by warning us that the kettle is hot or that the washing machine is full of water.

Discuss light sources that the children may use only occasionally, such as candles or fireworks. These are fun lights, but they can be dangerous. Talk about how we can keep ourselves safe while still having fun. Show the children the pretend birthday cake with real candles, and ask them what things they think could be dangerous about the lighted candles. Do they realise that trailing hair could easily catch fire, or that an unfixed candle could fall over and set things on fire? *How would you keep the birthday party safe?*

Set up a role-play situation with the birthday cake and candles on a small table. Have some paper napkins, 'matches' (an empty matchbox), streamers, paper hats and paper cups and plates on another table. Ask the children to choose the things that would be safe to put on the table with the lighted candles. Ask them to explain why the streamers, napkins or paper hats could be dangerous if they got too near the lighted candles. *Who should light the candles? Where and how should they sit or stand? Should they lean over the cake if they have long hair?* Remind the children that they should never play with matches or candles, and should always ask a grown-up to light candles.

GROUP ACTIVITIES

1. Individuals or pairs can draw up a set of rules for keeping safe at a birthday party.
2. Individuals can design a poster about the dangers of looking at the Sun.

DIFFERENTIATION

1. Some children might work together in a larger group to support each other, drawing up a set of rules between them.
2. All the children should be able to do this activity. Some may need help to write words on their poster.

ASSESSMENT

Watch the children as they set the party table. Are they able to explain why they have chosen the things they have? Assess the suitability of the rules and posters that they have made.

PLENARY

Remind the children of the need to use light sources sensibly. It is important to stress that light sources are useful and necessary, and we normally benefit from them; but they hold dangers if we are careless in using them.

OUTCOME

● Know some of the dangers associated with some light sources.

LINKS

Unit 5, Lesson 3: how to use electricity safely.
Unit 8, Lesson 1: the dangers of looking directly at the Sun.

LESSON 6

Objectives	● To know about the dangers associated with bonfires and fireworks. ● To know how to call the emergency services.
Resources	Pictures of bonfires, an old (unconnected) telephone.
Main activity	Many cultures celebrate festivals with bonfires and fireworks. Discuss when the children would see these. *What do you like best about a bonfire and firework party? What are the rules for keeping safe? Should everyone, including grown-ups, take notice of these rules?* Talk about keeping well back from fire. Stress that the children should never handle fireworks, except a sparkler given by a responsible adult. No one should ever put fireworks in someone's pocket. They should always be kept in a metal box, away from matches. *What should you do if there is an accident?* The children should learn the procedure for calling the emergency services (when at home): dial 999 and give their name and address. They can practise by role-playing with a telephone.
Differentiation	All the children need to be aware of these safety rules.
Assessment	During the Plenary session, ask the children to tell you some of the rules about bonfires and fireworks. Note which children know how to call the emergency services.
Plenary	Remind the children of the dangers of playing with fire and fireworks.
Outcomes	● Know how to avoid accidents at a bonfire or fireworks party. ● Know how to call the emergency services. ● Know their own address.

LESSON 7

OBJECTIVE

● To know that there are many different sources of sound in the school.

RESOURCES

Main teaching activity: Portable cassette recorders or clipboards and pencils.
Group activities: 1. Stiff paper or thin card (approximately 15cm × 40cm). **2.** Drawing and colouring materials, photocopies of a map of the school.

PREPARATION

For Group activity 2, you will need photocopies of a simple map or plan of the school buildings.

BACKGROUND

It is important for children to develop their listening skills. Sounds can tell us much about our surroundings, and listening is an important observational skill. Children, as we know, often hear things without actually listening! The children may have gone on a listening walk in Reception and identified some of the sounds in the environment; but this time, encourage them to think a little more about what is making each sound and what the sound can tell us. A portable cassette recorder will help the children to recall the sounds heard, and act as a stimulus for further discussion back in the classroom.

INTRODUCTION

This part of the lesson will need to be done with the whole class, since everyone will need to be quiet. Tell the children to sit, very quietly, with eyes closed, and listen.

MAIN TEACHING ACTIVITY

Ask the children to put a hand up when they hear a sound. *What is the sound? Who or what is making it? What does it tell you?* For example: 'I can hear footsteps. It sounds like the secretary, Mrs Calendar. She wears high heels. She might be going to her office.' Repeat for two or three sounds, so that the children get the idea of trying to explain the sound.

Divide the children into mixed-ability groups of four. Provide each group with a clipboard and pencil or cassette recorder. Explain that each group will have to report back on the sounds they heard to the whole class, so they need to write down or record each sound to help them remember. Set off on a walk around the interior of the school. If you have extra adult help, you could send some of the groups on an alternative route to avoid congestion. Encourage the children to listen to all the sounds they usually take for granted. *What sounds are coming from that classroom? What are they doing there? Are there any noises coming from the office or school kitchen? What is making the sound? Is it a telephone, someone using a keyboard, someone mixing food in a bowl? What do the sounds tell us?* (Someone is perhaps taking a message, writing a letter or making a dessert.) Listen for sounds coming from the boiler room, the cupboard, the hall. *Can you hear any sounds from outside?*

When you get back to the classroom, give the children a short time to think about the sounds they have heard and get ready to report back in the Plenary session.

GROUP ACTIVITIES

1. Individuals can make a zigzag book to record what sounds they heard during the walk.
2. Pairs can use a simple map of the school and mark on it the sounds heard in each location visited on the walk. Could another class follow the map and hear the same sounds?

DIFFERENTIATION

1. Less able children could draw pictures of what they think is making the sounds. More able children may be able to record the sounds in sequence and add a sentence of explanation to each picture.
2. Most children will need some help with reading the map. More able children may be able to add names to the classrooms and label other rooms.

ASSESSMENT

Listen to the children as they report back on the sounds they heard. Are they able to say what made each sound and give some explanation of what was happening?

PLENARY

Invite each group to report back on the sounds they have heard. If they were using cassette recorders, they may be able to play some of the sounds again. Did every group hear exactly the same sounds, or did one group hear something different? Did every group have the same explanation for each sound?

OUTCOMES
- Know that there are different sources of sound in the school.
- Can offer some explanation for sounds they hear.

LINKS
Unit 1, Lesson 3: how we use our senses to be aware of our surroundings.
Geography: simple maps and routes.

LESSON 8

Objective	● To know that there are many different sources of sound in the locality.
Resources	Clipboards and pencils or cassette recorders.
Main activity	Take a walk around the school grounds or local area. Give each group a clipboard and ask them to record the sounds they hear. Listen for traffic, animals and people. *Is it dustbin day? Can you hear aeroplanes or other machines?*
Differentiation	Less able children could record in pictures alone. More able children may be able to record the sounds in sequence and add a sentence of explanation to each picture. Less able children could record the sounds and present their work (orally) using a cassette recorder.
Assessment	In the Plenary session, as the children report, note those who understand that they have recorded a range of different sounds.
Plenary	Each group should report back as in Lesson 7.
Outcomes	● Know that there are different sources of sound in the locality. ● Can offer some explanation for sounds they hear.

LESSON 9

Objective	● To identify some objects that make sounds.
Resources	Old catalogues or magazines, large sheets of paper, scissors, glue, spreaders.
Main activity	Talk about things we use that make sounds: CD players, radios, TV sets, microwave ovens, toys, a dog's squeaky ball and so on. The children work in groups to cut out pictures of similar things from old catalogues or magazines and stick them down on display paper. Ask them to describe the sound each thing makes and explain the purpose of the sound.
Differentiation	Some children might find a list of sounds that they can choose from helpful (for example: 'ring', 'ping', 'bleep', 'squeak').
Assessment	Listen while the children are describing the sound each thing makes. Can they explain the purpose of the sound?
Plenary	Talk about why things make sounds. For example: *The microwave pings to let us know that it has finished cooking; the dog's ball squeaks to encourage the dog to play with it and have fun.*
Outcomes	● Can identify some objects that make sounds. ● Can explain the purposes of some of the sounds.

LESSON 10

OBJECTIVES

- To know how we make sounds with our voices.
- To conduct a simple investigation.

RESOURCES

Group activities: 1. A cassette recorder, story books. **2.** A screen to hide a child.

Vocabulary

voice, vibrate, whisper, shout, sing, talk, speak, communicate, lips, tongue, teeth

BACKGROUND

We make sounds with our voices by passing air through our vocal chords to make them vibrate. Changing the shape of these chords allows us to alter the pitch of the voice, but we need to alter the shape of the mouth and nasal cavity to change the kind of sound we make. A round, open shape produces an 'Aahh' sound; drawing back the lips into a straighter line produces 'Eeee' sounds; 'T' and 'D' sounds employ the tongue and teeth; 'N' involves directing the sound through the nose rather than the mouth. We usually only make sounds when breathing out; by increasing or reducing the amount of air passing through the vocal chords, we can change the volume. Always encourage children to speak clearly and distinctly. Be sensitive to children with speech problems who may have difficulty in making some particular sounds. You may have children who are experiencing a temporary difficulty, such as the loss of their front teeth, and who may be willing to talk about why they now find certain sounds difficult.

INTRODUCTION

This is a fun activity, but rather noisy! Ask the whole class: *How do we communicate with each other?* We write letters, send e-mails, draw pictures – but mostly, we talk to each other. *How do we talk to each other?* Face to face, on the telephone, perhaps through a cassette recording or on video. Hopefully, the children will know that we use our voices when we talk.

MAIN TEACHING ACTIVITY

Where do our voices come from? Encourage the children to put their fingers gently against their throats. *All together, say 'Aahh'.* If the children do this quite loudly, they may be able to feel their throats vibrating as they make the sound. It is easier to feel a low vocal sound than a high one. Ask the children to close their mouths and make the sound again. *How has it changed?* 'Aahh' should have changed to 'Mmm'. Talk about the parts of the mouth that we have used to make these two sounds. Very simply, the difference was made by having our lips open or closed. So our lips are very important in making different sounds.

Ask the children which other parts of their mouths they think are important. Many children will appreciate that they use their tongues, but may not realise the importance of the teeth in helping them to speak clearly. Choose three or four children and ask them to repeat a nursery rhyme such as 'Twinkle, twinkle, little star' without moving their tongues. *How easy was it?* Could the other children understand what they were saying? Ask them to try again, but this time using their tongues. *Was that better?* Talk about where they put their tongues to make a 't' sound.

Experiment by changing the shape of the mouth to find out what other sounds can be made: clicks and clucks, whistles, hisses, kissing sounds, tuts and so on. Encourage the children to think about how the different parts of their mouths help them to make the sounds.

What happens to our voices if we hold our noses while we speak? Invite a different group of children to recite 'Twinkle, twinkle, little star' while holding their noses. *Which sounds were particularly difficult to make?* Remind the children how difficult it is to make 'n' or 'm' sounds if they have a bad cold (because the nose is blocked).

GROUP ACTIVITIES

1. Groups of about four can use their voices to make sound effects to accompany a story, and record this on a cassette to play back to the rest of the class. One child could act as reader or narrator.

2. Several children stand behind a screen. Each takes a turn to speak, and the rest of the children try to guess who is speaking.

DIFFERENTIATION

1 and 2. All the children should be able to take part in these activities.

ASSESSMENT

Do the children understand that they make sounds with their voices? In the Main teaching activity, ask them to describe how the shape of the mouth alters the sound coming out.

PLENARY

Listen to the children's story tapes. Ask each group to describe how they made the sound effects. Practise making some specific sounds (such as 'p') then learn a suitable tongue twister (such as 'Peter Piper picked a peck of pickled pepper'). Sing 'Old MacDonald had a farm' and make the appropriate noises.

OUTCOME

● Know that they can change the sounds they make with their voice.

LESSON 11

OBJECTIVE

● To know that there are different ways of making sounds.

RESOURCES

Main teaching activity: A variety of musical instruments (try to include instruments that are played in different ways – by banging, blowing, shaking, plucking or scraping); cellophane, paper, wooden blocks, coconut shells, a bell or buzzer, sandpaper, a bowl, a jug of water, a party blower; a set of labels (see Preparation). If real instruments are not available, you could use pictures, but it is better to use the real thing if at all possible.
Group activities: 1. Photocopiable page 177; scissors, glue, blank A4 paper (or colouring materials). **2.** Cellophane and other materials as used for the Main teaching activity, stories.
Plenary: A short extract from a recording of *Peter and the Wolf* by Prokofiev (optional).

PREPARATION

Make a set of labels with the words 'shake', 'bang', 'pluck', 'scrape' and 'blow'.

Vocabulary

shake,
pluck,
scrape,
bang, blow,
crackle, click

BACKGROUND

Sound is made by something vibrating. Vibrations may be produced in a variety of ways; in musical instruments, they are usually made by banging (or tapping), shaking, plucking, blowing or scraping part of the instrument. The speed of the vibrations affects the pitch of the sound. A short string will vibrate faster than a longer one, and will produce a higher note. Slower vibrations produce a lower sound. Similarly, a longer column of air will produce a lower note than a short column. This can be demonstrated quite easily using a school recorder: covering more holes creates a longer column of air, and the pitch of the note becomes lower. Sounds can also be made in such ways as scrunching paper, rubbing sandpaper blocks together, scratching a slate, dropping a lump of play dough and pouring water.

INTRODUCTION

Gather the children together on the carpet and look quickly at all the instruments you have collected. Ask the children whether they know what kind of thing all these objects are. Can they name any of the instruments?

MAIN TEACHING ACTIVITY

Ask the children to sit very still with their eyes closed. Clap your hands several times. *Can you tell me how I was making that sound?* Ask the children to close their eyes once more, and this time choose one of the instruments and play one or two notes. *Can you guess which instrument it was?* Now choose something like the cellophane and scrunch it up so that it crackles. *Can you guess what was making the sound this time?*

Ask the children to think again about the sounds they have just heard. *Can you all clap your hands? How did you make the sound?* Ask them to tap their legs and chests. *Did you make the same sound or is it different?* Ask them how you made the second sound. *Did I bang, blow, pluck or scrape the instrument? Are there any other instruments here that you would play in the same way?* Ask different children to identify these and play a few notes on each to demonstrate. *Are there any other instruments that would go in the same set?* Put that set of instruments to one side, then ask a child to choose another instrument from the collection and say how it would be played. Make another set that would be played in the same way. Continue in this way until you have sorted all the instruments.

Look at the 'bang', 'pluck', 'scrape' and 'blow' labels and help the children to read them. Ask the children to put each set of instruments back on the table by the appropriate label. *Is there anything left that did not fit into the sets you have already sorted? What about sound 3 – how was that made?* Look at the sound-making materials left, and talk about how they can be used to make a sound. *What does the sound remind you of?* Crinkly paper might sound like a fire burning; water pouring from a jug could be a fountain or waterfall.

GROUP ACTIVITIES

1. Ask the children, working individually, to cut out the pictures of instruments from a copy of page 177 and paste them into sets on blank paper according to how they are played. Alternatively, they could colour the instruments according to which set they belong in (for example, things that are shaken in blue and so on).
2. Groups of five or six can use percussion instruments, sound-making materials and voices to make sound effects for a familiar story. One child could act as reader or narrator.

DIFFERENTIATION

1. All the children should be able to do this activity. Some may need help with cutting.
2. Most of the children will be able to do this activity using a simple, familiar story. More able children might make up their own story.

ASSESSMENT

At the start of the Plenary session, give the children three or four different instruments from the collection and ask them to describe how each is played. Use the photocopiable sheet as an assessment tool.

PLENARY

Ask the groups to perform their stories with sound effects. You may choose to listen to a short excerpt from *Peter and the Wolf* and talk about the instruments used for the different characters. Sing 'Oh, we can play on the big bass drum' and make the instrument sounds (or use appropriate instruments).

OUTCOME

● Know that there are different ways of making sounds.

LINKS

Literacy: retelling a familiar story.

LESSON 12

Objective	• To make a simple musical instrument.
Resources	Plastic pots with lids, rice, buttons, foil, beads, lentils, cotton wool and so on; plastic lunchboxes or margarine pots, elastic bands in different sizes; paint, sticky paper for decoration.
Main activity	The children make shakers: put items in pots and investigate the sounds made by different fillings; then choose one to cover and decorate. They investigate the sounds made by different-sized rubber bands on a container, then make a 'guitar' to play at least three different notes. They invent and play a simple 'guitar' riff or sound pattern.
Differentiation	More able children could devise a way of writing their sound pattern down for others to copy.
Assessment	During the Plenary session, as the children demonstrate their sounds, note those who understand that different shaker fillings or different-sized elastic bands make different sounds.
Plenary	Demonstrate some sound patterns. Talk about why different shaker fillings or different-sized elastic bands make different sounds.
Outcome	• Can make a simple musical instrument.

LESSON 13

OBJECTIVES
● To know that a 'noise' is often an unpleasant sound.
● To know that loud noises can be harmful.

RESOURCES
Main teaching activity: Pictures of noises (for example, traffic, an aeroplane, a helicopter, birds, a baby laughing, workmen wearing ear defenders); ear defenders, a cassette recorder, a cassette of gentle music and another of loud noise (such as a pneumatic drill, traffic or an aeroplane), a personal stereo.
Group activities: 1. Drawing and writing materials. **2.** Photocopiable page 178, blank A4 paper; scissors and adhesive or colouring materials.

Vocabulary
noise, pleasant, unpleasant, damage, deafness, loud, ear defenders, volume (loudness)

BACKGROUND
Describing sounds as pleasant or unpleasant ('noise') is very often a matter of taste. To some of us, current pop music may well be a horrible noise, while to others it is bliss! Most people would agree that loud noises made by some types of machinery (such as drills, diggers and aeroplanes) are unpleasant and to be avoided if possible. Young children will not appreciate that a persistent loud noise can, over time, damage their hearing. Many use personal stereo headsets; and while those designed specifically for children often have limited volume, others have no such limits and can damage the hearing if worn regularly and played at full volume.

INTRODUCTION
Play a short tape of gentle, quiet music to the class.

MAIN TEACHING ACTIVITY
Ask the children whether they think the music was pleasant or unpleasant, nice or nasty. *Why do you think that? What does it remind you of?* Talk about other pleasant sounds that the children like. Do they like to hear people laughing, birds singing, bacon sizzling? What unpleasant sounds do they really dislike? Listen to a tape of unpleasant sounds such as an aircraft, a pneumatic drill or a dog barking. *Why do you dislike these sounds?* (They are too loud, they hurt their ears, they remind them of something unpleasant.) Say that

'sounds' are everything we hear, but sometimes we call the sounds 'noises'. These are often sounds that are unpleasant. Show the children some pictures of things that make pleasant or unpleasant sounds; ask them how they would react to the sounds.

Look at a picture of workmen wearing ear defenders and/or look at a pair of ear defenders. Ask: *Why do workmen wear ear defenders when they are using some kinds of machinery?* Talk about how very loud noises can damage the hearing. Show the children a personal stereo and ask whether they know what it is. Do any of the children have one? Talk about how it, too, can damage their hearing if they listen to it for a long time with the volume turned up very loud. Talk about what it means to be deaf, and how deaf people communicate words by signing.

Ask: *Where do we hear unpleasant sounds or noises in school? Do we scrape and clatter chairs when we put them under the table? Do we sometimes make too much noise in the corridors when we are moving about? Do people scream and shout in the playground? Do noises from outside stop us working properly? What could we do about these unpleasant noises?* Explain how soundproofing and double glazing can help to protect rooms from outside noise.

GROUP ACTIVITIES

1. Working in pairs, the children can make a set of rules for a quiet school. These might include: lifting chairs when putting them away; walking quietly in corridors and not shouting inside; no screaming (unless hurt). Your school may have particular noise 'trouble spots' that the children can identify and think about.

2. Give each child a copy of photocopiable page 178 and make sure that all the children understand what sound each picture represents. Ask the children to colour pleasant sounds in one colour and unpleasant sounds in another, or to cut out the pictures and paste them into sets under appropriate headings on a sheet of A4 paper. Some children may have different opinions about what is a pleasant or horrible sound. Compare the children's answers and ask them to give reasons for their choices.

DIFFERENTIATION

1. Less able children could work in a larger group with an adult to draw up a set of rules agreed by them all.
2. All the children should be able to take part in this activity.

ASSESSMENT

Use the photocopiable sheet to assess the children's understanding. If they have made an unusual choice, discuss with them their reasons for doing so. For example, some children may have put the barking dog in the 'horrible' category because they don't like dogs and are frightened when they bark; other children may have a dog at home and count its bark as a welcome.

PLENARY

Talk about the noises the children like or dislike. Remind them of the noises around the school, and discuss the rules they have suggested for making school a quieter place. Discuss the importance of protecting their hearing.

OUTCOMES
- Know that not all sounds are pleasant.
- Know that some loud noises can be harmful.

LESSON 14

OBJECTIVES
- To know that we hear with our ears, but that we can alter the amount of sound entering our ears.
- To be able to carry out a simple investigation and record the results.

RESOURCES

Main teaching activity and **Group activity:** Ear defenders (if possible); earmuffs (one set per pair), round plastic margarine pots (two per pair), newspaper, cotton wool, scraps of fabric, polystyrene packing, tissue paper; a chime bar, drum or similar way to make a standard sound; photocopiable page 179.

Vocabulary

noise, silence, direction, protection, ear defenders, earmuffs, test, same, fair, predict, find out, decide

BACKGROUND

The outer ear (the part we can see) collects sounds in the form of vibrations. These vibrations are transmitted by very small bones to the inner ear. From the inner ear, signals are sent to the brain, where they are interpreted as sounds. Wearing ear defenders or earmuffs can reduce the level of vibrations entering our ears, and so reduce the amount of sound that we hear. This can be useful for protecting our ears from prolonged loud noises, or for just blocking sounds if we need to sleep or to concentrate on something else.

Some children may suffer from a temporary condition known as 'glue ear'. This inhibits the vibration of the tiny bones in the middle ear, and thus causes a loss of hearing.

Animals often have a much better sense of hearing than humans. As well as being able to hear a wider range of sound frequencies (higher or lower sounds), they can often move their outer ears in order to pin-point the direction from which a sound is coming.

In these activities, the children carry out simple investigations to find out the effectiveness of different earmuffs or ear defenders and the difference it makes if you can 'waggle' your ears. Young children will still need considerable help to design an investigation, but they should be encouraged to think about how they can find something out and what might happen. Ask questions such as: *How do you think we could find out which are the best?*

INTRODUCTION

Gather the children around you and ask them to look at each other's ears. *Are they all the same?* Look at the earlobes. Some may be very small and 'fixed', while other children may have bigger, 'free' lobes. *What do we use our ears for?*

MAIN TEACHING ACTIVITY

Make a sound using the chime bar and ask the children to put up their hands if they can hear it. Ask them to turn round so that they are sitting with their backs to you, and repeat the sound. *Who can hear it now?* Ask the children to cover their ears with their hands. Repeat the sound, and ask again who can hear it. *If you could hear it, was it still as clear as before?*

Ask the children to turn round and face you again. Remind them what they learned in Lesson 13 about loud noises being harmful and why people wear ear defenders. Show them the collection of margarine pots and materials, and suggest that they make some ear defenders for themselves. Explain that they will need to find out what is the best material to pack them with. *What could we do? How could we find out?* If necessary, prompt them to say that they could put different materials in the pots and put them over their ears to see which blocks out the most sound. *Do we need to wear two pots? Why? Does it matter if we have one material in one pot and a different material in the other pot at the same time? Does it matter how much material we put in each pot?* Some children may be quite happy to use different materials and quantities at the same time, but others may be starting to appreciate that some factors need to be kept the same if they are going to get any useful results. If they test different materials in two pots at the same time, they cannot be sure which material was best overall.

GROUP ACTIVITY

Working in pairs, the children should investigate the effect of using different materials to pack their earmuffs. They should listen to a standard sound, such as a chime bar or drum, while holding the earmuffs over their ears. Ask which material they think will be the best and why they think that. They should listen to the sound without earmuffs to start with, and give that sound a score of 5. They can use a copy of page 179 to record the score for the sound as heard through different ear defenders, and to record and explain their prediction and conclusion.

DIFFERENTIATION

Less able children may need more help to decide what they are going to do. They may not be able to give a reason for their prediction or explain their findings, and may need help in interpreting their results. Some children may be able to give reasons verbally, but not be able to write them down themselves.

ASSESSMENT

Observe the children as they carry out the investigation. Are they thinking about what they are doing? Are they trying to be systematic in testing the different materials? Are they recording as they go along? Use photocopiable page 179 to assess their ability to interpret their findings.

PLENARY

Ask the children to report back on what they have found out. *Which material was the best for blocking out sound?* Some groups may have different results. Discuss why this might be. *Did you all put the same amount of the material in the pots? Did you all stand the same distance away from the sound? Was the sound always at the same volume?* Stress that none of the results were 'wrong'; but because the investigation was carried out in a slightly different way, the results were different.

OUTCOMES

● Know that we hear sounds with our ears, but that we can alter the amount of sound entering our ears.
● Can carry out a simple investigation and make a simple record.

LINKS

Unit 1, Lesson 3: how we use our senses to be aware of our surroundings.

LESSON 15

Objective	● To investigate how we know from which direction sounds are coming.
Resources	Simple 'ear trumpets' made from thin card (see diagram below).
Main activity	Talk about animals that can move their ears in order to collect and locate sounds. Ask the children whether they can move their ears. *We have to move our heads, not just our ears. Is it better if we use both ears or cover one up?* Blindfold a child and make a noise in front, behind, to the side, above them. Can the child tell where the sound is coming from? Now let the child use ear trumpets and move them to 'collect' sound. *Does that make it easier to tell where the sound is coming from?*
Differentiation	All the children should be able to do this activity. Some may be able to write about what they have discovered.
Assessment	During the Plenary session, note those children who can tell you why being able to move the ears is an advantage.
Plenary	Talk about how our ears help us to locate sounds. Discuss how animals need to be able to locate sounds in order to escape predators or catch prey. Remind the children how it was easier to locate sounds using both ears than with one covered up.
Outcomes	● Know how our ears help us to locate sounds. ● Can carry out a simple investigation with help.

LESSON 16

OBJECTIVES
● To know that loud sounds can be heard over a greater distance than quiet sounds.
● To carry out a simple investigation.

RESOURCES

Main teaching activity: Objects that make loud and quiet noises: cymbals, a triangle, a drum, crackly paper, a ticking clock, a portable cassette player with short pieces of very quiet music and very loud music, a sheet of paper (to tear), a bouncy ball and so on; three large boxes; the hall or playground.
Group activities: 1. Paper, writing and drawing materials. **2.** The hall or playground.

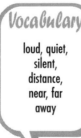

Vocabulary

loud, quiet, silent, distance, near, far away

BACKGROUND

Light and sound are thought to be similar in that both travel in waves. However, while light travels in straight lines from a source, sound travels in all directions. We can't see round corners, but we can hear! Sound travels rather like the ripples from a stone dropped in a pond: as the ripples travel away from the source, they decrease until they are no longer discernible. A bigger stone (a louder sound) makes bigger ripples that spread further before they die away.

INTRODUCTION

Working with the whole class, ask the children to whisper very quietly (perhaps recite a familiar nursery rhyme). Then ask them to shout 'Hooray'. Which sound do they think they would hear if they were on the other side of the playground or hall?

MAIN TEACHING ACTIVITY

Look at all the things you have gathered together and ask the children to think about what sort of sound each would make. *Would it be a loud sound or a quiet one? Which sounds would be easier to hear across the hall or playground?* Sort the things into two sets (boxes): 'easy to hear' and 'difficult to hear'.

Take the children and all three boxes into the hall or the playground and sit or stand them in a very large circle (as big as possible), facing outwards. Stand in the middle of the circle and use the things you have collected to make different sounds. Choose items randomly from each of the two sets. If the children think it is a loud sound, they should raise two hands; if they think it is a quiet sound, they should raise one hand. If they don't hear it at all, they will obviously raise no hands. Take a majority vote on each item and re-sort the items into three sets: 'loud, 'quiet' and 'silent'. As the children vote on each sound, if the result is different from that predicted by them, place the object in front of its new box. When you have used all the items, ask the children to turn round and move in towards the boxes. Look at the three sets of 'sounds'. Note the objects that have been moved into a different set from the one predicted. Try some of the sounds that the children did not hear again. *Can you hear them now that you are closer?*

GROUP ACTIVITIES

1. Ask each child to draw a picture of something that makes a sound that has to be heard some distance away, such as a fire engine, ambulance, police car, church bells, school bell or playground whistle, then write a sentence about why we need to hear that sound from a distance.
2. Stand all the children in the group in a circle, with one child in the middle. The child in the middle gives a simple message or phrase to one child in the circle, who repeats it back; both children use a normal to loud voice. Do this several times. The child in the middle should then use a very soft voice or whisper. Can the other children still repeat the message as accurately? This game could be played several times, changing the child in the middle each time.

DIFFERENTIATION

1. Some children may not be able to write a sentence without help. More able children may be able to draw and write about several things.
2. All the children should be able to take part in this activity. Be sensitive to any children whose hearing may be impaired.

ASSESSMENT

Make a quiet sound and a louder sound, then ask the children which one they think they would be able to hear from further away. Use the children's pictures and writing to assess their understanding.

PLENARY

Look again at the things you used to make the sounds. Ask the children: *Why do you think we couldn't hear all the sounds when we were in the big circle?* Talk about the difference in volume between the sounds, and the difference this makes to the distance over which they can be heard. Did the children make reasonable predictions? Were there some sounds that they thought would be easy to hear, but that they didn't hear at all?

OUTCOMES

● Know that loud sounds can be heard over a greater distance than quiet ones.
● Can carry out a simple investigation.

LESSON 17

OBJECTIVE

● To know that sounds get fainter as they travel away from a source.

RESOURCES

Main teaching activity: The hall or playground, beanbags, a buzzer or cassette player (with a music cassette).
Group activity: Reference books about means of communication.

Vocabulary

louder,
quieter,
distance,
volume

BACKGROUND

Sound waves travel in all directions from a source. They are often likened to the ripples on a pond. While this is a reasonable analogy, since sound waves travel in all directions the model should really be a sphere. As the ripples (waves) travel away from the source, they decrease until they can no longer be seen (or heard).

Some children's hearing may be less acute than others', for various reasons. It is important not to let any child feel inadequate. Stress that we are all different.

INTRODUCTION

Talk to the children about playing in the playground. *If your friend is on the other side of the playground, how do you attract his or her attention? Do you shout or whisper? Why do you need to shout?* Remind them of what they learned in Lesson 16 about sounds and distances. *If your friend were much further away, would they still be able to hear you?*

MAIN TEACHING ACTIVITY

Take the children into the hall or playground. Stand them in a tight circle facing outwards, and give each child a beanbag. Turn on the buzzer. Tell the children to walk slowly away from the sound, then stop when they can no longer hear it and mark the spot with their beanbag. *Are all the beanbags the same distance away from the sound? Why might there be differences?* Remind the children that we all hear differently, and so it would be very strange if all the beanbags were the same distance from the sound.

Ask the children to leave their beanbags where they are and make a new circle, as large as possible. Now they should walk in towards the sound and stop when they begin to hear it. *Have you reached your beanbag, or are you in a different place? Why might the distance be different?* Some children may have gone further when walking away from the sound because they 'remembered' it even when they could no longer hear it.

GROUP ACTIVITY

Working in pairs or individually, the children can use reference materials to find out how people send messages if they are too far away to hear. They can make a list of different means of communication: Morse code, semaphore, telephone, letter, e-mail and so on.

DIFFERENTIATION

The children could work in mixed-ability pairs to make a list. Some children may only be able to use very simple, pictorial reference books.

ASSESSMENT

Note which children can describe what happens as they move further away from a sound.

PLENARY

Talk about what the children noticed as they walked away from the sound. *Was the sound just as loud the whole time? Did it suddenly stop, or did it gradually get quieter?*

OUTCOME

● Know that sounds get fainter as they travel away from a source.

LESSON 18

OBJECTIVE

● To know that our hearing helps to keep us safe.

RESOURCES

Main teaching activity: A kitchen timer, an alarm clock (or a timer that rings), an old or toy telephone; pictures of traffic, an ambulance and a fire engine.
Group activities: 1. Reference books or CD-ROMs about animal sounds or animal warning signals. **2.** A simple 'roadway' (use chalk or ropes) in the hall or playground, two or three ride-on wheeled toys, road safety posters (available from RoSPA).

Vocabulary

danger,
warning,
alarm,
emergency,
siren, bells,
vehicles

BACKGROUND

Our sense of hearing is important for keeping us safe. We hear traffic approaching, alarm bells and sirens, and perhaps warning sounds from animals. Your local police force may be willing to come into school and bring model traffic lights, crossings and so on. You could perhaps arrange to have a fire drill as part of the lesson.

INTRODUCTION

Have all the children sitting together on the carpet. Set the timer or alarm clock to ring in a few seconds. Listen to it ring, then switch it off.

MAIN TEACHING ACTIVITY

Ask the children: *When might we hear that sound? What is it telling us?* Perhaps that it is time to get up, or that the cake is ready to take out of the oven. *Do we have a school bell? What does it tell you?* These are sounds that remind us of something or give us a gentle warning: don't oversleep, don't let the cake burn and so on. *What other 'warning' sounds might we hear at school or at home?* (The cooker, the microwave and so on.)

Some sounds give us a stronger warning, and it is important that we listen to them and act. *What does it mean when you hear the fire bell? Do you all know the fire drill? Do you have a smoke alarm at home? Do you know what to do if you hear it?* Use an old or toy telephone to practise making a 999 call and giving the correct information. Emphasise that such calls should only be made in a genuine emergency. Talk about the sounds made by emergency vehicles. *Why do they need to make a special noise?*

Ordinary traffic can also be very dangerous, and we need to use our ears as well as our eyes. Take the children to the school gate or somewhere where they can observe traffic safely. Ask them to close their eyes and listen carefully. *Can you tell when something is coming? Can you tell whether it is a bus, a car or a lorry? Can you tell how fast it is going?*

GROUP ACTIVITIES

1. Pairs of children can use reference books or CD-ROMs to find out about animals that use warning sounds. *When might you hear a dog growling or a cat spitting? Have you ever heard a blackbird's alarm call? What sound does a rattlesnake make, and how?*
2. The children can practise crossing the road in a role-play situation, focusing on listening for traffic as well as looking. Go through the rules of road safety for pedestrians with the children. Organise the groups according to the available space and resources (for example, the number of wheeled toys). Possible roles could include a crossing patrol person, a traffic police officer, shoppers, children playing, drivers and cyclists.

DIFFERENTIATION

1. Some children may need help with reading the reference books.
2. All the children should be able to take part in this activity.

ASSESSMENT

During the Plenary session, ask the children to describe some situations where our hearing is important in keeping us safe.

PLENARY

Talk about how important sounds are for keeping us safe. Go through the road safety rules again, and make sure the children know them. Ask one or two children to show how they would make an emergency telephone call if they had seen a road accident.

OUTCOME

● Know that our sense of hearing helps to keep us safe.

LINKS

Unit 1, Lesson 3: how we use our senses to be aware of our surroundings.
Unit 4, Lesson 4: identifying different materials by sound.

ASSESSMENT

LESSON 19

OBJECTIVES

● To know that there are many sources of light.
● To know there are many sources of sound.

RESOURCES

Photocopiable pages 180 and 181, pencils, colouring materials.

INTRODUCTION

You may wish to start the lesson by asking the children to remember some of the things they have learned in this unit. Before they do Assessment activity 1, remind them that we use our eyes to see, but that we also need a light source before we can see anything. Tell them that they are going to look for sources of light on the sheet and colour them in. Before they do Assessment activity 2, ask them to tell you which body part they use to hear. Ask them to name some familiar sounds that they might hear every day.

ASSESSMENT ACTIVITY 1

Give each child a copy of page 180. Go through the pictures and make sure the children know what each object is. Read out the words. Ask the children to complete the sheet.

Answers

The teddy bear, mirror, chair and spoon are not sources of light.

Looking for levels

Most children should be able to identify four of the light sources correctly and complete the sentence at the bottom with at least one suggestion. More able children will identify all the light sources and complete the sentence with several more. Less able children may not identify many of the light sources, and may include some non-light sources in their answer. They may also be unable to write the names of any further light sources.

ASSESSMENT ACTIVITY 2

Give each child a copy of page 181. Read through the words with the children and make sure they understand what they have to do.

Answers

The answers will vary, but anything that is a source of sound in the appropriate environment is acceptable. The missing word in the sentence is 'sound'.

Looking for levels

Most children should be able to complete the sheet successfully and write the word 'sound' to complete the sentence. They may only offer one more suggestion. Some children may have difficulty in completing more than two of the boxes, and may not write anything at the foot of the sheet. More able children will complete the sheet and offer three or four extra sources of sound.

Name

Light Lotto

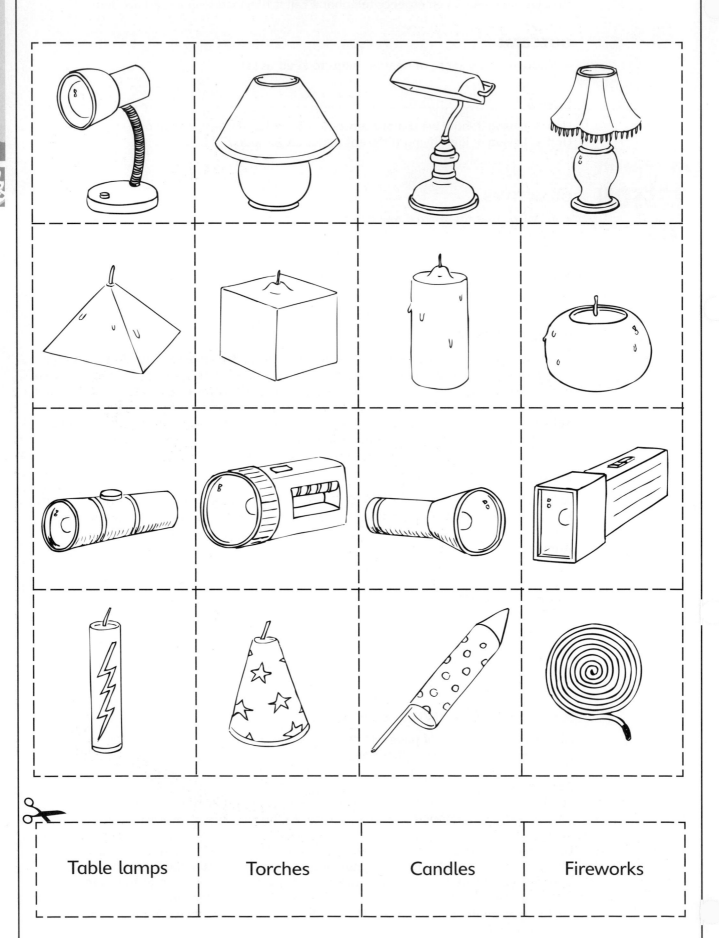

Table lamps | Torches | Candles | Fireworks

How is it played?

Bang, shake, pluck, blow or scrape?

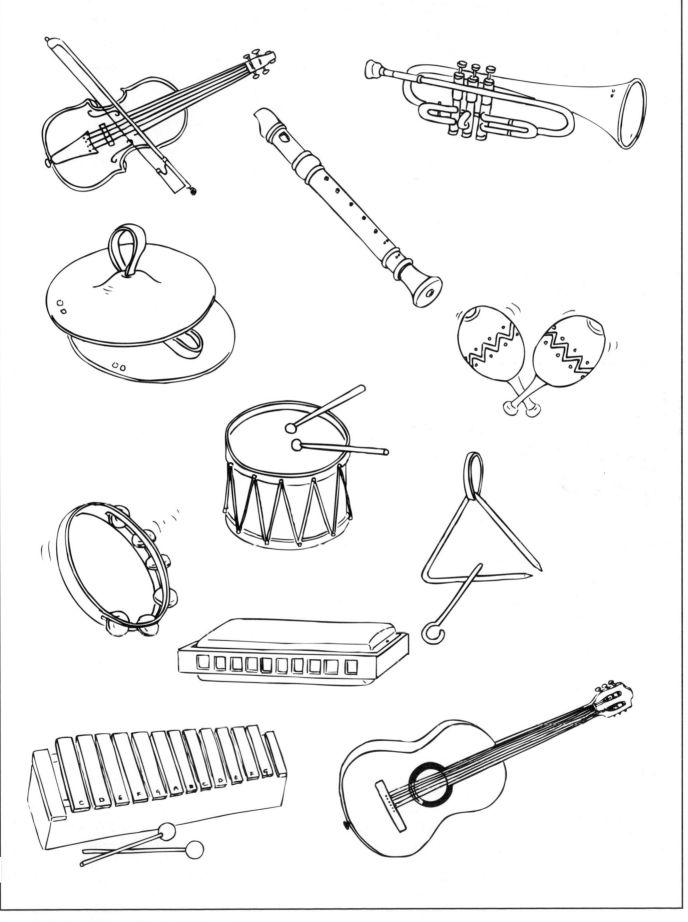

Pleasant or unpleasant?

UNIT 7 LIGHT & SOUND

Blocking out sound

I think the best material for blocking out sound will be _____

_____

_____

because _____

_____

_____

Stuffing in the earmuffs	Loudness: 1 (quiet) to 5 (loud)
none	5
fabric	
cotton wool	
newspaper	
tissue paper	

I found out that _____ blocked out the most sound.

I think this is because _____

_____

Name

Sources of light

Colour in all the things that are sources of light.

Write the names of some more sources of light:_____

_____

_____

Sources of sound

Draw a picture in each box.

I hear
at home.

I hear
at school.

I hear
in the park.

I hear
in the street.

All these things are sources of _____ . How many more

can you think of? _____

_____

Stargazing

ORGANISATION (6 LESSONS)

	OBJECTIVES	MAIN ACTIVITY	GROUP ACTIVITIES	PLENARY	OUTCOMES
LESSON 1	● To know that the Sun is a sphere and that we see it in the daytime. ● To understand the dangers of looking directly at the Sun.	Look at pictures of the Sun; discuss its shape and nature. Watch a tealight burn.	Write about sunshine activities. Make a large collage of the Sun, using the colours seen in the tealight flame.	Discuss the importance and dangers of sunlight.	● Know that we see the Sun during the day. ● Know about the dangers of looking directly at the Sun.
LESSON 2	● To know that the Moon is a sphere and we see it at night-time. ● To know that the Moon appears to change its shape.	Discuss why the Moon's shape appears to change. Demonstrate using a ball and OHP. Observe the Moon in the sky.	Identify different shapes that represent phases of the Moon. Make a large collage of the Moon.	Review ideas about the phases of the Moon, and when we can see the Sun and the Moon.	● Know that the Moon is a sphere. ● Know that we see it best when the sky is dark. ● Know that the Moon appears to change its shape.
LESSON 3	● To distinguish the Sun and Moon from the stars.	Watch a tealight burn. Discuss the nature and location of the Sun and the stars. Make a stars mobile.		Compare the Sun, Moon and stars; discuss when each can be seen.	● Can distinguish the Sun and Moon from the stars.
LESSON 4	● To know that the pattern of day and night affects animals.	Discuss which animals are active at night and why. Talk about how humans cope with working night shifts.	Make a zigzag picture diary of their own day and night. Identify nocturnal animals from a selection of pictures.	Discuss the various reasons why animals (including people) may need to be active at night.	● Know the difference between day and night. ● Know that some animals prefer to come out at night.
LESSON 5	● To know that the pattern of day and night changes with the seasons.	Discuss the seasonal changes in daylight hours. Use a display to represent the changes.	Draw summer and winter pictures. Draw or paint pictures of daytime or night-time activities.	Ask questions to help the children interpret the graph display.	● Know that the pattern of day and night changes according to the season.

	OBJECTIVES	ACTIVITY 1	ACTIVITY 2
ASSESSMENT 6	● To distinguish the Sun from the Moon. ● To know the pattern of day and night changes with the seasons. ● To know that the pattern of day and night affects living things, including humans.	Complete sentences and draw pictures to show the sky in the daytime and at night.	Complete sentences to describe the seasonal pattern of daylight hours. Know and draw some nocturnal animals.

LESSON 1

OBJECTIVES

● To know that the Sun is a sphere and that we see it in the daytime.
● To understand the dangers of looking directly at the Sun.

RESOURCES

Main teaching activity: Pictures of the Sun (both photographs and cartoons), a large ball (yellow if possible), a globe, a tealight, matches, a metal baking tray with sand, a small table, paper and drawing materials.
Group activities: 1. Photocopiable page 192, writing materials. **2.** A large circle of light-coloured paper (the size will depend on the size of the display area); tissue paper in shades of red, orange and yellow; gold foil, adhesive, spreaders.

Vocabulary

Sun, Moon, stars, gas, burning, shining, sphere, danger, orbit

BACKGROUND

Throughout this lesson, emphasise to the children that they should never look directly at the Sun, even through sunglasses: it can damage their eyes.

   The Sun is necessary for life on Earth to exist. It gives us warmth and light. Plants need light in order to make food by photosynthesis, and we depend on plants for food. We also need sunlight to remain healthy: our skin is able to manufacture vitamin D (which helps us to develop strong bones) in the presence of sunlight.

   The Sun is really just another star in the Universe, but it is very important to us. There may be other solar systems like ours, with planets that have life on them, but no one really knows. There is still a great deal of research going on to find out, and science fiction stories often speculate about what life might be like in other planetary systems. For your information (the children don't need to know this), the Sun is 93 million miles away from the Earth. Other stars are so far away that the distances are measured in light years. A light year is the distance travelled by a beam of light in one year (about six million million miles). After the Sun, the next nearest star is Proxima Centauri; this is 4.2 light years away, an almost unimaginable distance.

PREPARATION

Fill the tray with sand and place it on a small table.

INTRODUCTION

Working with the whole class, ask the children to draw and colour a picture of the Sun. Almost certainly, they will draw a stereotypical yellow disc with spikes or lines coming from it.

MAIN TEACHING ACTIVITY

Gather the children together on the carpet and talk about why they think the Sun is the shape they have drawn. Ask them to explain why they have drawn 'spikes' around it. We usually do this to indicate the rays coming from it. Look at some of the pictures you have and compare cartoon versions with actual photographs. *Which one is really the Sun?* Use a large ball to explain that the Sun is really a huge ball that is very, very hot, and is made of gases that are burning all the time. Emphasise that it is also very bright and can damage their eyes if they look at it, even through sunglasses. Introduce the word 'sphere' if the children have not met it before. Using a globe map, explain that the Earth is also (roughly) a sphere, but a much smaller one than the Sun. The Earth orbits around the Sun, and also spins – like a football that has been kicked at a slant so that its path will curve. At night, we cannot see the Sun because it is on the other side of the Earth. The Sun only seems small to us because it is so far away. Some children may find it difficult to accept that the Sun is a sphere. Talk about how we draw a ball as a circle, even though we know it is a sphere.

   Discuss all the colours that you might see in the Sun if you could look directly at it. Put the tealight in the middle of the sand tray on the small table, and make sure that the children are sitting well back. Light the tealight, watch it burning and discuss the colours you can see in the flame. Some children may never have encountered a 'living' flame, so take this opportunity to talk about the dangers of playing with fire and matches.

GROUP ACTIVITIES

1. The children can use photocopiable page 192 to record a sentence about what they like doing in the sunshine.

2. A group of four to six children can make a large collage of the Sun, using tissue paper in all the colours they have seen in the candle flame (plus gold foil).

DIFFERENTIATION

Both activities are accessible to most children. Less able children may need help with writing a sentence in Group activity 1.

ASSESSMENT

Ask the children when they see the Sun. Ask them to describe its shape, and to explain why the Sun is important to us.

PLENARY

Talk about the crucial role that the Sun plays in our lives: it gives us light and warmth. Discuss how most of us enjoy being out in the sunshine. Remind the children about the dangers of looking directly at the Sun, and talk about the need to wear a sunscreen to stop our skin from burning. *What other things can we do to protect ourselves from the Sun's harmful rays?* (Keep in the shade, wear a hat.) Ask the children to think about what it might be like if there were no Sun. Discuss the fact that it is colder at night, when we can't see the Sun in the sky.

OUTCOMES

- Know that we see the Sun during the day.
- Know about the dangers of looking directly at the Sun.

LINKS

Unit 3, Lessons 5–8: the four seasons.
Maths: solid shapes.

LESSON 2

OBJECTIVES

- To know that the Moon is a sphere and we see it at night-time.
- To know that the Moon appears to change its shape.

RESOURCES

Main teaching activity: Pictures or posters of the Moon (particularly a full Moon), a large ball, a strong torch or OHP, paper, pencils.
Group activities: 1. Photocopiable page 193, scissors, adhesive. **2.** A large paper circle (smaller than that for the Sun in Lesson 1), collage materials in shades of grey and black, silver foil, paper, adhesive, spreaders.

Vocabulary

Moon, stars, phases, half Moon, crescent, full Moon, reflected

BACKGROUND

The Moon is a satellite of the Earth. It moves in orbit around the Earth about once every 28 days. It has no light of its own, and shines only because it reflects the light of the Sun. The Moon appears to change shape because of the way we see the sunlight reflected from it. Young children can observe the changes in its shape, but understanding why these changes happen is too difficult for this age group. Until they have a firm grasp of how shadows are formed and can grasp the complexity of multiple movements, they cannot begin to understand why the Moon appears to change shape in such a regular pattern. Many adults find this difficult.

Choose the time when you do this lesson carefully. It is possible to see the waxing (growing) Moon in the late afternoon or early evening, and the waning (diminishing)

Moon in the early morning. The full Moon is only visible in the middle hours of the night, and the new Moon is in the sky in the middle of the day (when we can't see it, because the light from the Sun is too strong). What we call the 'new Moon' is really the first thin crescent that we see in a darker sky. What we call a 'half moon' is really a quarter Moon, since what we can see is a quarter of the whole sphere illuminated. The shape in between the 'half' and 'full' shapes is called a 'gibbous Moon' (see illustration below). It is not necessary for the children to know these names at this stage, but someone might ask! Some daily newspapers publish the phase of the moon along with the weather forecast and lighting-up times; if you choose to do the lesson during a waxing or waning period, you may be able to see the Moon while the children are in school.

While Moon-gazing, you may also be lucky enough to see a few stars. This may be difficult if you are in the middle of a town, where light pollution from street lamps and buildings may prevent you from getting a clear view. Many children do not appreciate that the stars are still in the sky during the daytime; it is just that the light from the Sun is so intense that we are unable to see the fainter light from the stars. The first bright 'star' to appear each evening, often called the Evening Star, is really the planet Venus and not a star at all. Planets, like the Moon, shine with the reflected light of the Sun; they shine steadily, whereas stars appear to flicker (because they are masses of burning gases).

   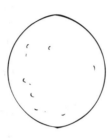

New Moon
In the sky in the middle of the day. Cannot be seen because of the brightness of the Sun.

Waxing crescent
Seen in late afternoon or early evening.

First quarter

Waxing gibbous

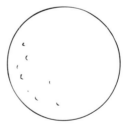 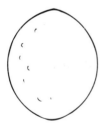  

Full Moon
Seen in the middle of the night.

Waning gibbous

Last quarter

Waning crescent
Seen in the early morning.

INTRODUCTION

Ask the children to draw a picture of the Moon. The majority will probably draw a crescent Moon, possibly with a face.

MAIN TEACHING ACTIVITY

Talk with the children about when we see the Moon in the sky. *Do you see the Moon every night?* Sometimes we cannot see the Moon because of clouds, but sometimes it is because of the phase of the Moon. Ask them whether the Moon is always the shape they have drawn. Look at some pictures or posters showing the full Moon. Show the children the large ball and say that the Moon is really a sphere or ball shape. Discuss the fact that we see the phases of the moon because of the way light is reflected from a sphere.

If possible, work in a dark place so that light and shadow are more pronounced. Sit the children with their backs to a bright light source, such as a strong torch or overhead projector. Move a large ball slowly from one side of the light beam to the other, in front of them. Can they always see the whole of the ball lit up – or do they sometimes, as the ball crosses the edge of the light beam, see a crescent shape?

If possible, go out each day and look for the Moon. The children should draw the shape they see. Remember that you will sometimes need to make observations as the children come into school, and sometimes as they go home. On some days you will not see the Moon at all, because it is only visible later in the night sky – or it is in the daytime sky, but cannot be seen because of the intensity of the Sun's light. If the Moon is coming towards full, the children may be able to make some observations at home before they go to bed and bring the results to school the next day.

GROUP ACTIVITIES

1. Give each child a copy of photocopiable page 193. They have to identify, cut out and stick down the different shapes that represent phases (shapes) of the Moon.
2. A group of four to six children can make a collage Moon to go with the Sun from the previous lesson. The Moon should be smaller than the Sun. They should collage most of the circle in black and grey, with a crescent of silver on one edge. This will help them to understand that the Moon is always complete, even though they can sometimes only see a small part.

DIFFERENTIATION

1. Some children may need help with cutting out the shapes. More able children could write the name of the phase under each picture.
2. All the children should be able to take part in this activity.
Some children may become very interested in this theme, and could keep their own 'Moon diary' as homework.

ASSESSMENT

Ask the children to draw a picture of the Moon or describe some of the Moon shapes they might see. Some children may find this a difficult concept: even though you have talked about it being a sphere, they may still draw the stereotypical crescent shape. More able children may understand that the Moon reflects the light from the Sun. Ask whether anyone can explain why we sometimes see a half Moon or crescent shape.

PLENARY

Look at the large ball and talk again about the Sun and the Moon really being spheres, even though we see and draw them as circles. Talk about why we sometimes see only part of the Moon. Ask the children to describe some of the shapes that we see. Discuss when is the best time to see the Sun or the Moon in the sky.

OUTCOMES

● Know that the Moon is a sphere.
● Know that we see it best when the sky is dark.
● Know that the Moon appears to change its shape.

LINKS

Maths: solid shapes.
Unit 7, Lesson 2: sources of light.

LESSON 3

Objective	● To distinguish the Sun and the Moon from the stars.
Resources	Pictures of the Sun, Moon and night sky (with stars), a tealight, a metal tray filled with sand, matches, silver foil, card, scissors, star templates.
Main activity	Observe a tealight burning (in the dark if possible). Remind the children of the Sun burning and glowing. The stars are like this, but so far away that they appear to be very, very small. Talk about when we can see stars, the Moon and the Sun. Go out and look for stars in the evening sky if possible. The children cut out silver stars to hang as mobiles in front of the collaged Sun and Moon display.
Differentiation	More able children could find out that some stars have names, or are grouped together in constellations that have names. Most of the children will be able to draw round a template to make their own stars, but some may need to have the shapes drawn for them.
Assessment	Take note of those children who contribute sensibly to the Plenary session.
Plenary	Talk about the things that are seen in the sky. Can the children identify the Sun, Moon and stars in pictures, and say when they are most likely to see each? Can they describe the differences between them?
Outcome	● Can distinguish the Sun and Moon from the stars.

LESSON 4

OBJECTIVE
● To know that the pattern of day and night affects animals.

RESOURCES
Main teaching activity: Pictures of nocturnal animals (hedgehogs, foxes, bats, owls and so on); picture books about nocturnal animals.
Group activities: 1. Thick paper or thin card, drawing materials. **2.** Photocopiable page 194, colouring materials.

PREPARATION
Make a zigzag book for each child from thick paper or thin card.

Vocabulary
day, night, dark, light, dawn, dusk, active, hunt, nocturnal

BACKGROUND
Sunlight is essential to life, and we might therefore expect living things to 'close down' at night, to sleep and await the dawn. Some creatures, however, started coming out at night to feed so that they had a better chance of avoiding their predators. But the predators responded by adapting their own feeding patterns so that they, too, came out at night. Many insects are most active at dusk, and some plants have adapted to attract the insects they need to pollinate them by producing their strongest scent at this time of day. Bats feeding on these insects are adapted to hunting in the dark, navigating by sound rather than sight. Owls have developed exceptional night vision, so that they can locate small creatures such as mice and voles in the dark. Some 'cold-blooded' creatures, such as lizards, need the warmth from the Sun in order to get their systems working. They may be seen soaking up the early morning sun before setting off on their hunt for food.

Humans are naturally diurnal, but many have needed to become nocturnal because of the work they do. Some people can adapt quite well to a nocturnal lifestyle, but others find it very difficult and may become ill.

Plants, too, are affected by the pattern of day and night. They are unable to photosynthesise in the dark. Since many of the insects they depend on for pollination are not abroad during the night hours, many plants close their flowers as night falls.

INTRODUCTION

Read a story such as *The Owl Who Was Afraid of the Dark* by Jill Tomlinson (Mammoth) or *Hoot* by Jane Hissey (Red Fox) to the class.

MAIN TEACHING ACTIVITY

Ask the children whether they know of any other animals that come out at night. Look at some pictures of nocturnal animals. *Why do you think they prefer to 'work' at night and sleep during the day? Why do they need to sleep?* Discuss the fact that many animals (including humans) need to sleep if they are to remain healthy and alert. Discuss with the children the kinds of animals they might see during the day. *What things are they doing? Are they feeding, playing or sleeping? What do they feed on? Does anything feed on them?* For example, talk about snails eating plants and birds eating snails.

Some of the children may have a family member who works at night. *How does working at night affect them? When do they sleep? When do they eat? Do they have their dinner in the middle of the night? What happens at the weekend or on their day off? Do you have to change your own behaviour if a parent is sleeping during the day? Do you have to be very quiet?*

GROUP ACTIVITIES

1. Give each child a zigzag book and ask them to make a picture diary of their own day and night. They should draw daytime activities on one side and night-time activities on the other.
2. Give each child a copy of photocopiable page 194. Ask the children to colour in the animals that come out at night and complete the sentence appropriately.

DIFFERENTIATION

1. More able children could write a short sentence to go with each picture.
2. All the children should be able to do this activity.

ASSESSMENT

Ask the children to describe some differences between day and night. Can they name some animals that come out at night? Use the photocopiable sheet to assess their understanding.

PLENARY

Discuss with the children what animals (including humans) do during their waking hours. All have to find food. Some animals may hunt directly; humans often work to earn money to buy food. Pets rely on us to provide their food. Talk about why and how some animals have adapted to become more active at night. *Why do some humans work at night?* For example, nurses and doctors are needed to look after people who are ill. Some people work at night to provide electricity and gas, which are needed at all times. Other people clean and repair public places ready for the next day.

OUTCOMES

● Know the difference between day and night.
● Know that some animals prefer to come out at night.

LINKS

Unit 2, Lesson 2: recognise and name some common animals.
Unit 2, Lesson 4: know how some animals move and feed.

LESSON 5

OBJECTIVE
● To know that the pattern of day and night changes with the seasons.

RESOURCES

Main teaching activity: A prepared display board; 'Bed in Summer' by Robert Louis Stevenson (in *A Child's Garden of Verses*, Puffin).
Group activities: 1. Photocopiable page 195, pencils. **2.** Drawing or painting materials, art paper.

PREPARATION

Use yellow and dark blue (or black) paper to cover a display board as shown below. If you choose to do this activity during the autumn term, you will need to cover the board as shown in the second diagram; otherwise, you should follow the first diagram.

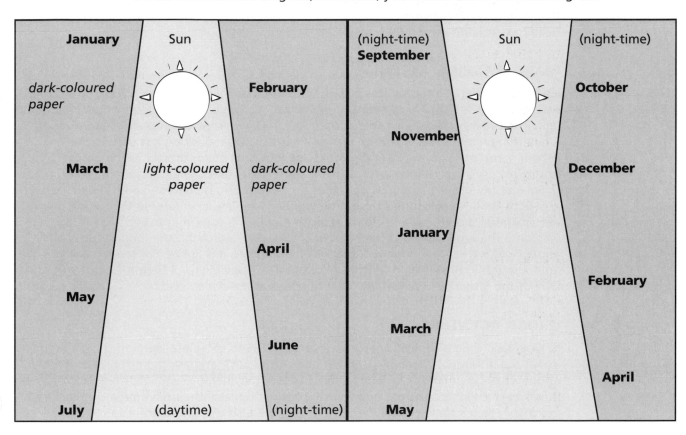

Make name labels for the months of the year from January to July. For the Plenary session, make a large arrow from card to pin to the display board in order to show the present month of the year.

BACKGROUND

The number of daylight hours varies considerably according to the season and the latitude (distance from the Equator) at which you live. At this stage, the children will just be observing or remembering that there is a change, and will not be expected to understand or explain the reasons for the change.

The variation is less in the tropics, but becomes more noticeable the nearer you get to the Poles. This is because the Earth is tilted on its axis. The angle and direction of this tilt does not change. This means that for part of the Earth's orbit the southern hemisphere is tilted toward the Sun, and for the other part the northern hemisphere is receiving more direct sunlight (see illustration overleaf). In summer in the northern hemisphere, that part of the Earth is tilted towards the Sun. The northern regions are thus exposed to sunlight for longer during each daily rotation than in the winter, when they are tilted away from the Sun.

Vocabulary

month, season, day-length, daylight, longer, shorter, evening, morning, spring, summer, autumn, winter

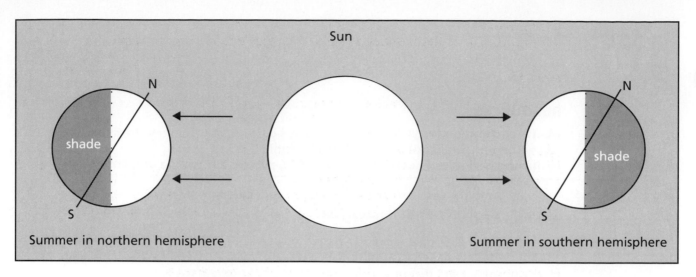

Sun

shade

N

S

Summer in northern hemisphere

N

shade

S

Summer in southern hemisphere

INTRODUCTION

Read Robert Louis Stevenson's poem 'Bed in Summer' to the class.

MAIN TEACHING ACTIVITY

Ask all the children whether it was dark this morning when they got up. *Do you think it will be dark when you go to bed tonight, or will you have to go to bed while it is still light? Is it always like this, or does it change? Can you remember [the opposite season], when things were different? Do you know what season it is when it is dark in the morning* **and** *at bedtime?* Talk about the daylight time being shorter in the winter. Briefly discuss other changes: it is warmer in summer, leaves fall in autumn, and so on.

Look at the display board. Explain that the yellow strip is daytime and the dark parts are night-time. Some of the shortest 'days' are in January, so where do they think the January label should go? Put the label at the top of the cone shape. Continue in this way until the June label is at the bottom of the cone, indicating the longest 'days'. Talk about how the days seem to get longer in the summer: it is lighter for longer, and it is light enough in the evening for the children to play outside until bedtime. *As the yellow part of the board becomes wider, what happens to the darker parts?*

GROUP ACTIVITIES

1. Give each child a copy of photocopiable page 195 to complete. Remind the children about the differences between summer and winter days, and ask them for some ideas about what they might draw on the sheet before they begin.
2. Ask each child to draw or paint a small picture of one of their daytime or night-time activities. Discuss some possibilities before they start, so that there are a variety of pictures. Add these to the display.

DIFFERENTIATION

1. More able children might add a short sentence to each of their pictures.
2. All the children can take part in this activity.

ASSESSMENT

Ask the children to describe the difference between getting up (or going to bed) in winter and in summer. Can they explain the display board?

PLENARY

Look at the display board and ask the children to explain it. Can they say why the yellow strip is narrower in January and wider in June? Pin the arrow to the board to indicate which month of the year you are in now. *What is going to happen to the day-length in the next few weeks? What shape would the display be if it went from June to December? What season is it when it is light for longest? Which season has the least daylight?*

OUTCOME

● Know that the pattern of day and night changes according to the season.

LINKS

Unit 3, Lesson 5: how the local environment changes with the seasons.

ASSESSMENT

LESSON 6

OBJECTIVES

● To distinguish the Sun from the Moon.
● To know that the pattern of day and night changes with the seasons.
● To know that the pattern of day and night affects living things, including humans.

RESOURCES

Photocopiable pages 196 and 197, writing and drawing materials.

INTRODUCTION

Look at the class display about day-length (from Lesson 5) and ask the children to tell you about it. *What does it show? What have you learned in the last few lessons?*

ASSESSMENT ACTIVITY 1

Give each child a copy of page 196 and ask them to complete the sheet. Make sure that they understand what is required.

Answers

'We see the Sun in the sky in the daytime'. Pictures could include the crescent Moon (see Looking for levels). 'We usually see the Moon at night'. Pictures may show either a crescent or a full Moon, and may also show stars.

Looking for levels

Most children should be able to complete the sheet successfully. Those with a better understanding will draw both the Sun and the Moon as circles (indicating spheres), and may colour one yellow and the other white or silver. Children with a less well-developed understanding may make more stereotypical drawings, such as the Sun as a circle with spikes and a crescent Moon (perhaps with a face). More able children with a very good understanding may include a crescent Moon in the daytime drawing.

ASSESSMENT ACTIVITY 2

Give each child a copy of page 197. Read through the sentences with them and make sure they understand that they have to complete each one. Some children may need to have the sentences read to them again as they work through them.

Answers

1. summer, 2. winter, 3. dark, 4. light, 5. summer, 6. winter, 7. day, night. 8. Any sentence that conveys an understanding that nocturnal animals are active at night either to avoid their predators or to hunt for their food (because that is when their food is available). The children's pictures should show nocturnal animals such as the badger, mouse, owl, hedgehog and so on. Pictures of foxes, rabbits, slugs and snails are acceptable, though these are mainly active at dusk and dawn.

Looking for levels

Most children should be able to answer questions 1–7 and give at least one reason to answer question 8. They should be able to draw three or four nocturnal animals. More able children may answer all the questions, giving two or three reasons to answer question 8 and identifying a range of nocturnal creatures. Less able children may answer question 1 or 2 (depending on the season in which this unit is being taught) and questions 5, 6 and 7, but only manage a verbal answer to question 8. They may know two or three nocturnal animals.

What do you do in the sunshine?

When the sun is shining, I feel _____

_____

I like to _____

_____

_____

_____

Draw what you like to do.

The Moon changes shape

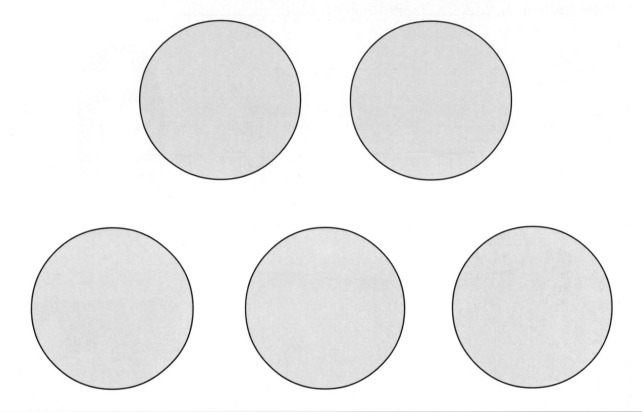

Choose the Moon shapes.
Cut them out and stick them in the grey circles to make Moon shapes.

Name

Nocturnal

I come out at _____ and sleep all _____ .

Winter or summer?

Draw a picture in each box.

When I get up, it looks like this:

winter	summer

When I get home, I play like this:

winter	summer

When I go to bed, it looks like this:

winter	summer

Stargazing

Fill in the missing word in each sentence, then draw a picture to show what you might see.

We see the _____ in the sky in the daytime.

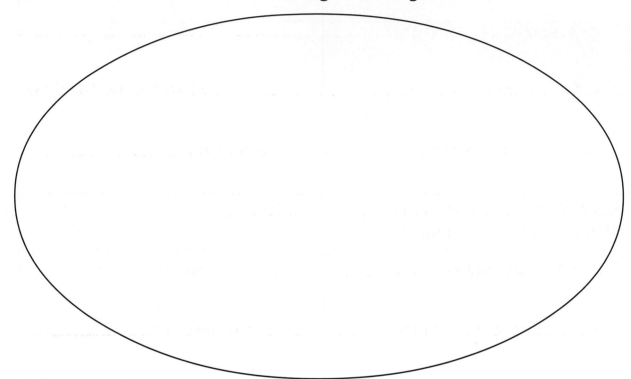

We usually see the _____ at night.

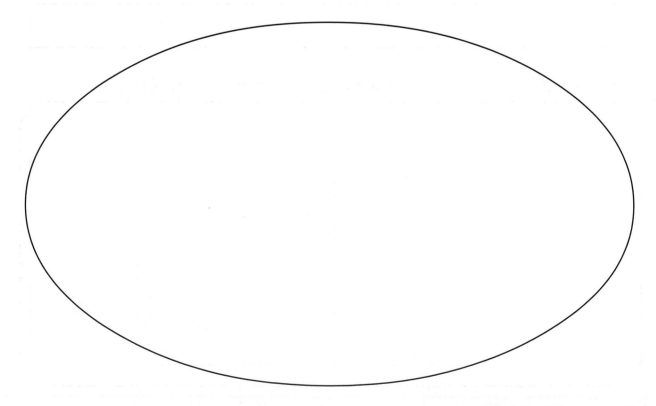

Stargazing

1. It is light enough to play outside until bedtime in the _____

_____ .

2. It grows dark early in the _____ .

3. In the winter it is still quite _____ when I come to school.

4. When I wake up early in the summer, it is already _____ .

5. It is light for longer in the _____ .

6. It is dark for longer in the _____ .

7. Most humans work in the _____ and sleep at _____ .

8. Some animals sleep all day because _____

_____

_____

Draw a picture of some of the animals that come out at night.

PROGRAMME OF STUDY SCIENCE KS1

National Curriculum in England

		Unit 1: Ourselves Me and my body UNIT 1A	Unit 2: Animals & Plants Growing and caring UNIT 1B

LINKS TO QCA SCIENCE SCHEME OF WORK

SC1 SCIENTIFIC ENQUIRY

	Unit 1A	Unit 1B
1 Ideas and evidence in science		
pupils should be taught that it is important to collect evidence by making observations and measurements when trying to answer a question	2	8, 9, 11
2 Investigative skills – Planning		
a ask questions and decide how they might find answers to them	2	8, 11
b use first-hand experience and simple information sources to answer questions		8, 11
c think about what might happen before deciding what to do		8
d recognise when a test or comparison is unfair		11
Investigative skills – Obtaining and presenting evidence		
e follow simple instructions to control the risks to themselves and to others		8
f explore, using the senses of sight, hearing, smell, touch and taste as appropriate, and make and record observations and measurements	1, 3, 4, 5, 6, 7	1, 2, 3, 4, 6, 7, 9, 10, 11, 12, 13, 14, 15
g communicate what happened in a variety of ways, including using ICT	2, 10, 11	11
Investigative skills – Considering evidence and evaluating		
h make simple comparisons and identify simple patterns or associations	1, 2, 8, 9, 11	5, 9, 11
i compare what happened with what they expected would happen, and try to explain it, drawing on their knowledge and understanding		8
j review their work and explain what they did to others	4, 5, 6	8

SC2 PROCESSES AND LIVING THINGS

	Unit 1A	Unit 1B
1 Life processes		
a the differences between things that are living and things that have never been alive		1
b that animals, including humans, move, feed, grow, use their senses and reproduce	3, 4, 5, 6, 7, 8, 9, 12	4
c to relate life processes to animals and plants found in the local environment		
2 Humans and other animals		
a to recognise and compare the main external parts of the bodies of humans and other animals	1, 2, 12	3
b that humans and other animals need food and water to stay alive	10	1
c that taking exercise and eating the right types and amounts of food help humans to keep healthy		
d about the role of drugs as medicines		
e how to treat animals with care and sensitivity		
f that humans and other animals can produce offspring and that these offspring grow into adults	8, 9	5
g about the senses that enable humans and other animals to be aware of the world around them		
3 Green plants		
a to recognise that plants need light and water to grow		9, 10, 11, 12
b to recognise and name the leaf, flower, stem and root of flowering plants		6, 10, (13), (14), (15), 16
c that seeds grow into flowering plants		8
4 Variation and classification		
a recognise similarities and differences between themselves and others, and to treat others with sensitivity		
b group living things according to observable similarities and differences		
5 Living things in their environment		
a find out about the different kinds of plants and animals in the local environment		2, 7, 16
b identify similarities and differences between local environments and ways in which these affect animals and plants that are found there		
c care for the environment		

SC3 MATERIALS & THEIR PROPERTIES

	Unit 1A	Unit 1B
1 Grouping materials		
a use their senses to explore and recognise the similarities and differences between materials		
b sort objects into groups on the basis of simple material properties		
c recognise and name common types of material and recognise that some of them are found naturally		
d find out about the uses of a variety of materials and how these are chosen for specific uses on the basis of their simple properties		
2 Changing materials		
a find out how the shapes of objects made from some materials can be changed by some processes, including squashing, bending, twisting and stretching		
b explore and describe the way some everyday materials change when they are heated or cooled		

SC4 PHYSICAL PROCESSES

	Unit 1A	Unit 1B
1 Electricity		
a about everyday appliances that use electricity		
b about simple series circuits involving batteries, wires, bulbs and other components		
c how a switch can be used to break a circuit		
2 Forces and motion		
a to find out about, and describe the movement of, familiar things		
b that both pushes and pulls are examples of forces		
c to recognise that when things speed up, slow down or change direction, there is a cause		
Light and sound		
3 Light and dark		
a to identify different light sources, including the Sun		
b that darkness is the absence of light		
4 Making and detecting sounds		
c that there are many kinds of sound and sources of sound		
d that sounds travel away from sources, getting fainter as they do so, and that they are heard when they enter the ear		

198   **100 SCIENCE LESSONS ● YEAR 1 / PROGRAMME OF STUDY SCIENCE KS1**

Lessons where curriculum content is the main objective are listed below. Lessons where content is included but is not the main focus are shown below in brackets.

Unit 3: The environment Environments and living things	Unit 4: Materials Properties of materials	Unit 5: Electricity Using and misusing electricity	Unit 6: Forces & motion Introducing forces	Unit 7: Light & sound Sources of light and sound	Unit 8: Earth & beyond Stargazing
–	UNIT 1C	–	UNIT 1E	UNIT 1D, 1F	–
2, 3, 4	8	4	3, 4	7, 8	
15, 16	8, 12	4	3	10, 14, 15	
15, 16	8, 12	4	3	10, 14	
	8	4	3, 4, 5	14	
	8, 12	4	3	14	
9				5, 6, 13	
1, 2, 3, 4, 9, 10, 11, 12, 15, 16	1, 2, 3, 4, 5, 6, 7, 8, 10	1, 2, 3	1, 2, 4, 7, 8	1, 2, 7, 8, 9, 11, 18	1, 3
2, 3					
2, 3, 4, 5, 6, 7, 8, 9, 13, 14	8, 7, 11, 13, 14, 15		3, 5, 6	3, 4, 12, 16, 17	2, 4, 5
	8		4, 5	14	
3, 4	8	4	3		
			1, 2, 3	18	
				18	
10, 11, 13, 14, 17					
12					
15, 16, 17					
	1, 3, 4, 11				
	1, 3, 4, 5, 6, 7, 8, 16				
	2				
	9, 10				
	13, 14, 15		4		
		1, 2, 3, 5			
		4			
			5, 6, 7, 8, 9		
			1, 2, 3, 9		
			1, 2, 3, 7		
				2, 3, 19	13
				1	
				8, 9, 10, 11, 12, 13, 14, 15, 19	
				16, 17	

The Northern Ireland Curriculum

		Unit 1: Ourselves Me and my body	Unit 2: Animals & Plants Growing and caring
INVESTIGATING AND MAKING IN SCIENCE AND TECHNOLOGY	Pupils should be encouraged to adopt safe practices when undertaking science and technology activities. They should be made aware of potential hazards and the appropriate actions necessary to avoid risks.		
	Planning		
	Pupils should have opportunities to participate in practical activities which involve them in talking to the teacher and each other about ideas, predictions and solutions to problems and planning what to make.		
	a respond to questions		
	b talk about what they are going to make and the materials they will use		
	c ask questions, discuss ideas and make predictions		8, 11
	d recognise a fair test		11, 12
	e suggest ideas which can be investigated and make predictions	10, 11	11
	f choose appropriate materials and components when planning what to make		
	Carrying out and making		
	Pupils should have opportunities to participate in practical activities which involve them in exploring familiar objects and materials in their immediate environment and recording what they have done.		
	a make observations using their senses	1, 3, 4, 5, 6, 7	2, 6, 7, 10
	b assemble and rearrange materials		
	c make observations noting similarities and differences	1, 2, 7, 8, 9	1, 3, 4, 5
	d record observations in a simple form	1	9
	e explore different ways of joining materials		
	f reinforce measuring skills using non-standard measures and progress to using standard measures	8	8, 9
	g develop manipulative skills using a range of materials and tools		
	h record what they have done or observed using appropriate methods	10, 11	
	Interpreting and evaluating		
	Pupils should participate in practical activities which provide them with opportunities to develop skills in reporting, presenting and interpreting results and evaluating what they have made.		
	a talk to the teacher and others about what happened or about what they have made		
	b comment on what happened or what they like or dislike about what they have made		
	c present their findings using appropriate methods		13, 14, 15
	d relate what happened to what they predicted		8, 11
	e talk about what they have made in terms of materials, colour, size or shape and make suggestions for improvement		

			Unit 1	Unit 2
KNOWLEDGE AND UNDERSTANDING OF SCIENCE AND TECHNOLOGY	**Living things**	**Ourselves**		
		a recognise and name the main external parts of the human body	1	
		b observe seasonal changes and talk about how these affect themselves		
		c explore similarities and differences between themselves and other children	2	
		d develop ideas about how to keep healthy, through exercise, rest, diet, personal hygiene and safety	7, 11	14, 15
		e be introduced to the main stages of human development	8, 9	
		f find out about themselves including how they grow, move and use their senses	3, 4, 5, 6, 7, 12	
		Animals and plants		
		a find out about the variety of animal and plant life both through direct observations and by using secondary sources	1	1, 7, 8, 9, 10, 11, 12, 13
		b sort living things into the two broad groups of animals and plants		
		c recognise and name the main parts of a flowering plant including root, stem, leaf and flower		6, 16
		d sort living things into groups using observable features		
		e find out about animals and their young		5
		f find out about some animals, including how they grow, feed, move and use their senses		2, 3, 4, 16
		g observe similarities and differences among animals and among plants		9, 10, 11, 12
		h discuss the use of colour in the natural environment		
		i find out ways in which animal and plant behaviour is influenced by seasonal changes		
	Materials	**Properties**		
		a work with a range of everyday materials in a variety of activities		
		b sort a range of everyday objects into groups according to the materials from which they are made		
		c explore the properties of materials including shape, colour, texture and behaviour		
		d find out some everyday uses of materials		
		e investigate similarities and differences in materials and objects; sort them according to their properties		
		Change		
		a find out about the effect of heating and cooling some everyday substances, such as water, chocolate or butter		
		b investigate which everyday substances dissolve in water		
		Environment		
		a identify the range of litter in and around their own locality		
		b find out how human activities create a variety of waste products		
		c find out that some materials decay naturally while others do not		
	Physical Processes	**Forces and energy**		
		a explore forces which push, pull or make things move		
		b explore devices, including toys, which move		
		c explore how pushes and pulls make things speed up or stop		
		d find out about the range of energy sources used in school and at home		
		Electricity		
		a find out about some uses of electricity in the home and classroom		
		b know that electricity can be dangerous		
		c know about the safe use of mains electricity and its associated dangers		
		Sound		
		a listen to and identify sources of sounds in their immediate environment		
		b explore ways of making sounds using familiar objects		
		c investigate how sounds are produced when objects vibrate		
		Light		
		a find out that light comes from a variety of sources		
		b explore the use of light including colour in relation to road safety		
		c explore how light passes through some materials and not others		

EMU and Cultural Heritage Pupils should have opportunities to develop an understanding of themselves and others by exploring similarities and differences between thee   s and other children, and developing a sense of their own individuality. They should appreciate the environment around them, the need to take care of it and how human ac..........can upset the natural environment. They should consider how some toys and devices work and know that the technology which drives them has been developed over a period of time.

Lessons where curriculum content is the main objective are listed below. Lessons where content is included but is not the main focus are shown below in brackets.

Unit 3: The environment Environments and living things	Unit 4: Materials Properties of materials	Unit 5: Electricity Using and misusing electricity	Unit 6: Forces & motion Introducing forces	Unit 7: Light & sound Sources of light and sound	Unit 8: Earth & beyond Stargazing
15, 16	12	4		1, 3, 10, 14	
15, 16	12	4		10, 14	
	12	4		14	
		4	5, 8	12	
10, 11	1, 2, 3, 4, 5, 9	1, 4	1, 2, 3, 6, 7, 8	1, 2, 3, 4, 7, 8, 11, 13	1, 4, 5
5, 6, 7, 8, 9, 12, 14	1, 2, 6, 7, 8, 10, 11	2			2, 3
2, 3, 4	12	4		15	
	12		1		
4	8			16, 17	
			3		
4	12	4	8	9	
	13, 14, 15	4	2, 3, 4, 6, 7, 8	1, 3, 5, 6, 18	
	13, 14, 15	4	2, 3, 4, 6, 7, 8	1, 3, 18	
13	12	3	3	14	2
	12		5, 8		
	3, 4, 5				
1, 10, 11, 12, 15, 16, 17					4
13					
5, 6, 7, 8, 9, 14, 17					5
	2				
	2, 10, 11				
	1, 3, 4, 5, 6, 7, 8, 12, 13, 14, 15, 16				
	9				
7					
			1, 2, 5, 6, 7, 8, 9		
			3, 4		
			1, 2, 9		
		1, 2, 4			
		3, 5			
		5			
				7, 8, 9, 13, 14, 15, 16, 17, 18, 19	
				10, 11, 12	
				1, 2, 3, 4, 5, 6, 19	1, 2, 3
Unit 3: The environment Environments and living things	Unit 4: Materials Properties of materials	Unit 5: Electricity Using and misusing electricity	Unit 6: Forces & motion Introducing forces	Unit 7: Light & sound Sources of light and sound	Unit 8: Earth & beyond Stargazing

PROGRAMME OF STUDY SCIENCE KS1

National Curriculum in Wales

	Unit 1: Ourselves Me and my body	Unit 2: Animals & Plants Growing and caring
SCIENTIFIC ENQUIRY		
1 The nature of science		
the link between ideas and information in science		
1 to ask questions about their ideas in science	10, 11	4, 8, 9
2 to obtain information from their own work and also, on some occasions, from other simple sources	2, 3, 4, 5, 6, 10, 11	4, 8, 9
3 to use their experiences and the information they obtain from their investigations to develop their own scientific ideas	3, 4, 5, 6, 10, 11	4, 8, 9
2 Communication in science		
presenting scientific information		
1 to describe their work clearly, in speech and in writing, using appropriate vocabulary	3, 4, 5, 6, 7	4, 5, 10, 13, 14, 15
2 to present scientific information appropriately in a number of ways, through diagrams, drawings, tables and charts	2	1, 2, 6, 10
3 to use ICT to enter and to present different kinds of information, when this is appropriate	2	13, 14, 15
4 to use non-standard and standard measures appropriate to their work	1	8, 9
handling scientific information		
5 to sort and classify scientific information, using ICT to do so on some occasions	2	13, 14, 15
6 to recognise that scientific information can be changed into different forms, and that ICT can help in doing this	2	13, 14, 15
3 Investigative skills		
planning an investigation		
1 to turn ideas suggested to them, and their own ideas, into a form that can be investigated		8
2 that thinking about, and if possible suggesting, what might happen, can be useful when planning what to do		
3 to decide what is to be observed or measured	1	3, 8, 9
4 to recognise that a test or comparison may not always be fair		11
5 to recognise hazards and risks in obtaining information		
obtaining information		
6 to explore using appropriate senses	3, 4, 5, 6, 7	1, 2, 7, 13, 14, 15
7 to follow instructions to control the risks to themselves		
8 to make observations and measurements		1, 2, 7, 9, 12
9 to make an appropriate record of observations and measurements considering information	10, 11	1, 2, 7
considering information		
10 to make simple comparisons	1, 2, 8, 11	5
11 to use results to say what they found out	10, 11	
12 to try to explain what they found out, drawing on their knowledge and understanding		
13 to evaluate their work		
LIFE PROCESSES AND LIVING THINGS		
1 Life processes		
1 the differences between things that are living and things that are not		1
2 that humans and other animals have and use senses which enable them to be aware of the world around them	3, 4, 5, 6, 7, 8, 9, 12	4
3 that animals, including humans, move, need food and water, grow and reproduce	7, 8, 9, 10	
2 Humans and other animals		
1 to name the main external parts of the human body	1, 2, 12	
2 to recognise similarities and differences between themselves and other pupils	2	
3 to compare the external parts of human bodies with those of other animals		3
4 that taking exercise and eating the right types and amounts of food helps humans to keep healthy		
5 about the role of drugs as medicines		
6 that humans and other animals can produce offspring and these offspring grow into adults	8, 9	5
3 Green plants as organisms		
1 that plants need light and water to grow		9, 10, 11, 12
2 to recognise and name the leaf, flower, stem and root of flowering plants		6, 10, (13), (14), (15), 16
3 that flowering plants grow and produce seeds which, in turn, produce new plants		8
4 Living things in their environment		
1 to find out about the different kinds of plants and animals in the local environment		2, 7, 10
2 that animals and plants con be grouped according to observable similarities and differences		
MATERIALS & THEIR PROPERTIES		
1 Grouping materials		
1 use their senses to explore and recognise the similarities and differences between materials		
2 sort materials into groups, separating them on the basis of simple properties that can be seen or felt, including texture, shininess, transparency, and on whether they are attracted by a magnet		
3 recognise and name common types of material, and that some of these materials are found naturally		
4 find out about the uses made of a variety of common materials		
2 Changing materials		
1 that objects made from some materials can be changed in shape by stretching, squashing, bending and twisting		
2 to describe the way some everyday materials change when they are heated or cooled		
PHYSICAL PROCESSES		
1 Electricity		
1 know that many everyday appliances use electricity and that they should be used with care		
2 to construct and explore simple circuits involving batteries, wires, bulbs, switches and other components		
3 that electrical devices will not work if there is a break in the circuit, and that a switch in the circuit can be used to control an electrical device.		
2 Forces and Motion		
1 to describe the movement of familiar things		
2 that a push or pull can make something speed up, slow down or change direction		
3 that both pushes and pulls are examples of forces		
4 that forces are used in changing the shape of an object or breaking it into parts		
3 Light and Sound		
light and dark		
1 that light comes from a variety of sources, including the Sun		
2 that darkness is the absence of light		
making and detecting sounds		
3 that there are many kinds of sound and many sources of sound		
4 that sounds travel away from sources, getting fainter as they do so		
5 that sounds are heard when they enter the ear		

Lessons where curriculum content is the main objective are listed below. Lessons where content is included but is not the main focus are shown below in brackets.

Unit 3: The environment Environments and living things	Unit 4: Materials Properties of materials	Unit 5: Electricity Using and misusing electricity	Unit 6: Forces & motion Introducing forces	Unit 7: Light & sound Sources of light and sound	Unit 8: Earth & beyond Stargazing
2, 3, 4, 9	3, 4, 5, 6	4	3, 8	3, 4, 16, 17	
2, 3, 4, 9	3, 4, 5, 6	4	3, 8	3, 4, 16, 17	1, 2
2, 3, 4, 9	3, 4, 5, 6	4	3, 8	3, 4, 16, 17	2
1, 9, 12, 13, 16	12	3	6, 7	3, 16	
10, 11					5
			8	3	
2, 3, 4			3	3, 16, 17	
10, 11	1, 6	2	3, 8	4, 16, 17	
2	10, 11	2			
2, 3, 4	7, 8		3, 8	3, 16, 17	2
2, 3, 4		4	3, 8	3	
	12	4	3, 8		
				5, 6, 13	1
	1, 2, 3, 4, 5, 9		1, 2, 4, 8	1, 2, 7, 8, 9, 15, 18	1, 2, 3
	8			6	1
3, 4, 9	6, 7, 8, 12	1, 2	3, 8		
5, 6, 7, 8				14	
14	10, 11, 13, 14, 15	4	1, 2, 3, 5, 8	3, 4, 11, 12, 16, 19	3, 4
4					
15					
16					
(13), (14), (17)					
(1), 9, 10, 11, (12)					4
	1, 3, 4, 5				
	1, 3, 4, 5, 6, 7, 8, 12, 16				
	2, 11				
	9, 10				
	13, 14, 15		4		
		1, 2, 3, 5			
		4			
			1, 2, 5, 6, 7, 8		
			3, 9		
			3, 4, 7, 9		
			4		
				1, 2, 3, 4, 19	1, 2
				1, 4	
				7, 8, 9, 10, 11, 12, 19	
				16, 17	
				13, 14, 15, 18	

National Guidelines for Scotland

			Unit 1: Ourselves Me and my body	Unit 2: Animals & Plants Growing and caring
SKILLS IN SCIENCE: INVESTIGATING		**Preparing for tasks** Understanding the task and planning a practical activity. Predicting. Undertaking fair testing		
	A	● make simple suggestions and contribute to the planning of simple practical investigations	4, 5, 6	11
	B	● plan simple approaches by asking questions and making suggestions		11
		● make suggestions about what might happen		
		● recognise when a test or comparison is unfair		8, 11
		Carrying out tasks Observing and measuring. Recording findings in a variety of ways.		
	A	● carry out simple observations and measurements	1, 3, 4, 5, 6, 7	1, 3, 5, 7, 9, 10, 11
		● record observations in a simple form		
	B	● use simple equipment and techniques to make measurements		9
		● record findings in a range of ways	1, 10, 11	9
		Reviewing and reporting on tasks Reporting and presenting. Interpreting and evaluating results and processes.		
	A	● participate in the presentation of the findings through visual displays and oral reports		
		● answer simple questions about what happened	7, 8	2, 4, 6, 14, 15
	B	● make a short report of an investigation		
		● answer questions on the meaning of the findings		
		● recognise simple relationships and draw conclusions	8	
EARTH AND SPACE		**Earth and space** Developing an understanding of the position of the Earth in the Solar System and the Universe, and the effects of movement and that of the Moon.		
	A	● identify the Sun, the Moon and the stars		
		● link the pattern of day and night to the position of the Sun		
	B	● associate the seasons with differences in observed temperature		
		● describe how day and night are related to the spin of the Earth		
		Materials from Earth Developing an understanding of the materials available on our planet, and the links between properties and uses.		
	A	● recognise and name some common materials from living and non-living sources		
		● give examples of uses of some materials based on simple properties		
		● give the main uses of water		
	B	● make observations of differences in the properties of common materials		
		● relate uses of everyday materials to properties		
		● explain why water conservation is important		
		Changing materials Developing an understanding of the ways in which materials can be changed.		
	A	● make observations of the ways in which some materials can be changed by processes such as squashing, bending, twisting and stretching		
	B	● describe how everyday materials can be changed by heating or cooling		
		● give examples of everyday materials that dissolve in water		
		● give examples of common causes of water pollution		
ENERGY AND FORCES		**Properties and uses of energy** Developing an understanding of energy through the study of the properties and uses of heat, light, sound and electricity.		
	A	● give examples of sources of heat, light and sound		
		● give examples of everyday uses of heat, light and sound		
		● give examples of everyday appliances that use electricity		
		● identify some of the common dangers associated with use of electricity		
	B	● identify the sun as the main source of heat and light		
		● link light and sound to seeing and hearing		
		Conversion and transfer of energy Developing an understanding of energy conversion in practical everyday contexts.		
	A	● –		
	B	● give examples of being 'energetic'		
		● link the intake of food to the movement of their body		
		Forces and their effects Developing an understanding of forces and how they can explain familiar phenomena and practices.		
	A	● give examples of pushing and pulling, floating and sinking		
	B	● describe the effect that a push and pull can have on the direction, speed or shape of an object		
		● give examples of magnets in everyday use		
		● describe the interaction of magnets in terms of the forces of attraction and repulsion		
LIVING THINGS AND THE PROCESSES OF LIFE		**Variety and characteristic features** Developing an understanding of the characteristic features of the main groups of plants and animals including humans and micro-organisms. The principles of genetics are also considered.		
	A	● recognise similarities and differences between themselves and others	1, 2, 12	
		● sort living things into broad groups according to easily observable characteristics		1, 2, 3, 7, 14, 16
		● give some of the more obvious distinguishing features of the major invertebrate groups		2, 3
		● name some common members of the invertebrate groups		2, 3
		The processes of life Developing an understanding of growth and development and life cycles, including cells and cell processes. The main organs of the human body and their functions are also considered.		
	A	● name and identify the main external parts of the bodies of humans and other animals		
		● describe some ways in which humans keep themselves safe	3, 4, 5, 6, 12	
		● give the conditions needed by animals and plants in order to remain healthy		
	B	● give examples of how the senses are used to detect information	3, 4, 5, 6, 12	
		● recognise the stages of the human life cycle	8, 9	
		● recognise stages in the life cycles of familiar plants and animals		5, 8
		● identify the main parts of flowering plants		6, 10, 16

Lessons where curriculum content is the main objective are listed below. Lessons where content is included but is not the main focus are shown below in brackets.

	Unit 3: The environment Environments and living things	Unit 4: Materials Properties of materials	Unit 5: Electricity Using and misusing electricity	Unit 6: Forces & motion Introducing forces	Unit 7: Light & sound Sources of light and sound	Unit 8: Earth & beyond Stargazing
	3, 4	12	4		3, 10	
	3, 4	12	4		3, 10	
		12	4		3	
	1, 3, 4, 9, 12, 15, 16	1, 2, 3, 4, 5, 9	1, 2, 5	1, 2, 6, 7	1, 2, 4, 7, 8, 9, 11, 16, 17	1, 2, 3
	3, 4					
	5, 6, 7, 8, 10					
	13, 14	13, 14, 15	1, 2, 3	4	6, 15, 18	
				3, 5	12	4, 5
						1, 2, 3
	5, 6, 7, 8					4, 5
						5
		2, 10, 11				
		(10), (11)				
		1, 7, 8				
					1, 7, 8, 14, 15, 16, (17)	
					2, 3, 7, 8, 9, 19	
			1, 2			
			3, 5			
					2	
					1, 4, 7, 8	
				1, 2, 8, 9		
				3, 4, 5, 6, 7, 9		
	10, 17					
	10, 11					

	Unit 3: The environment Environments and living things	Unit 4: Materials Properties of materials	Unit 5: Electricity Using and misusing electricity	Unit 6: Forces & motion Introducing forces	Unit 7: Light & sound Sources of light and sound	Unit 8: Earth & beyond Stargazing

Living things and the processes of life continued overleaf

National Guidelines for Scotland

ENVIRONMENTAL STUDIES 5–14 SCIENCE

			Unit 1: Ourselves Me and my body	Unit 2: Animals & Plants Growing and caring
LIVING THINGS AND THE PROCESSES OF LIFE	LEVEL	**Interaction of living things with their environment** Developing an understanding of the interdependance of living things with the environment. The conservation and care of living things are also considered.		
	A	● recognise and name some common plants and animals		
		● give examples of how to care for living things and the environment	10, 11	4, 11, 12
		● give some examples of seasonal changes in the appearance of plants		
	B	● give examples of feeding relationships found in the local environment		
		● construct simple food chains		
		Developing informed attitudes Pupils should be encouraged to develop an awareness of, and positive attitudes, to:		
		A commitment to learning		
		● the need to develop informed and reasoned opinions on the impact of science in relation to social, environmental moral and ethical issues		
		● working independently and with others to find solutions to scientific problems		
		Respect and care for self and others		
		● taking responsibility for their own health and safety	10, 11	
		● participating in the safe and responsible care of living things and the environment		
		● the development of responsible attitudes that take account of different beliefs and values		
		Social and environmental responsibility		
		● thinking through the various consequences for living things and the environment of different choices, decisions and courses of action		
		● the importance of the interrelationships between living things and their enviroment		
		● participating in the conservation of natural resources and the sustainable use of the Earth's resources		
		● the need for conservation of scarce energy resources and endangered species at local and global level		

Lessons where curriculum content is the main objective are listed below. Lessons where content is included but is not the main focus are shown below in brackets.

Unit 3: The environment Environments and living things	Unit 4: Materials Properties of materials	Unit 5: Electricity Using and misusing electricity	Unit 6: Forces & motion Introducing forces	Unit 7: Light & sound Sources of light and sound	Unit 8: Earth & beyond Stargazing
12					
1, 15, 16, 17					
5, 6, 7, 8, 9, 14, 17					
13					
13					
		3, 5		5, 6, 18	1
15, 16					
15					
15					

Series topic map

Year/Primary	YR/P1	Y1/P2	Y2/P3	Y3/P4	Y4/P5	Y5/P6	Y6/P7
Unit 1: Ourselves	This is me!	Me and my body	Keeping healthy	Teeth and food	How I move	Growing up healthy	New beginnings
Unit 2: Animals & plants	Looking at animals and plants	Growing and caring	Growing up	The needs of plants and animals	Different sorts of skeletons	Life cycles	Variation
Unit 3: The environment	Out and about	Environments and living things	Life in habitats and change	How the environment affects living things	Habitats and food chains	Water and the environment	The living world
Unit 4: Materials	Exploring materials	Properties of materials	Materials and change	Natural & manufactured materials	Warm liquids, cool solids	Gases, solids and liquids	Reversible and non-reversible changes
Unit 5: Electricity	Making things work	Using and misusing electricity	Making circuits	Electricity and communication	Switches and conduction	Making and using electricity	Changing circuits
Unit 6: Forces & motion	Pushing and pulling	Introducing forces	Making things move	Magnets and springs	Friction	Exploring forces and their effects	Forces and action
Unit 7: Light & sound	Looking and listening	Sources of light and sound	Properties and uses	Sources and effects	Travelling and reflecting	Bending light and changing sound	Light and sound around us
Unit 8: Earth & beyond	Up in the sky	Stargazing	The Sun and the seasons	The Sun and shadows	The Sun and stars	Sun, Moon and Earth	The Solar System